EVE IN THE HEART OF HEART OF EDEN

UNDERSTANDING THE TREE OF KNOWLEDGE OF GOOD AND EVIL

EVE IN THE HEART OF EDEN

UNDERSTANDING THE TREE OF KNOWLEDGE OF GOOD AND EVIL

MARLA WHITMAN

Bridgewood Publishing
A Self-Publishing Imprint of Cedar Fort, Inc.
Springville, Utah

REL006060 RELIGION / Biblical Commentary / Old Testament / General
REL046000 RELIGION / Christianity / Church of Jesus Christ of Latter-day Saints (Mormon)
REL012130 RELIGION / Christian Living / Women's Interests

ISBN 13: 978-0-5784-6696-5

Published by Bridgewood Publishing, 2373 W. 700 S., Springville, UT 84663

Cover design © 2019 Marla Whitman
Edited and typeset by Sydnee Hyer

Printed in the United States of America

10 9 8 7 6 5 4 3 2 1

Printed on acid-free paper

CONTENTS

CONTENTS

INTRODUCTION
OUR LIFE BEGINS IN EDEN

My journey into the heart of Eden has been both fascinating and enlightening. I found it has also been a journey into the heart of the gospel of Jesus Christ. The purpose of my years of research have been to answer the questions we have all considered at times but do not yet fully comprehend. I have gained a love and understanding of Eve and the plan of happiness that continues to guide my footsteps through both desperate and joyous times. Adam and Eve show the pattern in which we must all travel. They gave us the tree of knowledge of good and evil, and understanding this tree gives us a unique and surprising comprehension of both heaven and earth.

Searching for the real Eve and the role she played in the beginning becomes a search for our own identity and role in life. Though Eve's story reads as a simple narrative, its interpretation varies through time. More often than not, we find negative, secular, and theological interpretations of her actions, rather than Eve's personal and spiritual oneness with God and Adam. Because Eve's part in the story of Eden has been vastly misunderstood, my goal is to see and tell Eve's story, and the truths therein, as I believe she would tell them.

While the Garden of Eden story in the scriptures is simple, vague, and full of metaphors and symbolism, it continues to stand at a pivotal time for us as we remain to experience the trials and gifts

1

of the Fall. It is through Eve that we came to be, and it is through Adam and Eve's story that we may connect these wondrous and final puzzle pieces of great knowledge that will aid us in preparing for the Second Coming of our Lord and Savior Jesus Christ.

It is understandable that many of us who have read, or at least heard, the Garden of Eden story from our youth have had varying misconceptions of the events that took place. We are often taught in our youth to picture a naive Eve standing naked in the garden, with a luscious red apple ominously cradled in her hand, being prompted by the serpent. Even when we get past these traditional interpretations and read the scriptural text for ourselves, questions still arise concerning Eve's actions in the partaking of the forbidden fruit.

To begin with, the commands given to Adam and Eve not to partake of "the tree of knowledge of good and evil" (Genesis 2:9) have caused some concern because of the apparent contradictions in the command, while the title of the tree makes the partaking seem necessary. "But of the tree of knowledge of good and evil, thou shalt not eat of it, nevertheless, thou mayest choose for thyself, for *it is given unto thee*; but, remember that I forbid it, for in the day thou eatest thereof thou shalt surely die" (Moses 3:17; emphasis added). This verse is complex and confusing; if taken literally, it is difficult to interpret and understand. Without research, many tend to fall back on the ominous words "forbid" and "die"—often leaving us bewildered over Eve's decision to partake.

Though we may take these transpiring events on faith, several questions persist. Did Adam and Eve understand God's command and the warning when they partook of the tree of knowledge of good and evil? Did they act for or against God's command? Had God laid an unfair and contradictory trap to accomplish His purpose? This quest for truth is spiritually necessary as we seek answers, and it need not be considered doubting to have these questions, because it becomes a vital aspect to our spiritual search. The incredible depth of the story of Eden cannot be fully comprehended without this introspective search. This principle of pondering is noted in the Book of Mormon as Jesus tells the people, "Ponder upon the things which I have said, and ask of the Father, in my name, that ye may understand" (3 Nephi 17:3). Pondering, as well as leaning on the scriptural words of ancient and latter-day prophets, aids us in receiving personal revelation. "Behold, I say unto you, that you must study it out in your mind; then you must ask me if it be right" (D&C 9:8). This is the spirit of revelation that you and I will utilize as we search for the truth in Eden. My hope is that this book, by examining Eden in the light of both ancient and modern-day revelation, will give greater understanding to an old story.

As we explore this simple yet complex story of the mother of all living, new insights and truths will begin to unfold. In the first two chapters, an overview of what took place in Eden and how Eve came to partake of the tree of knowledge of good and evil will help bring this remarkable story to life. Throughout the remainder of the book, truths will continue to emerge as we reach further into specific examples of Adam and Eve's journey that will bring us a valued understanding of their connective mission with us today and with our Savior, Jesus Christ.

In all of this we will discover the figurative implications of the dust of the earth and the conceptual infusion of the breath of life. We will recognize the needed preparatory events of the deep sleep, and the necessity of the veil and the forgetting. Adam and Eve's covenant of marriage, which was performed in Eden, also initiated a license to bear children in mortality "to be fruitful and replenish the earth"—becoming a foundation for the eternal family of God's children. In this new and everlasting covenant of Adam and Eve, we will find the powerful significance of the rib, symbolized as an equally shared priesthood between man and woman in its sealing power. Our first parents understood that this sealing power unto exaltation cannot be had if one of the three (man, woman, and Christ) are missing from this perfect triangle. The three must achieve *at-one-ment* in the eternal covenant of marriage, or we fall short of that coveted glory. We also find new insights into Paul's vocabulary toward women in his day and ours as he teaches us the connective rights of the priesthood between men and women. It all comes together as Eve stands valiantly in the heart of Eden. Adam and Eve, with faith in the atoning blood of Jesus Christ, took these necessary steps.

Through latter-day prophets, the tree of life and the tree of knowledge of good and evil become comprehensible. Both trees are necessary as they intertwine in purpose and become recognized as a complete order for our happiness. Only through the tree of knowledge of good and evil do we fully comprehend the tree of life. It is also through the metaphors for *fruit, forbidden*, and *eat* that the necessity of the partaking is explained. The acts of choice, sacrifice, and sorrow are imbued with meaning as sanctification is brought into play by the blood of Christ. It is through the words of modern prophets that the apron of fig leaves (see Genesis 3:7; Moses 4:13) is brought to light in relation to the "coats of skins" (Genesis 3:21; Moses 4:27), nakedness, and salvation. Cherubim and the flaming sword are better understood in regard to the forbidden fruit.

As Adam and Eve move into a mortal world, their companionship becomes evident when the words "rule over thee," and "thy desire shall be to thy husband" (Genesis 3:16; Moses 4:22) become beautiful expressions of oneness as secular and even theological interpretations of these scriptures are dispelled. In this perfect relationship, Adam and Eve's story qualifies as the greatest love story of all time as it also becomes exemplary for what we too may accomplish.

My personal reason for taking on this topic is not only to defend the character of Eve against misinterpretations that paint her as gullible and disobedient but also to open a vision of our origin as it instills within us our purpose. I find this story becomes a foundational witness for the basic principles of the gospel of Jesus Christ. We can then apply the story in Eden to our own lives as we also seek to live the gospel of Jesus Christ to its fullest. I implore you to read Eve's story that you may know her, and therein, you may also know yourself.

CHAPTER 1

ADAM AND EVE ARE
CALLED UPON TO ACT

"Thou mayest choose for thyself, for it is given unto thee."
—Moses 3:17

We all need the story of Adam and Eve, and we need it correctly interpreted, for it is Adam and Eve's example that directs our path toward the joy of our redemption. In the Doctrine and Covenants, we are reminded that truth encompasses all time. "Truth is knowledge of things as they are, and as they were, and as they are to come" (D&C 93:24). With that perspective, as we seek the truth in Eden, we are also seeking the fullness of the gospel of Jesus Christ through all time.

A new understanding begins with a needed overhaul of our past precepts. Many have assumed that when Adam and Eve partook of the fruit of the tree of knowledge of good and evil, they did so presumptuously, with little consideration for the consequences of the Fall. In this chapter, we explore the intricate details that led to the careful and educated path that they took toward complete compliance with God's laws. We will examine those godly laws with great care, as well as Satan's heart, mind, and purpose to deceive man. This can be done by considering the conditions in Eden, along with God's proposed advancement toward godhood. We will carefully examine the truths in Eden, because when truth is told, chaos and deceit are extinguished. Adam and Eve are exonerated, and once again we can claim that glorious inheritance our first parents so lovingly made available to each of us: the opportunity to attain our own "immortality and eternal life" (Moses 1:39), through the blood of Christ. Elder Jeffrey R. Holland wrote: "Adam and Eve made their choice for an even more generous reason than those of godly knowledge and personal progress. They did it for the one overriding and commanding reason basic to the entire plan of salvation and all the discussions ever held in all the councils of heaven. They did it 'that men might be.' . . . The privilege of mortality granted to the rest of us is the principal gift given by the fall of Adam and Eve."[1]

AGENCY

This they chose by their agency, "and in the Garden of Eden, gave I unto man his agency" (Moses 7:32). We would do well to lay groundwork for the importance of agency and its connection to Adam and Eve and the partaking of the forbidden fruit. It was not just the fruit that was placed before them but also a *choice*. The fruit is about choice: "Thou mayest choose for thyself, for *it is given unto thee*" (Moses 3:17; emphasis added). The process for that choice was intimate, intricate, God-given, and fully comprehended by both Adam and Eve. It was not easy, quick, or impulsive; a wealth of learning and growth preceded it (see Chapter 8, Did Eve Know). The choice to partake of "the tree of knowledge of good and evil" (Genesis 2:9) also carried heavy eternal consequences and opportunities, not just for Adam and Eve but also for every generation to follow. The Fall had to occur within preordained laws established in the councils of heaven and by individuals specifically chosen by God. Their choice could not be the least bit self-motivated, for all mankind depended on that choice. God said in accordance with His perfect tutelage, "Behold these thy brethren; they are the workmanship of mine own hands, and I gave unto them their knowledge, in the day I created them" (Moses 7:32). Without clear and concise instructions, it was impossible to choose what actions they should take. They were well instructed of the Father. "And God said unto [Adam and Eve], be fruitful, and multiply, and replenish the earth, and subdue it" (Genesis 1:28). Both obediently partook "that men might be" (2 Nephi 2:25). It was by their obedience that they exhibited the perfect protocol for mankind in choosing between good and evil. Elder Bruce C. Hafen said: "The experience of Adam and Eve is an ideal prototype for our own mortal experience. Their story is our story."[2] Robert L. Millet wrote, "The story of Eden, in fact, [is] a light that reveals the path all must travel to return to the divine presence."[3]

TWO TREES

Therefore, God placed two trees in Eden. To understand the choice that lay before our first parents, we must first understand the two trees planted in Eden by God. Both trees were needed in Eden because they both represented essential doctrine. In fact, agency in Eden was not fully activated until God placed them in the Garden. One was the *tree of life,* which Adam and Eve *partook of liberally;* the other was the tree of knowledge of good and evil. Yes, Adam and Eve partook of the tree of life along with all of the other trees in the garden. "And the Gods commanded the man, saying: Of every tree of the garden thou mayest freely eat, But of the tree of knowledge of good and evil, thou shalt not eat of it" (Abraham 5:12–13). The tree of life represented immortality and, specifically, being in the presence of God, which was enjoyed while in the garden. The tree of life also represented Christ as central to the immortal plan. It was not until the Fall of Adam that "they were cut off from the presence of the Lord" (2 Nephi 9:6) and the tree of life.

Returning to His presence is done only through Christ's "grace, and his great condescensions unto the children of men" (Jacob 4:7). Robert L. Millet wrote:

> Jesus Christ is the central figure in the doctrine of The Church of Jesus Christ of Latter-day Saints. The Prophet Joseph Smith explained that 'the fundamental principles of our religion are the testimony of the Apostles and Prophets, concerning Jesus Christ, that He died, was buried, and rose again the third day, and ascended into heaven; and

all other things which pertain to our religion are only appendages to it.' Latter-day Saints believe that complete salvation is possible only through the life, death, resurrection, doctrines, and ordinances of Jesus Christ and in *no other way*.[4]

The tree of life, which represents the Atonement of Jesus Christ, also represents our promised return from a mortal probation.

In Eden, Adam and Eve were His *immortal children but not yet* as God the Father. They had physical bodies without the impurities of mortal blood. As the children of immortality, they were pure, perfect, and innocent, both physically and spiritually. There was no need for salvation at that time because there was no sin or imperfection in them. To be in the presence of God and be *as God* the Father, to gain a perfect wisdom in all things, however, required the gauntlet of mortality—they would need to partake of the *tree of knowledge of good and evil*. That was the plan.

The tree of knowledge of good and evil came from God. It represented independent choice and accountability, allowing Adam and Eve to know good from evil, as did the Father, bringing forth a full maturation for godhood. This tree, however, also represented mortality, death, trials, laws, and a need for salvation. The full plan of happiness was based on the requirements of *both* trees, but only one could be enjoyed at a time, because mortality and immortality are two vastly different worlds. This tree of life meant being in the presence of God; the tree of knowledge meant being sent forth into a mortal world while being forbidden to enter into God's presence for a time. The presence of the two opposing trees invoked a pivotal choice for Adam and Eve.

Because Adam and Eve desired advancement into godhood, the tree of knowledge was given that they might know how to act in the laws of godhood. The knowledge of good was given by commandments to school them, that they might combat the ominous evil they would certainly face in a required mortal world, "Wherefore the law [commandments] was our schoolmaster to bring us unto Christ, that we might be justified by faith" (Galatians 3:24; emphasis added). The words *commandments* and *knowledge* are synonymous terms. God lovingly armed Adam and Eve with the knowledge that, through commandments, Christ would bring them safely back into His presence as gods. There is no happenstance here; Heavenly Father meticulously prepared them for their crucial journey. "Wherefore, he gave commandments unto men, they having first transgressed the first commandments" (Alma 12:31). The tree of knowledge of good and evil is about the applicable laws of godhood. By faith, were they then sent forth into a mortal world to act upon those commandments and laws in the face of evil. To facilitate Adam's fall, "God gave unto them commandments, after having made known unto them the plan of redemption, that they should not do evil, the penalty thereof being a second death, which was an everlasting death as to things pertaining unto righteousness; for on such the plan of redemption could have no power, for the works of justice could not be destroyed, according to the supreme goodness of God" (Alma 12:32).

Satan waited at the tree to provoke Adam and Eve before they entered into mortality. His plan was to sway them from the knowledge God had given them and to carefully lead them away from Christ and into diverse paths to destroy their agency—their knowledge of truth—just as he had attempted in the premortal world (Moses 4:3); for without the knowledge of truth (commandments), we cannot be agents unto ourselves.

It is in opposition to evil that the good is comprehended. Alonzo L. Gaskill writes,

> The pairing of these opposites, good and evil, is what is known as *merism*—a literary figure by which totality is expressed by the first and last in a series or by opposites. It is a Hebrew idiom meaning *all things*. Thus, the fruit of the tree of knowledge of good and evil represents the totality of the mortal experience: agency, trials, faith, knowledge, and experience. Minus the knowledge of good and evil, the plan would be void and mankind would be incapable of the growth requisite for exaltation. This is not to imply that we need to sin in order to become like God. Rather, we need the opportunity and enticement of sin, that we can overcome it and master the flesh, thereby becoming like God.[5]

After choosing the tree of knowledge of good and evil, Adam was sent out from the garden. "Wherefore, I, the Lord God, caused that he should be cast out from the Garden of Eden, from my presence, because of his transgression" (D&C 29:41). The words *cast out,* as noted in this scripture, seem harsh and feel like punishment, but Alma speaks of the fall in much gentler terms. "The Lord God sent our first parents forth from the garden of Eden, to till the ground, from whence they were taken—yea, he drew out the man" (Alma 42:2). Alma gives the impression that their exit is less of a punishment and more of a chosen journey, which God had sent them on, to fulfill all that they had purposed to do. It was, therefore, by their choosing that they were sent forth.

THE CHOICE

The choice given in Eden was this: If God gave the tree of knowledge of good and evil unto man in order that he should act for himself, should man then partake of the tree of knowledge of good and evil and thus become mortal and die? Mortality is where we make our biggest choices. It is where we find our biggest opposition. It is where we are enticed and where we experience the sweet and the bitter. The tree of knowledge of good and evil, then, becomes a door whereby man may freely act for himself. But was opening that door a command, or was the mortal world forbidden? If I were Eve, would I have walked through that door? Why or why not? It was given to Eve to act for herself. Can we know and understand the complexity of Eve's thoughts as she was faced with such a consequential decision? It seems that she pondered these things, because she chose mortal death—that man might be and that man might therefore transcend to a greater state of perfection, "that by his natural death he might be raised in immortality unto eternal life, even as many as would believe" (D&C 29:43). This is the plan that Adam and Eve chose for us, "that [we] might have joy" (2 Nephi 2:25).

In the book of Abraham, the scenario for mortality seems to be a planned arrangement: "And the Gods said: We will bless them. And the Gods said: We will *cause them* to be fruitful and multiply" (Abraham 4:28; emphasis added). The Gods caused that man should act intelligently by providing for them the tree of knowledge of good and evil. Therefore, it became evident to Eve, the mother of all living, that the command to be fruitful could be accomplished only in a mortal world; there was no other way. Eve understood that both trees were required to complete the plan of happiness. Elder Bruce C. Hafen writes, "Neither tree—neither force—is sufficient unless completed by the other."[6] It is only through the tree of knowledge of good and evil that we fully comprehend the tree of life. A Fall was needed.

Adam and Eve, in their immortal state, had been obedient up to the point that they were given a new door to open. They were offered a choice for mortality as "the Lord God planted the tree of life also in the midst of the garden, and also the tree of knowledge of good and evil" (Moses 3:9). "Wherefore, the Lord God gave unto man that he should act for himself" (2 Nephi 2:16). However, man cannot act for himself unless he is sufficiently instructed. Therefore, God forbade Adam of partaking, "lest [he] die" (Moses 4:9; see also 3:17), thus giving Adam a thumbnail sketch as to what he should expect if he should partake of the tree of knowledge of good and evil.

While yet immortal, they were given other godly promises before entering into mortality. Our first parents were promised posterity and that they would "be fruitful, and multiply, and replenish the earth" (Genesis 9:1). Also, in reference to the world or even worldliness, they were promised godhood with the command to "subdue it: and have dominion over . . . every living thing" (Genesis 1:28; see also Moses 2:28 and Abraham 4:28). Most important was the promise of salvation by the *mortal blood* of Jesus Christ should they partake: "There is *no other way* or means whereby man can be saved, only in and through Christ" (Alma 38:9; emphasis added; see also Mosiah 3:17; Helaman 5:9).

If Eve had not partaken, they would have had no challenges, no sin, and no joy. "And they would have no children; wherefore they would have remained in a state of innocence, having no joy, for they knew no misery; *doing no good, for they knew no sin*" (2 Nephi 2:23; emphasis added). You and I would not be here. In that light, there would perhaps have been more condemnation in Adam and Eve *not* partaking of the tree of knowledge of good and evil than in partaking of it; for in not partaking, there would be no godly advancement for them or for us. The risks are clearly spelled out in both choices.

They would *act* on the choices presented: live in Eden for all eternity in innocent confinement or progress through mortal trials and accountability toward the thrones of godhood.

The words "choose for thyself, for it is given unto thee" (Moses 3:17) indicate that for Adam and Eve, there was no wrong choice; it was entirely up to them whether to choose an immortal life or a mortal life. It had to be a *free will choice*; if the effects of that choice had not been clearly stated it could not have been a choice based on their God-given knowledge and agency (see Moses 7:32).

Jeffrey R. Holland said, "They were willing to transgress *knowingly and consciously* (the only way they could "fall" into the consequences of mortality, inasmuch as Elohim could not force innocent parties out of the garden and still be a just God) only because they had a *full knowledge* of the plan of salvation, which would provide for them a way back from their struggle with death and hell."[7] In essence, Adam and Eve were expected to become mortal and thus become fruitful as God had commanded them, but they were forbidden to be acted upon or influenced by the powers of Satan's lies and deceit. They were to choose good in the midst of evil—in the midst of mortality.

Adam and Eve had to act. The word *act* in this case is to keep God's commandments despite opposition, while to be *acted upon* refers to the temptations of Satan (see 2 Nephi 2:13–26). Therefore, they transgressed the comfortable law of immortality and became subject to mortality—a fragile condition of opposition, trial, and death. They became subject to the will of the devil in that they became subject to being acted upon by Satan. "And it *must needs be* that the devil should tempt the children of men, or they could not be *agents unto themselves*; for if they never should have bitter they could not know the sweet" (D&C 29:39).

"Wherefore, it came to pass that the devil tempted Adam, and he partook of the forbidden fruit and transgressed the commandment, wherein he became subject to the will of the devil, because he yielded unto temptation" (D&C 29:40). Though "transgressed the commandment" and "yielded unto temptation" sounds like a negative choice, the Lord points out that "it must needs be," and that it was clearly the only way they could become "agents unto themselves" (D&C 29:39) and know the bitter from the sweet. It was the only way they could become as the Gods.

President Brigham Young explained the need for bitter and sweet or good from evil:

> I will tell you a truth; it is God's truth; it is eternal truth: neither you nor I would ever be prepared to be crowned in the celestial kingdom of our Father and our God, without devils in this world. Do you know that the Saints never could be prepared to receive the glory that is in reserve for them, without devils to help them to get it? . . . Refer to the Book of Mormon, and you will find that Nephi and others taught that we actually need evil, in order to make this a state of probation. We must know the evil in order to know the good. There must need be an opposition in all things.[8]

That opposition was good and evil, bitter and sweet, darkness and light. Only through the tree of knowledge of good and evil would they experience this needed opposition.

OUT OF THE DARK

It was needful that Adam and Eve should experience the darkness to know the light. In their immortal life in Eden, the pure light of the Father and the Firstborn surrounded them, for "no unclean thing can enter into his kingdom" (3 Nephi 27:19). They, though taught by the Father, were surrounded by His pervasive light *without a comparative darkness to learn by.* "He is . . . a light that is endless, that can never be darkened" (Mosiah 16:9). This permeating light while in the presence of God is similar to the light that will rest upon the earth after it attains its celestial glory. We are also promised that this celestial light, both physical and spiritual, will descend upon the earth and rest upon the New Jerusalem. "And I John saw the holy city, New Jerusalem, coming down from God out of heaven. . . . And the city had *no need of the sun, neither of the moon, to shine in it*: for the glory of God did lighten it, and the Lamb is the light thereof" (Revelation 21:2, 23; emphasis added).

Only in mortality would they experience the darkness, in which they must now seek the light. After the Fall, their need was to transition from darkness back into the light: "For God, who commanded the *light to shine out of darkness,* hath shined in our hearts, to give the light of knowledge of the glory of God in the face of Jesus Christ" (2 Corinthians 4:6; emphasis added). A new awareness is given "to open their eyes, and to turn them from darkness to light, and from the power of Satan unto God" (Acts 26:18). We can also see this comparison in the Book of Mormon, as scriptures are prophesied to come into the light and out of the darkness: "And blessed be he that shall bring this thing to light; for it shall be brought out of darkness unto light, according to the word of God; yea, it shall be brought out of the earth, and it shall shine forth out of darkness, and come unto the knowledge of the people; and it shall be done by the power of God" (Mormon 8:16).

We find similarities in the comparing of good and evil and light and dark. Regarding the tree of knowledge of good and evil, Satan tells Eve, "For God doth know that in the day ye eat thereof, then your eyes shall be opened, and ye shall *be as gods,* knowing good and evil" (Genesis 3:5; emphasis added). Eve had to be tempted by Satan to know good from evil. She had to experience a comparative darkness to comprehend the light, a comparative evil to comprehend the good, and a comparative lie to understand truth. Until then, truth and light did not fully exist in her mind as truth and light. Wherefore, upon being beguiled by Satan, Eve might well have said, as did Moses, "Where is thy *glory* [light], that I should worship thee?" (Moses 1:13; emphasis added). It was through the serpent that Eve first recognized a lie, and a darkness; it wasn't until then that Eve was able to make a comprehensive choice between the two.

A TRANSGRESSION WAS NEEDED

A transgression was needed; a choice had to be made. Between the fruit of the two trees in the Garden of Eden (one offering immortality in God's presence and the other offering a door into mortality outside His presence), only one choice could be made at a time. Therefore, a transgression was needed to experience the "second estate" (Abraham 3:26) known as mortality. The fruit of these two trees could not bring forth their individual experience at the same time; the immortal and mortal estates had to be partaken of in *sequential* steps.

The word *transgression*, as we generally understand it, means to trespass, go beyond the bounds, break the law, or violate a command. The meaning of *transgress,* however, changed for me slightly as I broke the word down into two parts: *trans*, meaning across, beyond, or on the opposite side; and *gress,* meaning to step. The word base, *gression*, can indicate a backward movement, as in *regression,* or a forceful movement, such as in *aggression.* To me, it represented a forward movement such as in the word *progression.* Though Adam and Eve's transgression was seemingly a backward movement, when they became mortal and subject to death, it was also a forward movement required for godhood. Elder Orson F. Whitney said, "The Fall had a two-fold direction, downward, yet forward."[9]

According to the book of Abraham, mortality was a positive choice: "And they who keep their first estate shall be added upon; and they who keep not their first estate shall not have glory in the same kingdom with those who keep their first estate; and they who keep their second estate shall have glory added upon their heads for ever and ever" (Abraham 3:26). The promise of mortality is therefore reassuring. If we follow the example of our first parents and endure it well, we will have that promised immortal glory added upon our heads for ever and ever.

After being tempted of the devil, both Adam and Eve wisely chose the portal into mortality. We are reminded in Alma 12:31 that mortality is a step toward godhood. "Wherefore, *he gave commandments unto men*, they having first transgressed the first commandments as to things which were temporal [mortal], and *becoming as gods,* knowing good from evil, *placing themselves in a state to act,* or *being placed in a state to act* according to their wills and pleasures, whether to do evil or to do good" (Alma 12:31; emphasis added). This act does not sound like they were in defiance of God or that they acted out of ignorance. Nor does it sound like an easy choice. We can also safely conclude that "becoming as gods" indicates that *Adam and Eve did, in fact, choose the good over the evil.* Accordingly, it seems that by transgressing from immortality into mortality or from the tree of life to the tree of knowledge of good and evil, they also gained the advantage of "becoming as gods."

GOD'S WILL

This act of transgression was made available to Adam and Eve. In God's command to be fruitful and replenish the earth, we read, "by the power of his word man came upon the face of the earth, which was created by the power of his word" (Jacob 4:9). Joseph Smith said, "Adam *did not commit sin* in eating the fruits, for God had decreed that he should eat and fall."[10] Joseph also testified that "[God] foreordained the fall of man, but all-merciful as He is, He foreordained at the same time a plan of redemption for all mankind."[11] It was by God's *will* that man partook of the tree of knowledge of good and evil and fell, for Alma says, "It was appointed unto men that they must die" (Alma 12:27). "And thus did I, the Lord God, appoint unto man the days of his probation—that by his natural death he might be raised in immortality unto eternal life, even as many as would believe" (D&C 29:43). We also read, "Eve . . . was glad, saying: Were it not for our transgression we never should have had seed, and never should have known good and evil, and the joy of our redemption, and the eternal life which God giveth unto all the obedient" (Moses 5:11).

LEST YE SHALL DIE

"Lest ye shall die" was the warning. By her faith, Eve willingly ushered in the need for and the power of the Atonement, even the full plan of happiness. Their willingness to sacrifice eternal bliss for death, "lest ye shall die" (Genesis 3:3), in order to obey the will of the Lord to "be fruitful and replenish the earth" (Genesis 9:1) compares only to the sacrifice of the Savior, "who so loved the world that he gave his own life, that as many as would believe might become the sons of God" (D&C 34:3). According to God's command, "Adam fell that men might be; and men are, that [through Christ] they might have joy" (2 Nephi 2:25). "Greater love hath no man than this, that a man lay down his life for his friends" (John 15:13). In this perfect plan, Adam, Eve, and

Christ willingly chose to die that men might be, that men might have joy.

WE TOO

We too have willingly trespassed into mortality to learn to keep the laws of God, that we might know the good from the evil. Remember, to act in accordance with the commandments of God is key to the power of creation; all else is chaos. By keeping the ordinances of God, the Word of Wisdom, the law of tithing, the Ten Commandments, as well as His other commandments, we too can become as the gods, by applying the laws of God in opposition to the nature of man or the nature of evil. To act and not be acted upon is the full power of creation and becomes the fullness of joy. It is in the context of obedience that "men are, that they might have joy" (2 Nephi 2:25).

CHAPTER 2
"THOU SHALT NOT EAT OF IT"
—ABRAHAM 5:13 (12–13)

If the tree of knowledge of good and evil was required,
how then was it also forbidden?

Was there a double standard in the partaking of the fruit— was it forbidden or commanded? President Joseph Fielding Smith expressed these ideas as follows:

> Why did Adam come here? Not subject to death when he was placed upon the earth, there had to come a change in his body through the partaking of this element— whatever you want to call it, fruit— that brought blood into his body; and blood became the life of the body instead of spirit. And blood has in it the seeds of death, some mortal element. Mortality was created through the eating of the forbidden fruit, *if you want to call it forbidden*, but I think the Lord has made it clear that *it was not forbidden*. He merely said to Adam, if you want to stay here [in the garden] this is the situation. If so, don't eat it.[12]

Here we see the word *forbidden* as more of an interpretive term. We will further examine his revealing insight.

Because Adam and Eve were commanded to be fruitful and replenish the earth, we have established that they were, in essence, also commanded to partake of the tree of knowledge of good and evil. Mortality was the command. Why then was it forbidden?

Sacrifice, trial, and temptation were the command. Though it was a command to replenish the earth by eating the fruit, hadn't it also been vehemently forbidden? "Remember that I forbid it," God said, "for in the day thou eatest thereof thou shalt surely die" (Moses 3:17; emphasis added). This was a fair and distinct warning that man would be shut out from the presence of God. He uses direct and stunning words of foreboding; the heart stops at the words *forbid* and *die*. Adam and Eve, no doubt, took these words to heart. Surely it would take a great deal of contemplation to consider crossing over such lines. Satan is quick to step up and provide a contemplative consideration for entering into his forbidden world. His job of persuasion, however, would not be easy. Though seemingly controversial, God's command to not partake of the tree of knowledge of good and evil held no double standard. It was Satan who tempted Adam and Eve to indulge in forbidden paths. Christ, on the other hand, would pave their way back into the presence of God. These are evident in the scriptures, but the language of the scriptures is often presented metaphorically. We can best perceive the depth of these metaphors by the Spirit.

SPEAKING METAPHORICALLY

Symbols, parables, and metaphors are often used in the scriptures. To comprehend the use of these metaphors, "you must study it out in your mind; then you must ask me if it be right" (D&C 9:8). Metaphors are used in the scriptures to illuminate the intended spiritual concepts of a command or teaching. Though initially confusing, they cause our minds to search and ponder the deeper spiritual truths and meanings within a teaching, as they also help us to visualize ourselves within those concepts. The Ten Commandments are literal in the letter of the Mosaic Law, but symbols, parables, and metaphors prompt a spiritual understanding of the law, inducing a more personal evaluation of their meaning.

Jesus often spoke in parables. "Therefore speak I to them in parables: because they seeing [literal law] see not; and hearing [literal law] they hear not, neither do they understand" (Matthew 13:13). Paul tells us, "So then faith cometh by hearing [spiritual concepts], and hearing by the word of God [under the influence of the Holy Ghost]" (Romans 10:17; emphasis added). It is through the Spirit that we receive His word and comprehend the meaning. "Not that we are sufficient of ourselves; but our sufficiency is of God" (2 Corinthians 3:5). It was only through the Spirit that Peter received a witness of Christ. Of Peter, Jesus asked, "But whom say ye that I am? . . . Thou art the Christ, the Son of the living God. . . . Blessed art thou . . . for flesh and blood hath not revealed it unto thee, but my Father which is in heaven" (Matthew 16:15–17).

Though the fruit was forbidden—it is by prayer and faith that we understand the deeper meanings of the following metaphors used in the partaking for Fruit, Eat, and Forbidden.

FRUIT: CHOICE AND WORKS

Understanding the fruit on the two trees, metaphorically, helps us to better understand the choice that stood before Eve in the garden. The fruit on the two trees in Eden was both physical and spiritual (see chapter 32, Tree of Life). For instance, it is universally understood that fruit is a product of something; in literal terms it is an edible product of a tree or a vine. In the scriptures, however, the word *fruit* often metaphorically refers to the product of one's actions. "Wherefore by their fruits ye shall know them. [Conclusively,] not everyone that saith unto me, Lord, Lord, shall enter into the kingdom of heaven; but he that doeth the will of my Father which is in heaven" (Matthew 7:20–21; emphasis added).

The fruit of choice and good works is also represented in Lehi's dream as the tree of life (or the fruit thereof), which represents the love of God and is referred to as the greatest of all the gifts of God (see 1 Nephi 8; 11:21–22, 25; 15:36). Lehi admonished his family, saying "with a loud voice that they should come unto me, and partake of the fruit, which was desirable above all other fruit" (1 Nephi 8:15). Lehi eagerly attempted to persuade his family to choose the love of God, which is Christ, and follow in His good works.

We also find that the word *fruit* is the base to the word *fruitful*, as in "be fruitful and replenish the earth" (Genesis 9:1). The word *fruitful* is the adjective equivalent of the word *fruit*. The seeded fruit, by its nature, becomes prolific (to replenish the earth). We too can plant good or evil seeds in the hearts of those around us. "You can count the seeds in an apple, but you can't count the apples in a seed. When you teach, you never know how many lives you will influence . . . you are teaching for eternity."[13] Our actions are naturally prolific as we have a pervasive effect upon others for good or evil, intended or not. If we are not careful, negative choices can become cancerous in their negative productivity. Fruit, or our actions, therefore produces either a productive (eternal) or nonproductive (temporal) consequence.

Good works are a product of good choices. We read in Matthew that "the tree is known by his fruit" (Matthew 12:33; emphasis added)—meaning a man is known by his works. To illustrate, "Even so every good tree [man or woman] bringeth forth good fruit [works]; but a corrupt tree bringeth forth evil fruit" (3 Nephi 14:17).

In the scriptures we see other examples of fruit as the Lord demonstrates consequences upon the house of Israel due to their idolatry, such as with the fig tree: "Master, behold, the fig tree which thou cursedst is withered away" (Mark 11:21). Elder James E. Talmage tells us, "The leafy, fruitless tree was a symbol of Judaism."[14] Because of the idolatrous choices Israel often made, the metaphoric representation of the fig tree demonstrates spiritual consequence. "Trees whose fruit withereth, without fruit, twice dead" (Jude 1:12) represents the second death, which is spiritual death. These comparative teachings using fruit persuade us to contemplate our own works and the result of those consequences or blessings. As we make good choices, we are also partaking of the good fruit that leads us back to the tree of life.

Immortal and mortal are not the same as eternal and temporal. Adam and Eve, in partaking of the fruit, changed their realm of existence to mortal, but obediently clung to their eternal marriage covenants in Eden to be fruitful and replenish the earth. Though they were now in the world, they were still not "of the world" (see 1 John 2:15–16). While yet in a temporal world they continued to make eternal choices, that they might be redeemed, through faith in Jesus Christ.

In conclusion, the word *fruit* is synonymous with a product of choice. Thus by commandment, in choosing the fruit of the tree of knowledge of good and evil, Adam and Eve also became fruitful, to replenish the earth as God commanded them.

EAT: COVENANT KEEPING

The word eat is another metaphor with deeper meaning in the scriptures than first appears. While the meaning of the word *fruit* can become more comprehensive to us as we read scriptures, we should also more closely examine the word *eat*, as in "Thou shalt not eat of it" (Genesis 2:17). The word *eat* carries a great deal of biblical significance. "And as they did eat, Jesus took bread, and blessed, and brake it, and gave to them, and said, Take, eat: this is my body" (Mark 14:22; emphasis added). In the scriptures, the word *eat* often represents covenant keeping. This is symbolized in the Last Supper: "This is my body which is given for you: this do in remembrance of me" (Luke 22:19 [19–20]). "I am the bread of life: he that cometh to me shall never hunger. And he that believeth on me shall never thirst" (John 6:35). "I am the living bread which came down from heaven: if any man eat of this bread, he shall live for ever: and the bread that I will give is my flesh, which I will give for the life of the world" (John 6:51). In the scriptures, the word *eat* represents accepting and internalizing Jesus Christ and all His teachings, and keeping all His covenants.

While Adam and Eve were expected to eat of the fruit, become mortal, and thus gain salvation through the blood of Christ, what were they not to eat? They were not to "eat, drink and be merry," having the attitude that "tomorrow we die; and it shall be well with us." They were not to commit "a little sin," "lie a little, take the advantage of one because of his words, [or] dig a pit for [their] neighbor" (2 Nephi 28:7–8). They were not to become of the world. These indulgences of Satan are scattered throughout the scriptures. They tempt us to commit worldly acts, to rationalize sin, and to internalize lustful idolatries that lead us away from Christ and into the hands of Satan. I believe Eve was commanded not to eat of the fruit of worldly indulgence, which Satan offered her at the tree of knowledge, for there was a spiritual death to consider. Adam and Eve, on the other hand, were given a command to eat of the Lord's flesh and blood and to remember Him above all else. This sacred covenant became symbolized in the partaking of the sacrificial lamb (see chapter 25, Coats of Skins), and again in the bread and wine: "And when he had given thanks, he brake [bread], and said, Take, eat: this is my body, which is broken for you: this do in remembrance of me" (1 Corinthians 11:24).

Similar to the word *eat*, consider these words: "Blessed are they who do hunger and thirst after righteousness" (Matthew 5:6; emphasis added). "He that cometh to me shall never hunger" (John 6:35; emphasis added). "Feast upon the words of Christ; for behold, the words of Christ will tell you all things what ye should do" (2 Nephi 32:3; emphasis added). "In the day ye eat thereof, then your eyes shall be opened" (Moses 4:11; emphasis added). Along with being sent out of God's presence, the forbidden portion of the fruit (see Moses 3:17) was the choice to follow after Satan in his temporal world. While the words *hunger* and *thirst* indicate a desire to seek after, the word *eat* is in reference to covenant making. Who we seek after and who we choose to covenant with is critical.

While Adam and Eve were still in the garden, God clearly stated what should and should not be eaten, or internalized, as covenants were made between Him and man. They were well prepared and instructed for mortality (see Moses 7:32); they were given specific commandments regarding how to return to God's presence. "This is the plan of salvation unto all men, through the blood of mine Only Begotten, who shall come in the meridian of time" (Moses 6:62). "Keep yourselves in the love of God, looking for the mercy of our Lord Jesus Christ unto eternal life" (Jude 1:21). So when they were told to not eat of the forbidden fruit, they were instructed to not become of the world. Their instructions were to become as gods through Christ, in a required mortal journey. Covenants with God are needed throughout our journey to keep us on the straight and narrow path back to God (see 2 Nephi 33:9). But as cherubim and a flaming sword was a guarded forbidding, those doors were *not* forever closed.

FORBIDDEN: CLOSED DOORS

Choosing the forbidden fruit, in the case of the tree of knowledge of good and evil, produced a mortal world, in which mortal man had become impure and was therefore forbidden from entering into God's immortal presence. This prompts us to rethink the meaning of the word forbidden. For it was by the partaking of the forbidden fruit that Eve was then forbidden from partaking of the fruit of the tree of life, when cherubim and a flaming sword were placed in the way to guard the tree. If Eve chose to partake of the fruit of one tree, then the fruit of the other tree became forbidden. There is a guarded forbidding between these two worlds. *Forbidden* then becomes synonymous with closed doors. Eve could not partake of immortal and mortal fruit at the same time. If she partook of one tree, the other was then forbidden. This conceptual view of fruit changes the perspective of Eden's notorious forbidden fruit (see D&C 29:40).

The word *forbidden* can be defined as any unclean thing that cannot enter into the kingdom of God. "And he set the porters at the gates [see chapter 33, Cherubim] of the house of the Lord, that none which was unclean in anything should enter in" (2 Chronicles 23:19; emphasis added). Though mortality is required and even commanded, mortals are forbidden from entering into God's presence because the mortal, impure body is suffused with blood, and "flesh and blood cannot inherit the kingdom of God" (1 Corinthians 15:50; emphasis added) (see chapter 26, Blood). This explains why the spirit can ascend to heaven while the body must remain in the earth until it is cleansed through the resurrection, at which time blood will no longer be the life of the body. It is impure because it is weak and temporal and will succumb to death. It is unclean because it is tainted by succumbing to Satan and his beguiling lies. Lies are perishable (temporal) because they are unsustainable. Only truth is eternal; only truth is pure. All that is of God is eternal; His promises are eternal. All that is of Satan must perish; his words, his lies are not sustainable in an immortal world.

Deceptions do not come from God. As Ether said, "thou art a

God of truth, and canst not lie" (Ether 3:12). It was Satan's bidding that led to the mortal lusts of the earth. As for the evil portion of the tree of knowledge of good and evil, which Satan presented to Eve and which he presents to all of us, "God hath said—Ye shall not eat of it, neither shall ye touch it, lest ye die" (Moses 4:9).

"Let no man say when he is tempted, I am tempted of God: for God cannot be tempted with evil, neither tempteth he any man: But every man is tempted, when he is drawn away of his own lust, and enticed" (James 1:13–14). Thus, it is not God that deceives man; rather it is through Satan and the lusts of man, that evil comes into play.

When Satan presented the evil in opposition to the good, Eve made her choice and partook that men might be. Adam and Eve were then sent out of God's presence and became mortal, or physically perishable. Thus, God "placed at the east of the Garden of Eden, cherubim and a flaming sword, which turned every way to keep the way of the tree of life" (Moses 4:31). As a result, Adam and Eve would be forbidden from entering immortality from mortality until after they had been washed clean through the mortal blood of Christ. President Joseph Fielding Smith defined the forbidden fruit and its application this way: "The 'forbidden' aspect was not in the partaking, but instead had reference to Adam and Eve's not being able to remain in the garden if they partook. This explanation suggests that the Lord wanted the Fall to occur."[15]

Elder Bruce R. McConkie expressed these ideas as follows: "We do not know the real meaning of the term forbidden fruit. We do know that Adam and Eve transgressed, literally meaning to step over, in systematic fashion, the law of continuance in the garden. They complied with the law which enabled them to become mortal beings." He added: "And this course of conduct is termed eating the forbidden fruit."[16] Vivian M. Adams summarized these concepts: "Of one thing we may be assured: to gain the fullness of either tree, Adam and Eve could not stay in the garden; they must partake of the one to gain the fullness of the other. The two trees together comprised the eternal plan of salvation."[17] The partaking of the fruit of the tree of knowledge of good and evil was, therefore, a transgression rather than a sin.

OPENING A FORBIDDEN DOOR

To better understand the forbidden fruit we need to perceive Christ's mortal mission. Even Jesus Christ, as a mortal, did not ascend to the Father until all was accomplished and paid for. To Mary at the tomb, "Jesus saith unto her, Touch me not; for I am not yet ascended to my Father: but go to my brethren, and say unto them, I ascend unto my Father, and your Father; and to my God, and your God" (John 20:17). In perfect victory over mortal death and sin, the Savior ascended to the Father to enter into His presence as a resurrected, perfect, and immortal being. This insight helps to clarify the words of Christ when He said, "These things I have spoken unto you, that in me ye might have peace. In the world ye shall have tribulation: but be of good cheer; I have overcome the world" (John 16:33; emphasis added). Christ represents the tree of life, in that He opens the way for us to return to God's presence—gaining that prized immortality and eternal life with the Father (see Moses 1:39).

Elder McConkie stated, "When the veil of the temple was 'rent in twain' at the death of Jesus Christ (Matthew 27:51), it was a dramatic symbol that the Savior, the Great High Priest, had passed through the veil of death and would shortly enter into the presence of God."[18] Elder McConkie wrote further that "in addition to the Savior entering the presence of the Father, the Holy of Holies is now open to all, and all, through the atoning blood of the Lamb, can now enter into the highest and holiest of all places—that kingdom where eternal life is found. . . . The Apostle Paul taught that just as the torn veil of the temple allowed symbolic entrance into the Holy of Holies, it is the torn flesh of Jesus Christ that opens the way for us to enter into the presence of the Father (Hebrews 10:12, 19–20)."[19]

Promises kept, the forbidden doors are now open. We too can enter, "Then said Jesus unto his disciples, If any man will come after me, let him deny himself [of the world], and take up his cross [covenants], and follow me" (Matthew 16:24). "Be of good cheer, for I will lead you along. The kingdom is yours and the blessings thereof are yours, and the riches of eternity are yours" (D&C 78:18). In this, Adam and Eve accomplished all that they had proposed to do in the partaking of the forbidden fruit.

CHAPTER 3

DOES SATAN REPRESENT THE TREE OF GOOD AND EVIL?

Eve perceived the lies of Satan.

When Eve encountered Satan at the tree of knowledge of good and evil, his ploy was to deceive her. Who was Eve that she should be called upon to open up the realm of mortality unto the children of God? Did God not realize the danger here? If Satan had succeeded in his evil plot, then "our spirits must have become like unto him, . . . to remain with the father of lies, in misery, like unto himself" (2 Nephi 9:8, 9).

This was a critical responsibility for Eve to be placed in. Had she not been perceived as weak and disobedient? Did God not understand the risk involved? Did God make a mistake in calling Eve to be the mother of all living? (Genesis 3:20) The answer is simple: God does not make mistakes. The *Babylonian Talmud* "teaches that the Holy one, blessed be He, endowed the woman with more understanding than the man."[20] Brigham Young would agree, "Women are more ready to do and love the right than men."[21] He insisted, for women are "altogether of a finer nature" with "strong moral inclinations."[22]

"So came Eve," wrote J. Reuben Clark, "without whom the whole creation of the world and all that was in the world would

29

have been in vain and the purposes of God have come to naught."[23] In the words of President Gordon B. Hinckley, God created Eve as "the crowning of His glorious work," even "His masterpiece."[24] In this it would seem that Satan was seriously outclassed.

Preordained, Eve was set at the forefront of mortality. It was she who was required to discern the command, "But of the tree of knowledge of good and evil, thou shalt not eat of it, neverthe-less, thou mayest choose for thyself, for it is given unto thee; but, remember that I forbid it, for in the day thou eatest thereof thou shalt surely die" (Moses 3:17).

What of Satan? Did he represent the "tree of knowledge of good and evil" as Christ represented the "tree of life"? Satan set claim upon the tree of knowledge of good and evil as soon as he tried to sell it to Adam and Eve as his own. Though not mortal himself, Satan claimed godhood to the temporal world and to the mortal souls who inhabit it. Likening himself to God, he deceitfully became the opposite of all that is godly. His perverted truths became a snare to deceive and lead the children of God away from the Light of Christ.

In this chapter we will consider five of Satan's persuasive lies as he presented himself to Eve, even as the Christ (see Colossians 1:15). Rodney Turner speaks of Christ as "being the first-born of the human family, Jesus is rightly regarded by Latter-day Saints as our Elder Brother."[25] Satan also presents himself as the "god of this world" (2 Corinthians 4:4), and then proceeds to tell Eve, "Ye shall not surely die" (Genesis 3:4; Moses 4:10). In addition, he presump-tuously proclaims, "ye shall be as gods" (Moses 4:11), and that he (Satan) has "priesthoods" (Abraham 1:27). By examining these lies, we can better understand Eve's wisdom in the partaking.

As Eve evaluated each of Satan's subtle lies in contrast to God's commands, she was able to make her choice, for the Father had told her, "Thou mayest choose for thyself, for it is *given unto thee*" (Moses 3:17; emphasis added). Thus by *consent*, and after consid-eration, she accepts the fruit of the tree of knowledge, which God placed before her and Adam in the garden. "And when the woman saw that the tree was good for food, and that it was pleasant to the eyes, and a tree to be desired to make one wise, she took of the fruit thereof, and did eat, and gave also unto her husband with her; and he did eat" (Genesis 3:6). This verse does not allude to an instantaneous decision on Eve's part: "*when* the woman *saw*." Here the word *saw* depicts an in-depth consideration such as "your eyes shall be opened, and ye shall be as gods, knowing good and evil" (Moses 4:11). Often the word *saw* in the scriptures depicts a revelatory experience, such as when Lehi saw the tree of life (see 1 Nephi 11:3) and when Daniel "saw in a vision" (Daniel 8:2). Ezekiel says, "I saw, even according to the vision" (Ezekiel 43:3). Multiple revelatory examples of the word *saw* in the scriptures are easy to find. Eve partook of the fruit, not because of Satan's deceptive ploy, but because she saw her prophetic role in that choice. Elder Dallin H. Oaks declared, "It was Eve who first transgressed the limits of Eden in order to initiate the conditions of mortality. [As] Latter-day Saints, we celebrate Eve's act and honor her wisdom and courage in the great episode called the Fall."[26]

Satan aggressively targeted Eve, "wherefore he sought to destroy the world" (Moses 4:6). Why would he target the woman? "And when the dragon saw that he was cast unto the earth, he persecuted the woman which brought forth the man *child* [Christ]" (Revelation 12:13, emphasis added; see also chapter 5, Enmity). As the mother of all living, she perceived the lies of Satan as he desperately attempted to beguile her away from the Promised Messiah.

I AM ALSO A SON OF GOD

Among Satan's deceptive lies, he profanely claimed to be the Christ. To Eve and her children, Satan proclaimed his innocence by professing "I am also a son of God" (Moses 5:13–14, 28). According to *Tales of the Prophets,* "Eve did not recognize Satan when he approached her in Eden; she asked 'Who are you?' To which Satan replied, 'He created me, as He created you two, with his own hand and breathed his breath into me'—which is tantamount to saying, 'I am your brother.'"[27]

As the Firstborn of the Father, Jesus was Lucifer's older brother (see Colossians 1:15; D&C 93:21). "Satan was the spiritual offspring of Deity. He was a spiritual brother to the Chosen, the one whom we have come to know as the Savior, the Lord Jesus Christ."[28] As Lucifer desired to usurp his elder brother's birthright, according to Latter-day Saint doctrine, he proclaimed himself as that brother. Satan knew that "Jesus, as man's *elder brother* in the spirit life, was appointed to be man's God, and . . . in giving him the divine endowments that lead ultimately to eternal life, or glory."[29]

We continue to find Jesus thus characterized as an elder brother when we read the words of President Joseph F. Smith: "He [Jesus] declared that all power had been given unto Him, and He sits upon the right hand of the Almighty, and is our Mediator, our *Elder Brother*, and we must follow Him and *nobody else*."[30] In this, Satan would feign claim Christ's birthright as his own.

Jesus Himself uses this specific title: "Inasmuch as ye have done it unto one of the least of these *my brethren,* ye have done it unto me" (Matthew 25:40: emphasis added). In Mark 3:34, He says, "Behold my mother and my *brethren!*" (emphasis added). And in John 20:17, He says, "Go to *my brethren,* and say unto them, I ascend unto *my Father, and your Father*, to my God, and your God" (emphasis added).

Satan's claim of being the Christ was not uncharacteristic of him, given his statement to Moses: "I am the Only Begotten, worship me" (Moses 1:19). We find that Satan's claim as the Christ goes back to premortal life. "Satan . . . is the same which was from the beginning, and he came before me [the Father], saying—Behold, here am I, send me, *I will be thy son* [to us, I will be thy brother]. I will redeem all mankind, that one soul shall not be lost, and surely I will do it; wherefore give me thine honor" (Moses 4:1; emphasis added).

Even as a serpent, Satan claims the image of Christ. Alonzo L. Gaskill states,

> The Hebrew word translated as 'serpent' in the Genesis account is related to the Hebrew word for 'luminous' or 'shining.' Thus, some have suggested that the Genesis account should not read 'serpent' but rather 'angel of light.' In addition, it is believed that prior to the Fall the serpent was a symbol or type of Christ—hence its use in Numbers 21:8, Alma 33:19–20, and Helaman 8:13-15. Thus, associating the serpent with the devil would simply suggest that in Eden, Lucifer was seeking to usurp the role of Christ by appearing to Adam and Eve as an angel of light (see 2 Nephi 9:9).[31]

The phrase *angel of light* is also used in Doctrine and Covenants 128:20 and 129:8, as well as 2 Corinthians 11:14. Alonzo Gaskill explains, "The sin is not in wishing to become like God. The sin is in attempting to do so without God, in attempting to usurp His position over us, and in attempting to do so aside from the path He has laid out for us through entrance into covenants and obedience to commandments."[32]

The close proximity in which Satan mimicked Christ is truly deviant. By appearing and speaking to Eve as a serpent, Satan craftily claims the symbol, shadow, and type of Christ. This symbol is typified by Moses, who used a brass serpent as the symbol of Christ: "And Moses made a serpent of brass, and put it upon a pole, and it came to pass, that if a serpent had bitten any man, when he beheld the serpent of brass, he lived" (Numbers 21:9). This shows the opposition between the representation of a poisonous serpent that deceives and destroys and a serpent of light and truth that heals and saves. For us it becomes a matter of choice as to what and whom we seek.

The serpent played another role in Moses's time, when Moses was commanded to go to Pharaoh and show forth God's power and authority. "Aaron cast down his rod before Pharaoh, and before his servants, and it became a serpent. . . . For they cast down every man his rod, and they became serpents: but Aaron's *rod* swallowed up their *rods*" (Exodus 7:10, 12; emphasis added). The false serpents could not stand up to the true serpent, or power of God, which is Christ.

By mimicking both the rod and the serpent (priesthood of God; see Exodus 17:9, "rod of God in mine hand"), Satan's design was to obtain all Christ's power, just as he had demanded of the Father (see Moses 4:1). In all of Satan's deceptions before Eve, she comparatively viewed him as fraudulent. Continuing in faith, "Adam and Eve, his wife, called upon the name of the Lord" (Moses 5:4) seeking His guidance in all things.

"YE SHALL NOT SURELY DIE"

Satan pitched yet another false claim to Eve in the garden: "ye shall not surely die" (Genesis 3:4; Moses 4:10). This conversation between Satan and Eve was introduced by Satan with a question:

"Yea, Hath God said—Ye shall not eat of every tree of the Garden? (And he spake by the mouth of the serpent)" (Moses 4:7). Eve responded as taught by the Father, "We may eat of the fruit of the trees of the garden; but of the fruit of the tree which thou beholdest in the midst of the garden, God hath said—Ye shall not eat of it, neither shall ye touch it, *lest ye die*" (Moses 4:8–9; emphasis added). Satan responded, "Ye shall not die, but ye shall be as God, knowing good and evil" (2 Nephi 2:18).

In the Book of Mormon we can better see what Satan was proposing to Eve. Satan's choice of words, however clever, seems to point to God as the liar, "Ye shall not surely die: For *God doth know* . . . ye shall be as gods" (Genesis 3:4–5; emphasis added). All the while, Satan persuasively pointed to himself as "the god of this world" (2 Corinthians 4:4). He would disannul all of God's words of truth and light to set himself up as our preferred god. "I am also a son of God . . . and they [the children of Adam and Eve] loved Satan more than God" (Moses 5:13).

In spite of Satan's claim, "Ye shall not die," he had to know of the two deaths in mortality: (1) physical death of the mortal body and (2) spiritual death or separation from God. Both are *sure* in mortality, and both are redeemed through Christ. The resurrection of the body is promised to all who receive a body of flesh and blood. The spirit of redemption must also be obtained through Christ by choosing the good over evil. Partaking of Satan's plan is forbidden, while partaking of Christ's atoning sacrifice is commanded. "And we will prove them herewith, to see if they will do all things whatsoever the Lord their God shall command them" (Abraham 3:25). Satan is the author of death and sin, but through Christ and the Atonement, the stains of mortality—including the two deaths of mortality—are removed. Satan's goal was never to exalt man but to use his power to captivate and bring man down, "for he seeketh that all men might be miserable like unto himself.

"YE SHALL BE AS GOD" AND "GOD OF THIS WORLD"

Again, Satan speaks a shrouded truth: "Ye shall be as God, knowing good and evil" (2 Nephi 2:18). In truth, the Gods had advanced through this same mortal path of choice. The Father is a resurrected and exalted being, having Himself passed through the gauntlet of mortality—a choice that is required to obtain immortality and eternal godhood. Surely, this example of the Father was a determining factor in Adam and Eve's decision to partake of the fruit of the tree of knowledge. It is true that we may become as gods: "Unto Adam also and to his wife did the Lord God make coats of skins, and clothed them. And the Lord God said, Behold, the man is become as *one of us,* to know good and evil" (Genesis 3:21–22; emphasis added).

Satan's words to Eve that "ye shall be as gods" (Moses 4:11), though borrowed from the Father, were self-inclined. As Satan plays his deceit upon man, he would have us believe that he is the giver of good gifts, not Christ. Truth becomes a lie as Satan wittingly sets himself up as our alternative god. For Satan, "ye shall be as gods" is specifically pointing to himself as "god of this world." According to Paul, Satan is "the god of this world" who "hath blinded the minds of them which believe not, lest the light of the glorious gospel of Christ, *who is the image of God,* should shine unto them" (2 Corinthians 4:4; emphasis added). Satan's entire purpose is to block the image of God and man's potential for godhood. As "the god of this world," Satan claims the image of God as he blatantly mimics Christ's power.

Satan's dark and introverted image becomes the god of those who will worship him, but he has no power to save us. Satan's power cannot exceed his own false claims. Satan's claim as the Savior is a deceptive mockery of truth, light, and salvation. We must answer Alma's question and choose which image we will bear before the world. "And now behold, I ask of you, my brethren of the church, have ye spiritually been born of God? Have ye received his image in your countenance? Have ye experienced this mighty change in your hearts?" (Alma 5:14). He gives all of us that opportunity if we will seek Him. All are invited; all can come follow Him (see 1 Nephi 8:6).

SATAN'S CLAIM TO THE PRIESTHOOD

Satan's powers and priesthoods in the premortal life were refuted when "Satan rebelled against me, and sought . . . that I [the Father] should give unto him mine own power" (Moses 4:3). Satan's claim for priesthood was another perverted truth, unless you consider the powers of darkness and deceit as a type of power or priesthood. Of the devil, his angels, and the wicked, the Lord has said: "And now, behold, I say unto you, never at any time have I declared from mine own mouth that they should return, for where I am they cannot come, for *they have no power*" (D&C 29:29 [28–29]; emphasis added).

Having been stripped of power and priesthoods, whatever Satan claimed might well be a residue of that which was given him in the beginning. President Harold B. Lee wrote, "Satan, that illustrious one, was one of the first of our Father's creations in the very morning of His creation, one of the oldest, a chief, and one of great power."[33] "Thou art the anointed cherub that covereth; and I have set thee so: thou wast upon the holy mountain of God; thou hast walked up and down in the midst of the stones of fire. Thou wast perfect in thy ways from the day that thou wast created, *till iniquity was found in thee*" (Ezekiel 28:14–15 [12–15]; emphasis added).

We might wonder how this transformation from the son of the morning (see Isaiah 14:12) to the devil could have taken place. Consider King Saul, who was chosen to be the first king of Israel. "And Samuel said to all the people, See ye him whom the Lord hath chosen, that there is none like him among all the people" (1 Samuel 10:24). Nevertheless, disobedience transformed Saul's countenance: "And Samuel said to Saul, Thou hast done foolishly: thou hast not kept the commandment of the Lord thy God. . . . Now *thy kingdom shall not continue*: the Lord hath sought him a man after his own heart" (1 Samuel 13:13–14). Afterward, jealousy raged in King Saul's heart: "And Saul was very wroth . . . and he said, They have ascribed unto David ten thousands, and to me they have ascribed but thousands: and what can he have more but the kingdom?" It was then "that the evil spirit . . . came upon Saul" (1 Samuel 18:8, 10), and Jonathan warned David, "Saul my father seeketh to kill thee" (1 Samuel 19:2). In this, we can easily relate the covetous rivalry of Saul toward David's ordained crown to the ongoing battle of Satan for Christ's infinite power. Indeed, David's ordained crown was linked to Christ infinite power as the proclaimed son of David, even the king of the Jews (Matthew 12:23; 2 Chronicles 13:5–8), the very Son of God.

When Satan sets his own claim upon the powers of the priesthood, darkness reigns with its abhorrent evils. An example of this occurred in Abraham's time: "Now, Pharaoh being of that lineage by which he *could not* have the right of Priesthood, notwithstanding the Pharaohs would *fain claim it* . . . therefore my father was led away by their idolatry" (Abraham 1:27; emphasis added). "Now, at this time it was the custom of the priest of Pharaoh, the king of Egypt, to offer up upon the altar which was built in the land of Chaldea, for the offering unto these strange gods, men, women, and children" (Abraham 1:8). A feigned claim to the priesthood is in defiance of God and becomes the difference between the Light of Christ and Lucifer's darkest endeavor for power.

MAN'S AGENCY

Despite his self-ascribed power, Satan has no power to destroy any of God's work or any of man's godhood; he is left to seek to employ us in the destruction of man's agency. For Satan's work to move forward, it requires our willing participation. Perhaps we could say, as did the Father, that Satan sought "that I should give unto him mine own power" (Moses 4:3), my knowledge, my agency—that which was given to me by the power of the Only Begotten. Agency is a power given to all, even to Satan, by God. It is interesting that Satan rebelled against "the agency of man" (Moses 4:3), yet ironically he is the catalyst to that agency by providing opposition and thus choice.

Speaking to Cain, God patiently explained, "If thou doest well, thou shalt be accepted. And if thou doest not well, sin lieth at the door, and Satan desireth to have thee; and except thou shalt hearken unto my commandments, I will deliver thee up, and it shall be unto thee according to his desire. *And thou shalt rule over him*" (Moses 5:23; emphasis added). Satan has no power to rule over man. Man has been given the power to rule for himself. That power is man's agency to choose, given by God. "In the Garden of Eden," God says, "gave I unto man his agency" (Moses 7:32). Satan would remove that agency (knowledge of good), but he is powerless to do so. We, however, can freely give Satan our agency through addiction and wickedness. But he cannot take it, except we should choose to believe him over Christ.

Keeping the commandments and becoming like Christ takes a determined effort. Sometimes we find it much easier to slide down than to climb up, but it is always our choice, and the Lord has promised help: "Behold, my grace is sufficient for you; you must walk uprightly before me and sin not" (D&C 18:31). It is by the love of God that we overcome sin. "And it came to pass that there was no contention in the land, because of the love of God which did dwell in the hearts of the people" (4 Nephi 1:15). "For whatsoever is born of God overcometh the world: and this is the victory that overcometh the world, even our faith" (1 John 5:4). Therefore, seek the love of God, the tree of life, and live.

By Satan's agency, we find in him the absence of light, love, and faith. We find in him darkness, hate, and fear. Christ, on the other hand, is the light that cannot be dimmed: "He is the light and the life of the world; yea, a light that is endless, that can never be darkened; yea, and also a life which is endless, that there can be no more death" (Mosiah 16:9). It is by God's perfect love that we have the power of agency, the power of choice. It is also by obedience to His commandments that we may retain our agency through all time.

Satan works hard to bring us into his power and would hold us fast and not let go, thus bringing on a painful process for repentance. It is not Christ that brings on the pain of repentance; rather it is the desperate grasp of sin that would withhold that agency from us as we begin to move toward Christ. Therefore, we must be willing to see and receive the light of Christ. As hard as it may be, we must choose and act on our desired outcome of freedom or confinement. President Dieter F. Uchtdorf urges us to endure in this insightful message:

> The most important thing is to keep trying—sometimes it takes several attempts before people find success. So don't give up. Don't lose faith. Keep your heart close to the Lord, and He will give you the power of deliverance. He will make you free. . . .

I testify that the cleansing power of the Atonement of Jesus Christ and the transformative power of the Holy Ghost can heal and rescue mankind. It is our privilege, our sacred duty, and our joy to heed the Savior's call to follow Him with a willing mind and full purpose of heart. Let us "shake off the chains with which [we] are bound, and come forth out of obscurity, and arise from the dust."

Let us be awake and not be weary of well-doing, for we "are laying the foundation of a great work," even preparing for the return of the Savior. Brethren [and sisters], when we add the light of our example as a witness to the beauty and power of restored truth, we will not sleep through the Restoration.[34]

KEEPING THE DEVIL IN CHECK

President Joseph F. Smith explained, "Priesthood is the authority and the power which God has granted to men on earth to act for Him."[35] This kind of priesthood is not granted unto Satan. Whatever powers and priesthood he might claim, it is not a godly priesthood, for that comes by the Holy Order of God. "Behold it was by faith that they of old were called after the Holy Order of God" (Ether 12:10). The power of darkness, which Satan seems to hold, is an absence of the Order of the Son of God. It is, in fact, the priesthood of God that dictates the extent of Satan's power. For example, because of Job's righteousness, the Lord clearly dictated to Satan the extent to which Job could be tried: "And the Lord said unto Satan, Behold, all that he hath is in thy power; only upon himself put not forth thine hand. So Satan went forth from the presence of the Lord" (Job 1:12). For it is Satan who must *obey the confines of his power* through the priesthood of God. Author Larry E. Dahl wrote:

> In a vision, Enoch saw that when Satan had temporarily succeeded in the days of Noah, "he looked up and laughed, and his angels rejoiced in his power. The devil does have power . . . within limits, as Joseph Smith taught:[36]
>
> The Prophet also gave this succinct explanation: "*The devil has no power over us only as we permit him. The moment we revolt at anything which comes from God, the devil takes power.*"[37] It appears that, for the most part, we can avoid being overcome by the power of the devil

by being submissive to God. There are times, however, when Satan attempts to overstep his bounds and must be held in check by someone with more power than he has. ... Adam was that someone.

Satan "disputed [with Michael, the Archangel] about the body of Moses,' meaning that he sought the mortal death of Israel's lawgiver so that he would not have a tangible body in which to come . . . to confer the keys of the priesthood upon Peter, James, and John"[38] (see Matthew 17:1–13).

He [Satan] is emphatically called the prince of the power of the air [Ephesians 2:2]; and, it is very evident that they possess a power that none but those who have the priesthood can control.[39] [It is not that they (Satan) have the priesthood, but that only those who have the priesthood can control them (Satan).]

By the power of the priesthood, Moses was translated that he might confer the key to Peter, James, and John. It is a comfort to know that Adam (Michael) still steps in to protect his righteous posterity, by the keys which he holds, "Michael . . . the great prince which standeth for the children of thy people" (Daniel 12:1). It is he, Adam, who shall in all finality, defeat the devil (see Revelations 12:7–9).

WHAT IS THE FORBIDDEN?

Satan is "the forbidden fruit" (Alma 12:22). Knowledge of good and evil isn't forbidden; on the contrary, obtaining knowledge was part of Adam and Eve's mission. Moreover, the command to be fruitful persuades us to believe that mortality was indeed required, not forbidden. To do that which is forbidden is to do evil or to rebel against God's laws, as did Satan. Satan, then, becomes the opposition to God and the conceivable representative of the forbidden fruit that would exist in the world.

The word *forbidden* is a direct reference to Satan, for he had been cast out, cast down, and forbidden from entering into the presence of God. When God spoke directly to Satan, He commanded him to depart (see D&C 29:28). Satan and his ways then became the *forbidden fruit* of which Adam and Eve were commanded not to partake.

Satan's demise is sure, "And the dragon fought and his angels, and prevailed not: neither was their place found any more in heaven"

(Revelation 12:7–8). "Neither was there place found in heaven for the great dragon, who was cast out; that old serpent called the devil, and also called Satan, which deceiveth the whole world; he was cast out into the earth; and his angels were cast out with him" (JST Revelation 12:8). "And in his hot displeasure, and in his fierce anger, in his time, [the Lord] will cut off those wicked, unfaithful, and unjust stewards, and appoint them their portion among hypocrites, and unbelievers; even in outer darkness, where there is weeping, and wailing, and gnashing of teeth" (D&C 101:90–91).

"Wherefore, because that Satan rebelled against me, and sought to destroy the agency of man, which I, the Lord God, had given him, and also, that I should give unto him mine own power; by the power of mine Only Begotten, I caused that he should be cast down" (Moses 4:3). Jesus says, "Now is the judgment of this world: now shall the prince of this world be cast out" (John 12:31). We can safely conclude that to be in the world is not forbidden but to partake of Satan's wiles and ways is.

ESSENTIAL DOCTRINE

Two trees stood in the presence of Eve in Eden, both essential and important factors in the plan of happiness. Eve perceived Satan's lies as she turned to God for truth. By his tempting lies, Satan became the evil opposition to good. While the tree of life continued in God's presence, the tree of knowledge of good and evil led to a mortal probation in which Satan became the self-proclaimed god of that temporal world.

Satan's desire to rule, control, and destroy man's temporal body, his agency, and his path to godhood is obsessive, and he constantly entices us to physical and spiritual self-destruction. As "the father of all lies," he desires "to deceive and to blind men, and to lead them captive at his will, even as many as [will] not hearken unto [God's] voice" (Moses 4:4). Satan would have our souls. Adam and Eve knew, and we must remember, that their souls could be held secure only through Jesus Christ, by obedience to his word.

CHAPTER 4

CHRIST'S TEMPTATIONS PARALLEL THE TEMPTATIONS IN THE GARDEN

Thou shalt not tempt the Lord thy God.

Matthew 4:7; Luke 4:12

In mortality, Jesus Christ was given three temptations that parallel the temptations given to Adam and Eve in the garden. Temptation becomes a defining factor throughout mortality. As we study the temptations in Eden and Christ's temptations in the wilderness, we find a consistent pattern in which Satan tries us. Satan uses three basic tactics in these scenarios. The first deals with the appetites of the flesh. The second is about defying or misusing God's power and authority. The third has to do with who we worship: God or Satan.

APPETITE

After Christ had fasted forty days in the wilderness, Satan tempted Him to hunger after the things of the world while also tempting Him to prove his divine role as the Savior. "And when the tempter came to him, he said, *if* thou be the Son of God, command that these stones be made bread" (Matthew 4:3; emphasis added). Ready to begin his selfless Messianic mission, Jesus looked to the Father for implicit instructions as He also recited those same

43

instructions to Satan, "It is written, Man shall not live by bread alone, but by every word that proceedeth out of the mouth of God" (Matthew 4:4). Had Christ listened to Satan and hungered after bread instead of after the word and will of God, His faith and obedience would have been compromised. And had Christ's self-will not been swallowed up in the will of the Father, the Savior could never have endured the requirements of the infinite Atonement. Through His masterful resignation to do the will of His Father, Christ remained without sin.

We can compare this experience to that of Adam and Eve in the garden, where Satan tempted them to eat of the forbidden fruit. For Satan, this temptation transformed into lusting after, eating of, and being of the temporal world. Though Adam and Eve partook so that man might be, they heeded not Satan's ploy to become *of* the world, "And Adam and Eve, his wife, ceased not to call upon God" (Moses 5:16). Instead, they covenanted with God the Father as coats of skins were placed upon their now-mortal bodies (Genesis 3:21; see also Moses 5:7).

Jesus's reply in the wilderness was simple and perfect: "But he answered and said, It is written, Man shall not live by bread alone, but by every word that proceedeth out of the mouth of God" (Matthew 4:4). Once again the words *bread, eat,* and *fruit* become directives for making choices. While Christ easily buffeted Satan's temptation, so did Adam and Eve when they chose to live in the world but not of the world—meaning they chose to make and keep their required covenants for salvation (see Genesis 3:21).

POWER

Satan told Christ, "If thou be the Son of God, cast thyself down: for it is written, He shall give his angels charge concerning thee: and in their hands they shall bear thee up, lest at any time thou dash thy foot against a stone" (Matthew 4:6). In other words, "*If* you are the Son of God," Satan taunted, "you shall not surely die." Compare this to Satan's words as he tempted Eve: "ye shall not surely die . . . [but] ye shall be as gods, knowing good and evil" (Genesis 3:4–5; Moses 4:10–11). Both Adam and Eve were tempted to become as

Satan, who from the beginning challenged God for power and honor as he claimed a feigned entitlement as the Christ. "Ye shall be as gods," meaning ye shall be as *me,* the god of this world.

Christ's reply in the wilderness was simply, "Thou shalt not tempt the Lord thy God" (Matthew 4:7). It seems that the Savior was confirming His own godhood as the Lord and rebuking Satan with a simple "tempt me not." As Adam and Eve made covenants with the Savior, and coats of skins were placed upon them, they confirmed similar words to Satan, saying, "Tempt us not, for we have covenanted with the Father" (see Moses 5:4, 16).

WORSHIP

According to the Bible, "the devil taketh [Jesus] up into an exceeding high mountain, and sheweth him all the kingdoms of the world, and the glory of them." Satan said, "All these things will I give thee, if thou wilt fall down and worship me." Though Christ created the world, it seems that Satan claimed it as his own dominion while offering a temporal reign to Christ. The Savior's reply in the wilderness was again exemplary: "Then saith Jesus unto him, Get thee hence, Satan: for it is written, Thou shalt worship the Lord thy God, and him only shalt thou serve. Then the devil leaveth him, and, behold, angels came and ministered unto him" (Matthew 4:8–11). Satan offered Jesus a temporal dominion, but Jesus was unimpressed. He later said, "My kingdom is not of this world" (John 18:36). In other words, "Ye are from beneath; I am from above: ye are of this world; I am not of this world" (John 8:23).

To Adam and Eve in the Garden of Eden, Satan claimed power, priesthood, and godhood. By claiming to be the god of this world, he was surely demanding to be worshiped and revered as the Only Begotten. But Adam and Eve's love of God the Father did not falter. In choosing the Father and the Only Begotten Son, Adam rebuked the tempter as he turned to God with solemn covenants. With impeccable consecration to God the Father, he explained when asked why he performed sacrifices, "I know not, save the Lord commanded me" (Moses 5:6). By so doing, Adam, like Jesus, was saying, "Get thee hence, Satan: for it is written, Thou shalt worship the Lord thy God, and him only shalt thou serve" (Matthew 4:10). As it was with Christ—"Then the devil leaveth him, and, behold, angels came and ministered unto him" (Matthew 4:11)—so it was with Adam:

> And it came to pass, when the Lord had spoken with Adam, our father, that Adam cried unto the Lord, and he was caught away by the Spirit of the Lord, and was carried down into the water, and was laid under the water, and was brought forth out of the water.
>
> And thus he was baptized, and the Spirit of God descended upon him, and thus he was born of the Spirit, and became quickened in the inner man.
>
> And he heard a voice out of heaven, saying: Thou art baptized with fire, and with the Holy Ghost. This is the record of the Father, and the Son, from henceforth and forever;
>
> And thou art after the order of him who was without beginning of days or end of years, from all eternity to all eternity.
>
> Behold, thou art one in me, a son of God; and thus may all become my sons. Amen. (Moses 6:64–68)

Christ's experience in the wilderness with Satan is similar to the experience Adam and Eve had with him in the garden, and their experiences are similar to ours. Their temptations are our temptations, and we can use their examples to avoid falling into the grasp of Satan's power. As we continually reject the temptations that beset us on a daily basis, we can remember it is Christ who helps us in our temptations. Similarly, it was He who said to His Apostles, "Ye are they which have continued with me in my temptations" (Luke 22:28). Satan's tactics are not new, which makes him predictable and easily discernible by the spiritual eye.

Adam and Eve walked with the Father and the Son before the Fall. They had been taught in preparation for their crucial decision regarding the partaking of the forbidden fruit. Their choice was comparable to, and even linked to, the choice Christ made. After fasting for forty days in the wilderness and being tempted, Christ, in perfect obedience to the Father, chose to move into his prophetic and active role as the Savior in preparation for partaking of the bitter cup. This was central to the plan of happiness, so then, by Adam man might be, and through Christ men might have joy.

There would have been no need for a Savior had there been no forbidden fruit. The advancement of the children of God into godhood would have been thwarted. Traveling from the tree of life to the forbidden fruit also becomes a need for the bitter cup. Christ partook of the bitter cup, that we might once again partake of the tree of life. This is full circle for the plan of happiness. There are no big surprises when we look at the simplicity and significance of the plan in its true perspective. The plan is not complicated; it has clear directives. But we can easily complicate our lives by choosing forbidden worldly paths. When we choose to follow Satan, we relinquish our agency to him and chaos ensues. Choosing Christ, however, frees us from chaos so that we can continue in a straight path of progress and power. James teaches us,

> Blessed is the man that endureth temptation: for when he is tried, he shall receive the crown of life, which the Lord hath promised to them that love him.
>
> Let no man say when he is tempted, I am tempted of God: for God cannot be tempted with evil, neither tempteth he any man:
>
> But every man is tempted, when he is drawn away of his own lust, and enticed.
>
> Then when lust hath conceived, it bringeth forth sin: and sin, when it is finished, bringeth forth death.
>
> Do not err, my beloved brethren.
>
> Every good gift and every perfect gift is from above, and cometh down from the Father of lights, with whom is no variableness, neither shadow of turning.
>
> Of his own will begat he us with the word of truth, that we should be a kind of firstfruits of his creatures.
>
> Wherefore, my beloved brethren, let every man be swift to hear, slow to speak, slow to wrath. (James 1:12–19)

By attempting to usurp God's honor, glory, and power, Satan represented opposition, contradicting all good as the father of lies in the world of mortality. Satan struggled from the beginning for ultimate power and claim as the Christ: "I will redeem all mankind, that one soul shall not be lost [removing their agency], and surely I will do it; wherefore give me thine honor [power]" (Moses 4:1). Satan, therefore, came upon the earth to claim all that was not, and could not, be his, as testified in this example.

CHAPTER 5

ENMITY AND SEED

"And I will put enmity between thee and the woman, and between thy seed and her seed; it shall bruise thy head, and thou shalt bruise his heel."

—*Genesis 3:15*

Eve was able to clearly comprehend the truth against a backdrop of opposition, thus challenging her to make real life choices. She acted while being acted upon by Satan. She chose the truth, the good fruit, the command to be fruitful and replenish the earth. She then partook of the fruit and gave unto Adam that men might be. It was in this scenario that she was also designated to receive two gifts: enmity and seed. This because of her foundational faith and integrity toward God.

Elder John A. Widtsoe added that the problem before Adam and Eve was whether "to remain forever at selfish ease in the Garden of Eden, or to face unselfishly tribulation and death, in bringing to pass the purposes of the Lord for a host of waiting spirit children. They chose the latter. This they did with open eyes and minds as to consequences. . . . The choice that they made raises Adam and Eve to preeminence among all who have come on earth."[40] To Satan's chagrin, amidst all his deceptive lies, Eve chose wisely. "The Church of Jesus Christ of Latter-day Saints strongly affirms that in partaking of the fruit of the tree of knowledge of good and evil, Eve along with Adam acted in a manner pleasing to God and in accord with his ordained plan."[41] This is the very reason "we should never blame Mother Eve, not the least."[42] Adam and Eve "accepted a great challenge. They chose wisely in accordance with the heavenly law of love for others."[43]

SEED OF THE WOMAN

Eve understood her role in the Fall. She understood that the Fall was not just about her; rather it was about doing good for all. So, "at the moment when it appears that Satan, "that old serpent, even the devil" (D&C 76:28), has been victorious through the Fall, he is told that the seed of the woman will be victorious over him; or, in effect, the apparent tragedy of the Fall will be overcome by the seed of the woman."[44]

What then is the seed of the woman? Elder James E. Talmage clarifies that the seed of the woman is a reference to the birth of the Son of God through mortal woman. "The only instance of offspring from woman dissociated from mortal fatherhood is the birth of *Jesus the Christ*, who was the earthly Son of a mortal mother, begotten by an immortal Father. He is the Only Begotten of the Eternal Father in the flesh, and was born of woman."[45]

Daniel H. Ludlow also wrote:

> Adam, the patriarch of the race, rejoiced in the assurance of the Savior's appointed ministry, through the acceptance of which, he, the transgressor, might gain redemption. [Eve] appears in the promise given of God following the fall—that though the devil, represented by the serpent in Eden, should have power to bruise the heel of Adam's posterity, through the seed of the woman should come the power to bruise the adversary's head. It is significant that this assurance of eventual victory over sin and its inevitable effect, death, both of which were introduced to earth through Satan, the arch-enemy of mankind, was to be realized through the offspring of woman,"[46] which brought forth the promised Messiah.

ENMITY

There are two promises given to Eve in Eden: the first is enmity (an abhorrence of evil) and the second is the seed of woman (Christ).

Speaking to Satan, God proclaims, "And I will put enmity between thee and the woman, between thy seed and her seed; and he shall bruise thy head, and thou shalt bruise his heel" (Moses 4:21). Eve is given wisdom as enmity stands between her and Satan. Daniel H. Ludlow explains, "He placed enmity (an abhorrence of evil) between Eve's seed and Satan and his followers."[47]

Adam and Eve diligently teach their children, "And Adam and Eve blessed the name of God, and they made all things known unto their sons and their daughters" (Moses 5:12). The following generations were clearly taught good from evil, as this knowledge was freely shared among them. Hugh Nibley tells us, "Adam and Eve brought up their children diligently in the gospel, but the adversary was not idle in his continued attempts to drive wedges between them. He had first to overcome the healthy revulsion, 'the enmity,' between his followers and 'the seed of the woman.'"[48] Eve's seed, therefore, "being pure and spotless before God, could not look upon sin save it were with abhorrence" (Alma 13:12).

Remember that the seed of the woman is Christ. While the woman is also representative of the Church of Christ (see JST Revelation 12:7, 17), enmity, being an abhorrence of evil, seems to be a consecration to the teachings of Jesus Christ and none else. To be clear, we are speaking of Eve's enmity, or between her seed and Satan's seed, not to be confused with man's enmity toward God. The seed of Satan will have enmity towards God but the righteous seed of the woman has enmity, an abhorrence of evil, toward Satan.

The confrontation between the seed of the woman (Christ) and the devil is presented in the second volume of *Studies in Scripture*,

> The offspring of Satan, those who choose to follow Satan as did the serpent, will become his sons and daughters. The Lord places *enmity* between those people and the offspring of the woman Eve. There is a natural division between those who exemplify the darkness of the world and those who maintain their inherent light of Christ (John 1:9). . . . The followers of Satan will have power to bruise the heel of Eve's other seed by leading them to sin; this will cause Christ to suffer for those sins and thus be a bruise in the heel which crushes out the sins of mankind.[49]

I believe that enmity here, as promised to the woman, is or becomes the church or kingdom of God, for that is what the woman in Revelation represents. "And the dragon prevailed not against Michael, neither the child (Christ), nor *the woman which was the church of God*, who had been delivered of her pains, *and brought forth the kingdom of our God and his Christ*" (JST Revelation 12:7; emphasis adjusted). "And the dragon was wroth with the woman, and went to make war with the remnant of her seed, which keep the commandments of God, and have the testimony of Jesus Christ" (Revelation 12:17).

By transgression, Eve conceived the need for a Savior. By giving birth to man, she, through her seed, also conceived the body of Christ. In enmity, her abhorrence to evil and consecration to Christ also becomes the symbolic reference for the church or kingdom of God. The symbolic relevance of Eve being represented as the body (the church) of Christ, and Adam being represented as Christ, or represented by the power of Christ, is what makes them clearly one in Christ. Symbolically, Adam is to Eve as the priesthood is to the gospel.

We can see this as "Jesus Christ is symbolized in the scriptures as the Bridegroom. The Church is His symbolic bride."[50] This may be why the covenanted Israelite nation, because of idolatry, was often referred to as a harlot: "Know ye not that your bodies are the members of Christ? Shall I then take the members of Christ, and make them the members of a harlot? God forbid" (1 Corinthians 6:15). Israel often succumbed to idolatry: "And the children of Israel remembered not the Lord their God, who had delivered them out of the hands of all their enemies on every side" (Judges 8:34). Christ, as the symbolic bridegroom, requires complete fidelity of his covenanted people, which are his symbolic bride. This insightful metaphor gives us a more compassionate view of the betrayed Christ as it relates to His covenant church (bride).

By enmity, the seed of the woman becomes the Church of God, and in faith brings forth the kingdom of God and His Christ. This similitude is not new, for the woman is compared as the bride of

Christ (church of God), and Christ is the bridegroom. This is taught to some degree in Ephesians as Paul explains the relationship of men and women in marriage, "For the husband is the head [keys of the priesthood] of the *wife*, even as Christ is the head of the *church*" (Ephesians 5:23 [23–24]; emphasis added), another way of saying "thy desire shall be to thy husband" (Moses 4:22), or to the priesthood of God through patriarchal order.

The gospel is of Christ; Eve is of Adam. Eve represents the gospel of Christ; she is not the least in the chain of creation, but in all, the crowning gift of life. *While Adam holds the keys of eternity, Eve holds the keys of life itself. Yet all must be shared equally or marriage has neither life nor eternity;* Eve to Adam, Adam to Christ, Christ to the Father, becoming one eternal round. One is not without the other. Being first or last, it is the same purpose and glory. They are one, or they do not exist. Christ speaks, "And the glory which thou gavest me I have given them; that they may be one, even as we are one" (John 17:22). Though He is directing His prayers about the apostles, we often see the number one in the scriptures, not as singular but as plural, or whole in the Christ, "There is neither Jew nor Greek, there is neither bond nor free, there is neither *male nor female*: for ye are all one in Christ Jesus" (Galatians 3:28).

AWAKE AND ARISE

As we look to Christ and His promised coming as the bridegroom, and to His church, we can relate to the comments of President Kimball: "Much of the major growth that is coming to the Church in the last days will come because many of the good women of the world . . . will be drawn to the Church in large numbers. This will happen to the degree that the women of the Church reflect righteousness."[51]

In relationship to the church of God and women, we can also appropriate remember these scriptures: "Yea, let the cry go forth among all people: Awake and arise and go forth to meet the Bridegroom; behold and lo, the Bridegroom cometh; go ye out to meet him; Prepare yourselves for the great day of the Lord" (D&C 133:10). "Then shall the *kingdom of heaven be likened unto ten virgins,* which took their lamps, and went forth to meet the bridegroom" (Matthew 25:1; emphasis added). "Awake, and arise from the dust, O Jerusalem; yea, and put on thy beautiful garments, O daughter of Zion; and strengthen thy stakes and enlarge thy borders forever, that thou mayest no more be confounded, that the covenants of the Eternal Father which he hath made unto thee, O house of Israel, may be fulfilled" (Moroni 10:31).

Elder Bruce R. McConkie observed: "After the fall *Eve continued to receive revelation, to see visions, to walk in the spirit.*"[52] "Eve, as the first and head, would have been first to lead and teach her faithful daughters in particular. Eve's knowledge of the gospel, her capacity, and her intelligence must have been, as with father Adam, unexcelled."[53]

Sisters, we have a unique role to play in the Lord's Second Coming, as do our brethren. As a covenant people, let us not miss such an incredible opportunity to serve Him in these last days. We will together courageously finish what Adam and Eve began, "the immortality and eternal life of man" (Moses 1:39) by passage of the tree of knowledge of good and evil. We can again direct our course to partake of the tree of life, through the Atonement of Jesus Christ.

CHAPTER 6

"THE WOMAN BEING DECEIVED WAS IN THE TRANSGRESSION" 1 TIMOTHY 2:14

"The eyes of them both were opened"

—*Genesis 3:7*

Most of our negative impressions of Eve are based on this one quote, "For Adam was first formed, then Eve. And Adam was not deceived, but the woman being deceived was in the transgression" (1 Timothy 2:13–14). When I listen to latter-day prophets, I am confused by Paul's words in 1 Timothy. Jeffrey R. Holland said, "They were willing to transgress *knowingly and consciously* (the only way they could "fall" into the consequences of mortality, inasmuch as Elohim could not force innocent parties out of the garden and still be a just God) only because they had a *full knowledge* of the plan of salvation, which would provide for them a way back from their struggle with death and hell."[54]

Because Eve understood what she was to do and made the correct choice, it's hard to consider her as having been deceived. As with the wording of many scriptures, I think it is important to focus less on the literal words of Paul and more on what he was saying, or rather what his spiritual message was to a particular group of people, within the brief and vague story of Eden and the Fall. For instance, most tend to believe Paul was speaking of Adam and Eve's comparative obedience or lack thereof. However, I believe Paul was speaking about the combined responsibilities of Adam and Eve as the first patriarch and matriarch in the priesthood, this being a more likely message by an Apostle of the Lord (see chapter 31; Priesthood Veil). The impactful events of the Fall are far more spiritually inclusive than words alone have expressed.

Though Paul's words towards Eve in 1 Timothy seem harsh, I found him to be very loving and Christlike throughout his apostolic journey. Paul and his dedication to our Savior Jesus Christ are without question. There was no hesitation as he stood resolute to his mission under the direction of Jesus Christ, "Whereunto I am ordained a preacher, and an apostle, (I speak the truth in Christ, and lie not;) a teacher of the Gentiles in faith and verity" (1 Timothy 2:7).

Paul is a dynamic figure in the New Testament. His teachings are as transitional and as abrupt as his conversion—transitional because he takes us out of the confinement of the Mosaic laws of Israel to open up the fulfilling gospel of Jesus Christ unto all the world (the gentile nations); abrupt because the explanations for the new law were unfamiliar, different from hundreds of years of tradition, difficult to articulate, and patently unwanted. Not only was he called to radically change his heart and mind in Christ, but also that of nations.

The scriptural story of the Garden of Eden in Genesis, Moses, and Abraham (especially the verses in 1 Timothy 2:13–14) perhaps needs some spiritual translation. The word *deceived* is a harsh word that might be interpreted as a mistake on Eve's part. Latter-day prophets have made it clear that Eve did not make a mistake in partaking of the fruit of the tree of knowledge of good and evil. That being said, one could still technically call her deceived. Paul is the only one in ancient scripture that refers to Eve as having been deceived and only in this particular passage; therefore, it is important to interpret his words correctly.

In speaking about the priesthood, and those individual responsibilities by Adam and Eve, I believe Paul is referring to the pattern in which the Fall came about in verse 13, "For Adam was first formed [in the priesthood], then Eve." Adam, being first to hold the keys of the priesthood, then called Eve as his companion, in marriage, to that same priesthood (see chapter 30, Deep Sleep). Elder Dallin H. Oaks says, "When men and women go to the temple, they are both endowed with the same power, which is priesthood power."[55] In verse 14, "And Adam was not deceived, but the woman being deceived was in the transgression." Because Adam, by those priesthood keys, called Eve as mother of all living (Genesis 3:20), he was also calling her to be the first in mortality. Thus, she was compelled to act, while being acted upon by the deceiver, that they might advance into mortality. After opening those mortal doors, as Mother Eve, Adam was then required by the Father to follow as her companion (Genesis 2:24). First the priesthood by Adam and then Eve; then Eve is called to open the door into mortality and Adam is commanded to follow as her companion—equal companionship with different responsibilities in the priesthood. Paul confirmed this, "Nevertheless neither is the man without the woman, neither the woman without the man, in the Lord. For as the woman is of the man [priesthood], even so is the man also by the woman [life]; but all things of God" (1 Corinthians 11:11–12).

Though Satan presented a deception to Eve, because of faith and obedience to her calling, she was clearly enlightened in the knowledge of good from evil. "And the eyes of them both were opened" (Genesis 3:7). We could, perhaps, compare Eve's beguiling with going to a magic show where we are deceived by a magician's illusions but we do not necessarily believe the illusions to be a reality. Instead, Eve recognized Satan as the deceiver.

Then in verse 15, Paul confirms God's saving approval if they should be obedient to their callings to be fruitful and replenish the earth, "Notwithstanding she [*they*, JST] shall be saved in child-bearing, *if* they continue in faith and charity and holiness with sobriety." I believe that here, Paul is referring them back to God's first command to replenish the earth, requiring that it be done in faith, charity, and holiness. In this they are cautioned that only by reverence to this holy act of childbearing can they be saved. This is the family order that Adam and Eve were called to: first the keys of the priesthood by God's authority, then marriage by that same authority, and finally, within that same authority, they are both charged to reverence their new creative power of procreation, "that man might be" (2 Nephi 2:25). Only then can families be sealed together in heaven as one. All three godly powers are needed to preserve the families of God, to bringing them safely back into the presence of God in covenants. In all caution, if we do not honor procreation, we have not honored, cannot honor the priesthood or the ordained marriage in the holy union of man and woman. We have not kept sacred covenants and must speedily repent or be cut off. To be sure, this holy order of the priesthood comes first from Christ to Adam, then to Eve, then on to all their posterity; through them *families* will receive it. Thus, by way of priesthood power, we are given the statement from Paul: "For Adam was first formed then Eve" (1 Timothy 2:13)— in the priesthood. This was Paul's message.

THE WORD *DECEIVED*

It is my opinion that Eve was not deceived. However, instead of contesting with Paul the Apostle, I would attempt to explain Paul's meaning for the word itself. We could perhaps even liken the word *deceived* to the word *forbidden* in a quote by President Joseph Fielding Smith, who said, "Mortality was created through the eating of the forbidden fruit, *if you want to call it forbidden [deceived]*, but I think the Lord has made it clear that *it was not forbidden*."[56] We have learned in chapter 2 that the word *forbidden* has a different connotation than previously thought. In that same setting, we will look at the word *deceived* and its correct meaning as put forth by Paul. Though Eve was beguiled by Satan, she had a clear understanding of the plan of salvation and, in fact, made the correct choice. I will compare this point to a story told by Matthew Holland, the son of Jeffrey R. Holland. Matthew was seven years old when his father invited him to go on a road trip:

> It was dusk, and we had only gone a bumpy mile or two when we came to a fork in the road. We stopped. Dad was not certain which trail we had come in on. He knew he had to make the right decision. There

wasn't much light left, light he desperately needed to ensure he could make the correct turns the rest of the way home. Wasting time on a wrong road now meant we would face the difficult task of making our way home in the dark.

As we did whenever we had a family problem or concern, we prayed. After we both said amen, Dad turned and asked me what I thought we should do. I answered and said, "All during the prayer, I just kept feeling, '"Go to the left."'"

Dad responded, "I had the exact same impression…"

We started down the dirt road to the left. We had traveled only about 10 minutes when our road came to a sudden dead-end. My father promptly whipped the truck around, roared back to that fork in the path, and started down the road to the right. Fortunately, there was still just enough light to help us navigate the web of dirt roads. . . .

My dad said, "The Lord has taught us an important lesson today. Because we were prompted to take the road to the left, we quickly discovered which one was the right one. When we turned around and got on the right road, I was able to travel along its many unfamiliar twists and turn perfectly confident I was headed in the right direction."

Sometimes in response to prayers, the Lord may guide us down what *seems* to be the wrong road—or at least a road we don't understand—so, in due time, He can get us firmly and without question on the right road. Of course, He would never lead us down a path of sin, but He might lead us down a road of valuable experience.[57]

When Matthew Holland and his father, Elder Jeffrey R. Holland, were impressed to go to the left in the fork in the road, were they deceived, or were they enlightened? Technically, you could say they were deceived because we term their choice as a 'wrong road'; but they concluded and we know in our hearts that they were enlightened. I believe Eve is under this same descriptive technicality as were Matthew and his father. It was not until after Adam and Eve partook of the forbidden fruit that "the eyes of them both were opened [enlightened]" (Genesis 3:7), as they gained a valued knowledge between good and evil.

This same type of scenario is familiar in many of our most popular scripture stories. Nephi and his brothers took several inspired actions before they were able to obtain the brass plates. I don't believe they were deceived in those seemingly unproductive and even disruptive actions; rather they needed to set up connective responses in which Nephi could clearly see Laban's evil intent. Inspired by God, because of faith and obedience to his calling, Nephi remembers, "Yea, and I also knew that he had sought to take away mine own life; yea, and he would not hearken unto the commandments of the Lord; and he also had taken away our property." Nephi then recognizes the Lord's command to kill Laban for the sake of a nation, "Behold the Lord hath delivered him into thy hands" (Nephi 4:11).

It was Abraham who was commanded to sacrifice his only son. Critical thinkers might feel that he was deceived in this test of faith, but for most of us, we see the revelatory relationship between the father and the son as truly enlightening (Genesis 22:2–18).

Joseph of Egypt was inspired to tell his family of his dream (Genesis 39–46). Was that a deception or part of the developing objective? In these stories, wrong paths are not always wrong and certainly do not proclaim the traveler as having sinned. If these men had given up before reaching their objective (like Laman and Lemuel desired), we could easily describe them as having been deceived, for they never would have reached their objective. However, the real deception would not have been in taking a wrong turn but in losing the needed faith to endure to the end of their desired objective.

Both Adam and Eve are exonerated in the words of Elder Oaks as he informs us, "[Eve's] act . . . was formally a transgression but eternally a glorious necessity to open the doorway toward eternal life. Adam showed his wisdom by doing the same. And thus Eve and Adam fell that men might be"[58] (see also 2 Nephi 2:25). Joseph Fielding Smith confirmed the same when he wrote, "This was a transgression of the law, but not a sin in the strict sense, for it was something that Adam and Eve had to do!"[59] Transgression into motherhood brought the salvation that is now available to all the sons of Adam, "if they continue in faith and charity and holiness with sobriety" (1 Timothy 2:15).

The word *deceived*, as Paul speaks of Eve to the people, was in response to her prophetic call, as mother of all living, to be *enlightened by the deceptive ploy of Satan*. Dr. Nehama Aschkenasy, a Hebrew scholar, said that in Hebrew the word which is translated as *beguiled* in the Bible does not mean 'tricked' or 'deceived,' as we commonly think. Rather, it is a rare verb that indicates an intense multi-level experience evoking great emotional, psychological, and/or spiritual trauma. As Aschkenasy explained, it is likely that Eve's intense, multi-level experience, this 'beguiling' by the serpent, was the catalyst that caused her to ponder and evaluate what her role in the Garden really was."[60]

Eve then turns to Adam, "and gave also unto her husband with her; and he did eat" (Genesis 3:6). "And Adam and Eve, his wife, ceased not to call upon God" (Moses 5:16). "And Adam knew his wife, and she bare unto him sons and daughters, and they began to multiply and to replenish the earth," (Moses 5:2) as commanded. Though ancient scriptures are often hard to interpret, by study and prayer we can see that both Adam and Eve followed proper protocol in transgressing from the tree of life to the tree of knowledge of good and evil.

CHAPTER 7
A CONTROVERSY ABATED

Man must put Eve's theoretical misconduct in Eden to rest.

In chapter 3, we detailed the controversies between Satan and Eve in the partaking of the tree. In this chapter, we will speak of the lies in which *Satan deceives man* regarding Eve's partaking. In countering those lies with prophetic defenses, we can better see, tell, and learn from the *Gospel Truth*s presented in Eden.

As in the previous chapter, the statement in 1 Timothy puts forth that Eve was deceived while Adam was not—which seems to have become the basis of all other secular, theological, and even LDS controversy that Eve was deceived rather than enlightened. My purpose is to face those accusations with solid defenses. To do so we must start by looking at the ordained oneness of Adam and Eve in the priesthood, marriage, and childbearing. They simply could not have fallen save by priesthood keys, marriage within those keys, and a promise to fulfill sacred and selfless procreation in that ordained partnership. The fall was preordained by God in the counsels of heaven or a Savior would not have been chosen (see Abraham 5:3–4). As Christ himself prayed, "Thy will be done on earth as it is in heaven" (3 Nephi 13:10).

In all of this, Eve was neither naive nor disobedient. That is a vile misconception of Eve's tremendous character and fortitude as both she and Adam willingly sacrificed that man might be. Though Satan engaged Eve in the partaking of the fruit, her purity of heart did not allow deceit. She calculated his motives and chose to obey God under the conflicting circumstances. Eve never hearkened unto Satan but looked steadfastly unto the Father for truth (see Moses 5:16). God could not have chosen a nobler, more honorable woman to be the mother of all living. Surely her nobility [preordained calling] and intelligence was fitted to that of Adam's. God himself chose her; and "after his own image and in his own likeness, created he *them*" (D&C 20:18). She was not, could not, be an accident waiting to happen. That was not the plan; *nobility was the plan.*

If we read Paul's statements correctly, it was not Paul who was targeting Eve. Paul united Adam and Eve in purpose and priesthood, for he reminds us, "Nevertheless neither is the man without the woman, neither the woman without the man, *in the Lord*" (1 Corinthians 11:11; emphasis added). It was Satan who had determined that woman shall be divided from man, accused and thus subjugated. "[Satan] sought also to beguile Eve," (Moses 4:6). But, if Satan could not deceive Eve, *he would cleverly deceive us*, in that he would cunningly accuse Eve of having been deceived, therefore subjecting her to a perceived inequality with Adam. With a presumed accusation, Satan could easily subjugate woman through man. In the conflict and competition between the man and woman he could then easily subject the world unto himself; for he knew full well that if the man and the woman were not equal as one "in the Lord" (1 Corinthians 11:11), they were his.

EVE'S IMPERATIVE ACTIONS

I wonder if Eve realized that she was risking being the brunt of so much controversy, even within the Church of Jesus Christ of Latter-day Saints, for her imperative actions. We will examine both sides of this issue through latter-day prophets, but let's start with some who have initially and literally taken to heart Paul's words in 1 Timothy that Eve was deceived.

Before I get into controversial statements in order to expel misconceptions, we need to recognize that even the very elect can experience misunderstanding (see Matthew 24:24). This comes as prophets and apostles also have human errors. This does not mean that a church authority that is mistaken on a subject should be disregarded in all their testimonies. Speaking of faith, Elder Henry B. Eyring advised, "My counsel . . . is that *you* have the capacity to receive revelation and to act on it fearlessly. It takes faith to do so." Then he added, "It takes even greater faith to believe that the Lord has called imperfect human servants to lead you."[61] It was Joseph Smith who in speaking of his most recent trial and accusations explained "Although I do wrong, I do not the wrongs that I am charged with doing." He said. "The wrong that I do is through the frailty of human nature, like other men. No man lives without fault."[62]

We are wisely given leadership of apostles, prophets, bishops and those in authority, but as God would have it, it is on us to know right from wrong. Even Nephi, who recognized his prophet father's human error, humbly went to his father, "And I said unto my father: Whither shall I go to obtain food?" (1 Nephi 16:23). His faith was undaunted as he continued to put his trust in his father's prophetic calling. Looking past human error to recognize God's perfect understanding takes faith. We in present time can easily see how foolish it would have been if Nephi had rejected all of Lehi's prophecies because of a misstep in his father's faith. The two of them were clearly watchmen for each other "in the Lord" (1 Corinthians 11:11).

I'm reminded of a wise idiom, "don't throw the baby out with the bathwater." We need to overlook human error while holding steadfastly to the prophetic teachings our leaders give us by the light of Christ. We need the Spirit, even by study and prayer, to help us distinguish between the two. Where there is misinterpretation, there is also an opportunity for enlightenment. As we recognize the mistakes of others, we can then recognize our own misinterpretations about Eve and correct them. Much like Eve, truth is best viewed in comparison to non-truth; we can then make our own insightful decisions.

Eve's actions are often misinterpreted. Even in the Doctrines of the Gospel student manual from 1966 we read: "The adversary,

Lucifer, through the serpent, beguiled Eve and deceived her and induced her to eat of the forbidden fruit. *It was not so with Adam. . . .* He knew that unless he did partake there would be an eternal separation between him and the partner that God had given to him, so he transgressed the law; . . . Because had he not partaken of the fruit, they would have been eternally separated."[63] "Adam voluntarily, and with full knowledge of the consequences, partook of the fruit of the tree of knowledge of good and evil that men might be; . . . For his service we owe Adam an immeasurable debt of gratitude."[64]

It is true that Adam's choice to partake of the fruit that men might be was paramount, and our gratitude goes out to Father Adam for that God-given choice. Remember, however, that it was Eve who gave him the fruit that he might partake. I do not believe Adam would have partaken without Eve's supplication, or without God's command to cleave unto his wife (Matthew 19:4–5). Even though Eve was beguiled in Genesis, Moses, and Abraham, we should not automatically conclude that she was also deceived. As acknowledged before, being tempted was a necessary part of choice making.

I can visualize Eve's selfless response concerning the rhetoric from 1 Timothy, as she might concede with Helaman, "But, behold, it mattereth not—we trust God will deliver us" (Alma 58:37). Or it might look something like the words of Pahoran to Moroni: "And now, *in your epistle you have censured me, but it mattereth not*; I am not angry, but do rejoice in the greatness of your heart. I, Pahoran, do not seek for power, save only to retain my judgment-seat that I may preserve the rights, and the liberty of my people. My soul standeth fast in that liberty in the which God hath made us free" (Alma 61:9; emphasis added).

In Eve's defense, she had declared unto us, "Were it not for *our* transgression *we* never should have had seed, and never should have known good and evil, and the joy of *our* redemption, and the eternal life which God giveth unto *all the obedient*" (Moses 5:11; emphasis added). Eve's magnificent and comprehensive declaration does not set up the partaking as a singular action on her part alone, but denotes an act of oneness between her and Adam.

It's interesting, however, that Adam was the first to proclaim the blessings of having transgressed into mortality, but his announcement seems to be a self-declaration of responsibility. "Blessed be the name of God, for because of *my* transgression *my* eyes are opened, and in this life *I* shall have joy, and again in the flesh *I* shall see God" (Moses 5:10; emphasis added). Out of their own mouths, clearly the Fall is not entirely on Eve's shoulders. In D&C 29:36, the Lord confirms Adam's words as we read, "And it came to pass that Adam, being tempted of the devil—for, behold, the devil was before Adam," and again in verse 40, "Wherefore, it came to pass that the devil tempted Adam, and he partook of the forbidden fruit and transgressed the commandment, wherein he became subject to the will of the devil, because he yielded unto temptation."

Perhaps as Adam claims joy upon himself for the wisdom of the Fall, he is claiming it for both him and Eve because they are *"one."* In this same concept, "and [God] called *their* name Adam" (Genesis 5:2; emphasis added). When the scriptures speak of Adam, they speak of Adam and Eve; when the scriptures speak of Eve, it is of Eve alone. Even when God questions Adam about the partaking of the forbidden fruit, Adam clearly connected his actions with Eve: "The woman whom thou gavest to be with me, she gave me of the tree, and I did eat" (Genesis 3:12). So it is with Eve as she connects her actions with Adam; the woman "gave also unto her *husband with her*; and he did eat" (Genesis 3:6; emphasis added). As God commanded, "They twain shall be one" (Mark 10:8). Once again we can see, by their own words, Eve was not alone in her choice as many have thought but was clearly in a patriarchal, matriarchal companionship with Adam in the partaking.

Bruce R. McConkie writes,

> Thus the name of Adam and Eve as a united partnership is Adam. They, the two of them together, are named Adam. ... Adam and Eve taken together are named Adam, and the fall of Adam is the fall of them both, for they are one. How aptly did Paul say: "Neither is the man without the woman, neither the woman without the man, in the Lord" (1 Corinthians 11:11). The fall of Adam is the fall of *The Man Adam* and the woman Eve.[65]

Simply stated, if Eve had not partaken, we would not be here. *Adam would not have partaken of the fruit without Eve's promptings* (Genesis 3:8). (see Chapter 30; Walking through the Scriptures.) She was called to be the mother of all living, in which she was also called to induce mortality that men might be. She had the faith, the wisdom, and the love of man to instigate the eternal plan of happiness that "men might be" (2 Nephi 2:25). It was because of the command to be fruitful and replenish the earth that she, with her husband, wisely took their first steps into mortality.

As we look to the Savior's Second Coming, the fullness of the gospel must go forward with a greater understanding of the paramount oneness of Adam and Eve and the partaking of the forbidden fruit. Whether in the beginning with Adam and Eve or in the final days of our mortal probation, "neither is the man without the woman, neither the woman without the man, in the Lord" (1 Corinthians 11:11). So simple yet so eternally comprehensive is this statement.

THE SAVIOR TEACHES

Even Christ openly rejected the traditional misunderstandings about the social value of women. The finest of these examples that Jesus put forth to magnify the cherished role of women was when he, as the risen Christ, first appeared unto Mary Magdalene, "Jesus saith unto her, Mary. She turned herself, and saith unto him, Rabboni; which is to say, Master. Jesus saith unto her, Touch me not; for I am not yet ascended to my Father: [then authorizing her as the first witness to His rising] but *go to my brethren, and say unto them*, I ascend unto my Father, and your Father; and to my God, and your God." As commanded, "Mary Magdalene came and told the apostles that she had seen the Lord, and that he had spoken these things unto her" (John 20:16–18; emphasis added). This purposeful inclusion of women by Christ indicates that His church (JST Revelation 12:7; see chapter 5, Enmity) cannot go forward without covenant women in the midst, as it was in the beginning, with Adam and Eve. Also in Luke: "It was Mary Magdalene, and Joanna, and Mary the mother of James, and *other women* that were with them, *which told these things unto the apostles* and their words seemed to them as idle tales, and *they believed them not*" (Luke 24:10–11; emphasis added). Even Cleopas and another [presumably Luke[66]] who had a witness of Christ on the way to Emmaus (see Luke 24:13–35) told these things to the brethren, and they believed not—"and as they thus spake, Jesus himself stood in the midst of them" (Luke 24:36): "Afterwards he [the risen Christ] . . . upbraided them with their unbelief and hardness of heart, because they believed not them which had seen him after he was risen" (Mark 16:14). In such times, the social standing of women was not to be credited; so it was with Eve and the part she played in Eden.

This experience may have been a benefit to the apostles, for after Christ ascended, the Apostles were sent forth as witnesses to the people that Christ lives. They were sent to teach that which they had not believed, though informed by witnesses—that Christ had risen. This might have better prepared them to understand the resistance they would certainly face in their apostolic journey, also showing forth that Christ does not come to the apostles only, but unto all who believe. As the Apostles had much to learn, we can patiently accept their learning curve in such circumstances, while we also learn with them.

JESUS COUNSELS THE TEMPTING PHARISEES

Jesus was approached by the prideful Pharisees on the subject of their wives. In Matthew 19:3–6, Jesus counseled the Pharisees, who "came unto him, tempting him, and saying unto him, Is it lawful for a man to put away his wife for every cause? And he answered and said unto them, have ye not read, that he which made them at the beginning made them male and female, And said, for this cause shall a man leave father and mother, and shall cleave to his wife; and they twain shall be one flesh? Wherefore they are no more twain, but one flesh. What therefore God hath joined together, let not man put asunder." Do not be deceived, in Christ's own words; Adam and Eve were one in the beginning, in the partaking of the fruit. They were sealed in Eden and commanded to be one in all things. As we can see, these laws have not been rescinded, and Jesus points that out to the Pharisees of His time.

The repetition of this declaration by Jesus confirms the divine truth of male–female union beyond contest. This is not just a physical or marital command but a spiritual command of oneness and unity of heart and mind: bound by the Father, in the Father, by the Holy Spirit of Promise, as it was performed in the Garden of Eden. The command to partake of the fruit and become fruitful was sealed in Eden by a marriage covenant. This celestial marriage is a culmination of the family unit, which enables husbands and wives to become gods, "by the new and everlasting covenant . . . as hath been sealed upon *their* heads, which glory shall be a fullness and a continuation of the seeds forever and ever. Then shall *they* be gods, because *they* have no end" (D&C 132:19–20; emphasis added).

In Matthew 19, Jesus continued, in verses 7 and 8, explaining man's propensity for pride and prejudice: "They say unto him, why did Moses then command to give a writing of divorcement, and to put her away? He saith unto them, Moses because of the *hardness of your hearts* suffered you to put away your wives: but *from the beginning it was not so*" (emphasis added). Indeed, it was not so with Adam and Eve, who chose to enter into a forbidden (see 2 Nephi 2:15, 18–19) world together. Not as Eve, not as Adam, but as one.

He who divides our first parents in intellect, intelligence, purpose, and obedience is without full comprehension of the original marriage covenant; and therefore those conclusions are derived from base, worldly, or social assumptions. Surely those assumptions are not "in the Lord" (1 Corinthians 11:11); but rather they come "because of the hardness of your hearts" (Matthew 19:8).

How do we become one with the Father? It is done by becoming one in heart, might, mind, and soul, as well as through the holy ordinance of marriage. Adam and Eve's marriage was performed before the partaking of the tree of knowledge of good and evil. It was performed in an immortal world, in God's presence, in all purity, and *specifically that men might be.* This is the oneness in which Adam and Eve obeyed the Lord. This is the commandment in which "men are, that they might have joy" (2 Nephi 2:25). How is it then that the aforementioned statements of Paul can be so misconstrued?

Perhaps we are not yet 'entirely one with our Lord'—perhaps the natural man still has some residence within our hearts. I believe, however, that as a covenant-making and temple-building people in these last days, we are heading toward that perfection.

MISCONCEPTIONS AFFECT THE RELATIONSHIP

Unfortunately, it seems to me that the misconception of men regarding Paul's statement—that Eve was somehow deceived while Adam was not—has brought on a plethora of misconceptions about the relationship between men and women, even in the Church, creating a division, separating their purpose, social and spiritual standing, and even creating a precept of marital inequality. Even the priesthood order was vastly misunderstood in ancient as well as latter-day times, as women were often perceived as exempt from the priesthood. Much of this is based on theological misunderstandings from 1 Timothy 2:14, "Adam was not deceived but the woman being deceived was in the transgression."

Perhaps in 1 Timothy, Paul is addressing a particular outgrowth of apostasy which had to be kept in check, and this is his verbal explanation of priesthood order for the family. Perhaps it could be likened to today when we hear of women protesting the church because they have not been ordained to the priesthood, wanting to possess the keys of the priesthood. These women also do not have a full understanding of the holy order of the priesthood. Yet, in this generation of restoration, instead of separating men and women in the priesthood, Elder Oaks combines them in that same authority. He speaks in a new and clearer tone than did Paul:

> When a woman—young or old—is set apart to preach the gospel as a full-time missionary, she is given *priesthood authority* to perform a priesthood function. The same is true when a woman is set apart to function as an officer or teacher in a Church organization under the direction of one who holds the keys of the priesthood." He also quoted President Kimball, saying "*When we speak of marriage as a partnership, let us speak of marriage as a full partnership.* We do not want our LDS women to be silent partners or limited partners in that eternal assignment! Please be a contributing and full partner.[67]

While Elder Oaks was speaking of the women of the church in these latter-days, Paul might have been addressing a specific, perhaps apostate, group in his comments toward women, for he knew of the Prophetess Deborah, the Prophetess Huldah, and the Prophetess Miriam in the Old Testament; as well, he would have known of Anna, the Prophetess in the New Testament. Paul, in his apostolic journey, also "entered into the house of Phillip the Evangelist, which was one of the seven; and abode with him. And the same man had four daughters, virgins, which did prophesy. And . . . [he] tarried there many days" (Acts 21:8–10).

As Elder Oaks stands as a strong advocate for Eve and the partaking, his plea for full partnership in marriage is without doubt inclusive in the fullness of the gospel in these last days. I believe the social standing and placement of women in such times as Paul experienced, the eventual apostasy, and perhaps even the influence Paul was under from having been taught as a Pharisee, may have influenced his writings concerning the role Eve played in the Fall. I believe, however, that much can be explained as we continue to study Paul's words as well as the setting from which he came. Paul's words open up in a much broader scope as we continue to view them by the spirit of revelation and in the concept of priesthood as a family order. Also keep in mind that, "because of the many plain and precious things which have been taken out of the book, which were plain unto the understanding of the children of men, according to the plainness which is in the Lamb of God— because of these things which are taken away out of the gospel of the Lamb, an exceedingly great many do stumble, yea, insomuch that Satan hath great power over them" (1 Nephi 13:29). The persuasion that Adam and Eve were separate and even opposing in the partaking of the fruit, is false. These false accusations have caused much confusion and "if possible, they shall deceive the very elect, who are the elect according to the covenant" (Joseph Smith—Matthew 1:22).

Perhaps that is why Paul's statement in 1 Timothy continues to be perpetuated in a less-than-positive light by others, such as in James E. Talmage's 1981 book, *The Articles of Faith*, a marvelous book of revelatory truth; however, in his exuberance to confirm Paul's statement in 1 Timothy, he writes,

> The woman was captivated by these representations; and, being eager to possess the advantages pictured by Satan, *she disobeyed* the command of the Lord, and partook of the fruit forbidden. She feared not evil, for *she knew it not.* . . . On the other hand, Adam would be disobeying another command by yielding to his wife's request. He deliberately and wisely decided to stand by the first and greater commandment; and, therefore, with a full comprehension of the nature of his act, he also partook of the fruit that grew on the Tree of Knowledge. The fact that Adam acted understandingly in this matter is *affirmed by the scriptures. Paul, in writing to Timothy,* explained that "Adam was not deceived; but the woman, being deceived, was in the transgression.[68]

Elder Talmage's influence on Eve's perceived actions has penetrated into church manuals, as noted in a preceding paragraph. Only recently, through modern prophets, has this influence been addressed and modified. I don't hesitate to use Elder Talmage's quotes throughout this book as he is a prolific writer and a profound witness of *Jesus the Christ.* I do, however, feel his comments on Eve's choice need to be addressed and considered in order to fully vet Eve in this controversy.

In contrast to Talmage's statement, Paul wrote, "In *Adam* all die" (1 Corinthians 15:22; emphasis added); and to the Roman Saints he declared: "Wherefore, as by *one man, sin entered into the world, and death by sin*; . . . for as by one *man's disobedience many were made sinners*" (Romans 5:12,19). Also, the second article of faith states: "We believe that men will be punished for their own sins and not for *Adam's* transgression" (emphasis added). This leads us to believe that the brief statement in 1 Timothy may have deeper meaning than first perceived. I now believe that, through study and prayer, Paul's words lead us to a far greater understanding of the gospel of Jesus Christ than first encountered, as it also brings us to a greater understanding of Adam and Eve's united partnership. We will continue to examine Paul's prophetic words in depth, that our minds might truly be enlightened (see chapter 31; Priesthood Veil).

I love James E. Talmage, a dynamic figure in the world and in

Church history. Born in 1862, ordained an Apostle in 1911, he died a dedicated Apostle of the Lord in 1933. Much like Paul, his life was centered in declaring the gospel of Christ while at the same time, he was also centered, as was Paul, in a great deal of social change as women's suffrage in the United States brought about the passage of the Nineteenth Amendment to the United States Constitution, which provided that "The right of citizens of the United States to vote shall not be denied or abridged by the United States or by any State on account of sex." In 1920, *this guaranteed all American women the right to vote.* This was a new social revolution that brought fear into the hearts of some men, as it seemed to be in defiance to God, according to noted biblical accounts.

Elder Talmage, however, has a high regard for Eve as he articulates priesthood in an advanced perspective pertaining to man and woman:

> In the restored Church of Jesus Christ, the Holy Priesthood is conferred, as an individual bestowal, upon men only, and this in accordance with divine requirement. It is not given to women to exercise the authority of the priesthood independently; nevertheless, in the sacred endowments associated with the ordinances pertaining to the house of the Lord, woman shares with man the blessings of the priesthood. When the frailties and imperfections of mortality are left behind, in the glorified state of the blessed hereafter, husband and wife will administer in their respective stations, seeing and understanding alike, and cooperating to the full in the government of their family kingdom. Then shall women be recompensed in rich measure for all the injustice that womanhood has endured in mortality. Then shall woman reign by divine right, a queen in the resplendent realm of her glorified state, even as exalted man shall stand, priest and king unto the most high God. Mortal eye cannot see nor minds comprehend the beauty, glory, and majesty of a righteous woman made perfect in the celestial kingdom of God.[69]

I agree with Elder Talmage that the "majesty of a righteous woman [is] made perfect in the celestial kingdom of God." I also believe that would apply to Eve in Eden, as they both dwelt in the presence of the Father, "in the *image* of God created he him; *male and female* created he them" (Genesis 1:27; emphasis added).

She would not be able to receive such splendor if it had not been accounted unto her in the beginning.

Elder Talmage, however, seems to take a different approach than Paul: "Let the woman learn in silence with all subjection. But I suffer not a woman to teach, nor to usurp authority over the man [keys of the priesthood], but to be in silence" (1 Timothy 2:11–12). Women are expected, as are men, to submit to the authority (priesthood) of Christ. Talmage, however, insightfully qualifies faithful, covenant women when he writes: "No special ordination in the Priesthood is essential to man's receiving the gift of prophecy; *The ministrations of Miriam and Deborah show that this gift may be possessed by women also.*[70] In Eve's prophetic calling, she was the first of all women who talked with God. "Adam and Eve, his wife, called upon the name of the Lord, and *they* heard the voice of the Lord from the way toward the Garden of Eden, *speaking unto them*" (Moses 5:4; emphasis added).

For in Eve, as well as in Adam, we find a well spring of latter-day prophecies which support their ongoing righteousness. A more recently published doctrinal manual explains, "If we correctly understand the role of Adam and Eve, we will realize that those who have labeled them sinners responsible for the universal depravity of the human family are *misguided*. The truth is that Adam and Eve opened the door for us to come into mortality, a step essential to our eternal progress."[71]

According to sacred teachings, it is Eve who explains to Adam why they must fall, "that men might be" (2 Nephi 2:25). Indeed, latter-day prophets that I quote throughout this book most assuredly assert Eve's courageous choice—that Eve took her rightful role as "mother of all living" (Genesis 3:20). "In all of this," wrote Elder Bruce R. McConkie, "Adam and Eve simply complied with the law which enabled them to become mortal beings, and this course of conduct is *termed* eating the forbidden fruit."[72]

Author Alonzo Gaskill wrote about Eve: "She is a heroine because she understood what was right and then chose to do exactly that, *not because she was deceived* into doing something that, in the end, benefited God's plan."[73] Then he concludes, "Thus, the traditional interpretation that Eve was somehow tricked is inaccurate."[74] In defense of Eve, Elder Dallin H. Oaks declared, "Some Christians condemn Eve for her act, concluding that she and her daughters are somehow flawed by it. Not the Latter-day Saints! *Informed by revelation*, we celebrate Eve's act and honor her wisdom and courage in the great episode called the Fall."[75]

Let us remove the shadows of deception that have long validated our misinterpretations of Eve. For it is not Eve who had been deceived. By revelation and the spirit of latter-day prophecy, we can more clearly understand the truth in Eden, and thus, more clearly discern our own path through their righteous directives.

Truth was brought forth from Eden. Eve's role in her companionship with Adam helps me to clarify my role in my companionship with the priesthood. I identify with Eve; she is my teacher, my exemplar, my mother. She is Mother Eve.

CHAPTER 8

DID EVE KNOW?

Adam knew what was required of him.
How does knowing pertain to Eve?

Many believe that Adam knew but that Eve did not (see 1 Timothy 2:11–12). Jeffrey R. Holland confirmed, "They had full knowledge of the plan of salvation during their stay in Eden."[76] Adam and Eve, in the immortal presence of God, received under His tutelage immense knowledge and understanding as they were prepared to become the parents of all mankind. As God said, "They are the workmanship of mine own hands, and I gave unto *them* their knowledge, in the day I created them; and in the Garden of Eden, gave I unto man his agency" (Moses 7:32; emphasis added). Our first parents walked and talked with God while they dwelt in Eden (see Genesis 3:8–10). President Brigham Young stated, "Adam was as conversant with his Father who placed him upon this earth as we are conversant with our earthly parents."[77]

Gospel scholar Alonzo Gaskill wrote, "The only knowledge Adam and Eve appear to have been void of during their stay in the Garden was experiential knowledge."[78] Gaskill continues,

> Alma suggests that prior to the Atonement, Christ was in a similar situation regarding sin. He stated: "Now the Spirit knoweth all things; nevertheless, the Son of God suffereth according to the flesh that he

might take upon him the sins of his people, that he might blot out their transgression according to the power of his deliverance; and now behold, this is the testimony which is in me" (Alma 7:13). Of this verse, Hugh Nibley once noted that although the Spirit could have shown Christ what being a sinner would be like, Jesus needed to experience this firsthand. He must "go through it himself." Elder Neal A. Maxwell added, "Jesus knew cognitively what He must do, but not experientially."[79] The Atonement provided Christ with this experiential knowledge. And so it was with Adam and Eve. In order to gain their eternal exaltation, they needed experiential knowledge as well as intellectual knowledge. The Fall would be the means of gaining that."[80]

To keep all the vital covenants of salvation and teach proper doctrine, we need to correctly understand the depth of that doctrine, and Adam and Eve can give us that—they brought us here under essential doctrines of priesthood, marriage, and procreation, as well as the salvation of Jesus Christ and taught it to their children. Though much has been lost, basic and vital doctrine can be found as we turn back to Eden for understanding. The joyous message of Adam and Eve's oneness has been taught by Christ and by latter-day prophets, but it takes time and determination to put out Satan's lies that lead us to traditional misunderstanding and teachings.

Adam and Eve were both given the command to multiply and replenish the earth. However, as Eve was named, she was specifically chosen by God and then named by Adam as the mother of all living (see Moses 4:26). Adam and Eve were taught by their immortal Father and surely tutored by Heavenly Mother as well. Thus, it was by command that they left *father and mother* (see Genesis 2:24) and came to a mortal earth that men might be. It had to be through Heavenly Father and Mother that the example of parenting was demonstrated before entering mortality. They would continue that same pattern as taught by their parents and thus teach it to their children.

Though my accolades are specific to Eve in this book, the correlation between Adam and Eve as equals is clearly stated. Eve knew her role and so did Adam. They were equally compatible as they enhanced each other in their designated callings and attributes.

In Eve's specified motherhood, she becomes the life of man. Would she not have been given necessary knowledge and direction for that calling? Being called of God and through the priesthood key first given to Adam, Eve was fully authorized to fulfill her name. By taking her preordained path, she helped pave the way for the Savior's infinite Atonement and our eternal salvation. This was not done in ignorance.

A calling does not come from God without direction from the Holy Spirit. Eve did know and had been taught what she must do: be fruitful, multiply, and replenish the earth so that "men might be" (2 Nephi 2:25). Certainly this was not the least of callings; to the contrary, Eve's actions were imperative to all mankind. She acted accordingly under the tutelage and keys of the priesthood, for it was "I, the Lord God, [who] called the first of all women, which are many" (Moses 4:26). Adam was the first man to hold the keys of salvation on the earth, Eve was the first mother, and through her seed the living Christ was prophesied to come (see Genesis 3:15). Yes, they had been taught. Therefore, they knowingly opened the door to a much higher agency, an experiential agency, even the knowledge of good and evil. We wisely agreed to follow in their parental footsteps.

CHAPTER 9

THE MOUTH OF THE SERPENT

Satan carefully manipulates a developing scenario
between Eve and the subtle serpent.

Satan was also in the midst of the Garden of Eden, probably skulking around the tree of knowledge of good and evil, maybe for eons, before Adam even came upon the earth. Satan coveted the power of God the Father and the eminent domain of the Son of God. As a result of Satan's defiant nature, he was cast down upon the earth and out of God's presence. In his profuse anger, Satan was determined to defy all that was godly and to reign as the lord of lords. With falsely imputed entitlement, he demanded of the immortal Father, "give me thine honor" (Moses 4:1; D&C 39:36). But it would not be given to him; it would be given to one who was in the perfect image of the Father.

If Satan's demands for power would not be met, he would surely feign it. Thus, he would claim for himself that earthly domain in which he was now confined. Pronouncing himself as the god of this world, he would also claim the souls of the children of God, who would be schooled upon his worldly domain for a time. Satan would craftily devise a plan to trap the children of men in his earthly mire until they could no longer escape him.

As Satan came upon the scene of Adam and Eve in the garden, his obsession was to possess the bodies (not having his own body) of

Adam and Eve (see 3 Nephi 7:19) by contradicting and destroying the knowledge given to them by God, and thus their agency. "Wherefore, because that Satan rebelled against me, and sought to destroy the agency of man, which I, the Lord God, had given him, . . . I caused that he should be cast down" (Moses 4:3). Having fallen to the earth, out of God's presence, Satan would continue his undaunted work of subtlety trying to obtain the agency of man.

DEVILS AND SWINE

As Satan is cast down to the earth, I find it a metaphoric representation in the story for which the demonic legions were also cast out of "two possessed with devils" and into a herd of swine (Matthew 8:28 [28–32]). Swine in such times were notably unclean animals. Similarly, Satan and his minions, being cast down upon the earth, pled for a fitting sanctuary (Revelation 12:9). Compare this with the devils' plea in Matthew:

> And, behold, they cried out, saying, what have we to do with thee, Jesus, thou Son of God? Art thou come hither to torment us before the time [before the final judgment]?
>
> So the devils besought him, saying, if thou cast us out, suffer us to go away into the herd of swine [the natural man].
>
> And he said unto them, go [upon the earth, where the battle for dominion continues]. And when they were come out [onto the earth], they went into the herd of swine: and, behold, the whole herd of swine ran violently down a steep place into the sea, and perished in the waters [eternal darkness]. (Matthew 8:29, 31–32)

As with the swine, Satan has become a demonic plague on a weak, perishable, mortal world.

In Eden, unlike Lucifer, Adam had been given an immortal body of flesh and bone and was under the personal tutelage of the Father. Because Adam and Eve were valiant disciples of Christ in the spirit world, it would not be easy for Satan to deceive them now. Adam, as Michael, had defeated him once before in the spirit world. This came as "there was war in heaven; Michael and his angels fought against the dragon; and the dragon and his angels fought against Michael; And the dragon prevailed not against Michael.

. . . For the accuser of our brethren is cast down, which accused them before our God day and night" (JST Revelation 12:6, 7, 10). Adam's power is far greater than that of the disobedient Lucifer, for "[Adam] received those [priesthood] keys in the Creation, according to the Prophet Joseph Smith, who added, "Christ is the Great High Priest; Adam next."[81]

It was Adam who Satan must defeat now. To Satan's advantage, however, Adam had forgotten his previous battles with Lucifer (see chapter 31, Veil). Having forgotten all such proceedings, Adam was childlike in his learning as the Father schooled him in the matters of faith for a mortal probation (Moses 7:32). Satan, on the other hand, knew that mortality would surely be Adam and Eve's weakness and his only possible chance to deceive them.

How long was Satan upon the earth in his spiritually fallen state? How long did it take him to impress his diabolical plan upon Adam and Eve, who were pure, innocent, and in the presence of God? How many times did Satan try and fail before he perfected his subtle plan? Satan, being without a physical form, needed a willing body through which to convey his plan. His subtlety, therefore, became the body and deceived heart of the serpent (Moses 6:4).

How could Satan infiltrate the affections of Adam and Eve that he might deceive them? Seeing that there was clearly an affectionate relationship between them and the animals, Satan saw his chance. He knew that Adam had been commanded to name and care for every beast: "I, the Lord God, formed every beast . . . and commanded that they should come unto Adam." Leaving Adam with implicit instructions, "Adam gave names to all cattle, and to the fowl of the air, and to every beast of the field" (Moses 3:19–20). Surely, the love and contact Adam and Eve had for and with the animals would prove advantageous for Satan. With malevolent persistence, Satan found a way to influence man: "Now the serpent was more subtle than any beast of the field which I, the Lord God, had made. And Satan put it into the *heart* of the serpent, (for he had drawn away many after him,) and he sought also to beguile Eve" (Moses 4:5–6; emphasis added).

Adam and Eve, as the children of God, held the dominative law of transgression in which the animals too would fall into a forbidden world. When Adam and Eve fell, the animals fell with them. President Joseph Fielding Smith wrote: "Adam [and, by extension, all of the animal creation] had no blood in his veins before the fall. . . . All forms of life to multiply and replenish the earth (see Moses 2:22, 28) could not be obeyed until man had fallen and until blood had entered the human and animal systems."[82]

Satan's plan was planted into the "heart" of the deceived serpent. Perhaps the serpent too presumptuously desired a mortal body, as well as the power to bring forth his own kind upon the earth (see Abraham 4:25). In any case, it seems that Satan employed the serpent in the act of beguiling Eve. So through the serpent, Satan, "who transformeth himself nigh unto an angel of light," appeared and "beguiled our first parents" (2 Nephi 9:9).

Perhaps it was because of the persuasion of the subtle serpent that Christ was then given the power to save all. For if the Fall had not occurred, neither would the redemption of man be necessary. In a strange way, the poisonous serpent afforded Christ the inherent and sustaining power to save and to heal. Thus you could say that the symbolism of a serpent also represents the power for which Christ will eventually reign upon this earth and bruise the serpent's head. In that sense, the chaotic anger of Satan is entirely ironic because it spelled his doom while creating a greater agency for man's godhood and Christ's eminent crown.

Satan would not have been able to approach Adam and Eve, save Christ should remove himself to allow the subtlety of Satan and the Serpent, being left to choose good or evil (Alma 13:3). Only then did Adam and Eve's agency fully emerge; "in the Garden of Eden, gave I unto man his agency" (Moses 7:32). Together, Satan and the subtle serpent effectively began to seek to beguile Eve: "And he [Satan] said unto the woman: Yea, hath God said— Ye shall not eat of every tree of the garden? (And he spake by the mouth of the serpent)," (Moses 4:7; see also Numbers 22:20–35). As Satan opened his dialogue to Eve with a question, which prompted thought and consideration about the forbidden fruit, he seemed to have caught her in a moment of contemplation over that which had been forbidden, for a pondering mind is an open mind. When Eve responded to his question, in his beguiling efforts, Satan deceitfully pointed to the pros and cons of mortal life. Eve, being fully motivated to consider the Father's commands to multiply and replenish the earth, she knew "there is no other way."[83] It was then that "she took of the fruit thereof, and did eat, and also gave unto *her husband with her*, and he did eat" (Moses 4:12; emphasis added). All this was done under the reassurance of redemption, should they remain faithful.

As God returns to them in the garden, "in the cool of the day; Adam and his wife went to hide themselves from the presence of the Lord God amongst the trees of the garden. And I, the Lord God, called unto Adam, and said unto him: Where goest thou?" (Moses 4:14-15; Genesis 3:8). Instructing Adam the Lord God said, "For this cause shall a man leave father and mother, and shall cleave to his wife: and they twain shall be one flesh?" (Matthew 19:5). "Therefore the Lord God sent him forth from the garden of Eden, to till the ground from whence he was taken (Genesis 3:23). Unto the woman God said, "I will greatly multiply thy sorrow and thy conception. In sorrow thou shalt bring forth children, and thy desire shall be to thy husband" (Moses 4:22). (See chapter 13, Sorrow; and 19, Eve and the Priesthood.)

Turning to the Serpent, "the Lord God said unto the serpent, "Because thou hast done this, thou art cursed above all cattle and above every beast of the field; upon thy belly shalt thou go, and dust shalt thou eat all the days of thy life" (Genesis 3:14) (Chapter 27, Dust). And to Satan God said; And I will put enmity between thee and the woman, and between thy seed and her seed; it shall bruise thy head. And thou shalt bruise his heel" (Genesis 3:15) (Chapter 5, Enmity).

After placing coats of skins upon Adam and Eve (Genesis 3:21), "did I, the Lord God, appoint unto man the days of his probation—that by his natural death he might be raised in immortality unto eternal life, even as many as would believe" (D&C 29:43).

As this writing follows Satan and the serpent, we can better understand what took place and how it may have played out. In this rendition, it is not hard to see how the serpent fits into Satan's plan. Though many scriptures are figurative, symbolic, and metaphorical to gospel principles, it's important to remember that these are true events. They are not made up; they are not mythical but are the works and word of God.

CHAPTER 10
WHEN THE HEART SPEAKS DECEIT

Only by knowing truth can we clarify a lie.

In Satan's efforts to deceive, "he sought also to beguile Eve, for he knew not the mind of God" (Moses 4:6). Satan knew not the mind of God because he knew not the heart of God. Satan was completely void of love, while "God is love" (1 John 4:16). God's intelligence is as wide as eternity (see Moses 1:35), while Satan's mind dwells singularly upon himself.

As the children of Adam and Eve continue to combat evil, it is needful to recognize what is true and what is false. As we learn from Eve, her truth becomes our truth. Their story is our story and our victory becomes their victory. As our mortal journey advances through the tree of knowledge of good and evil we need to look to the tree of life for truth, "which is the love of God" (1 Nephi 11:22).

The two trees in the Garden of Eden provided a full scope of choice. The trees were not opposite or contradictory but together became a needed spectrum to our agency. We were not left to ourselves; God provided us with the agency to choose between good and evil. In that He gave us sufficient instruction before and after entering into mortality. (Moses 7:32). Those instructions, if utilized, will safely guide us through the oppositions and trials of this life.

Opposition provides choice; it is a sure way to perfection, in that it allows us to use our agency to think, to choose good over evil, to act, and to create as God creates, gaining a needed maturity for godhood. Like Adam and Eve, it requires choosing one of two sides, or more specifically, choosing truth over the lies, because truth can be maintained eternally. *Contradiction* is trying to choose the lies, or the truth mingled with lies, becoming self-contradictory because it is not pure truth. It therefore becomes a lie and cannot be maintained. The simple conclusion here is that *opposition is choosing truth over lies, while contradiction becomes lies over truth.*

Opposition by way of choice is provided with clear godly instructions; by commandments we know that which is truth and, therefore, that which is a lie. Only by knowing truth can we clarify a lie. It is Satan who provides contradiction to truth, in that he masks over the truth with his lies, thus compromising the distinction between truths and lies.

It's important to recognize all of Satan's most effective tactics, starting with the deviant art of mingling truth with lies to suit his own purposes; doing so allows him to more perfectly deceive. "For many shall come in my name, saying, I am Christ; and shall deceive many" (Matthew 24:5). Satan masks and manipulates his diabolical lies by paralleling them with God's truth. "The purity of the gospel is lost when scripture is mingled with the philosophies of men."[84] When Joseph Smith inquired of the Lord which church was true, he learned that the churches of his day "draw near to me with their lips, but their hearts are far from me, they teach for doctrines the commandments of men, having a form of godliness, but they *deny the power thereof*" (Joseph Smith—History 1:19).

Cain is an example of having been deceived, for he rejected the Lord and hearkened unto Satan's lies, "Who is the Lord that I should know him?" (Moses 5:16). To be beguiled, one need be presented with lies for deception. To be deceived, one must accept those lies. Cain readily accepted the lies presented by Satan. Eve, on the other hand, understood that truth is what leads us unto Christ, for Christ is truth, light, and love. Lies are what lead us away from Christ, becoming darkness and confusion. Beguiled is to hear the lies: charm, enchant, captivate, engage, divert, tempt. Deceive is to accept the lies: swindle, cheat, defraud, mislead, or double-cross—this having been Cain's sure demise.

To apply our hearts to understanding, we must apply the first commandment, "Thou shalt love the Lord thy God with all thy heart, and with all thy soul, and with all thy mind" (Matthew 22:37). To know if we love the Lord, John tells us: "And hereby we do know that we know him [Christ], if we keep his commandments. He that saith, I know him, and keepeth not his commandments, is a liar, and the truth is not in him. But whoso keepeth his word, in him verily is the *love of God* perfected: hereby know we that we are in him" (1 John 2:3–5; emphasis added). Neither can we receive a testimony unless we put off the natural man, "The natural man receiveth not the things of the Spirit of God: for they are foolishness unto him: neither can he know them, because they are *spiritually discerned*" (1 Corinthians 2:14; emphasis added).

Many have been captivated by Satan as he fraudulently appears to them as one who is godly. Adam and Eve made that discernment when "the devil . . . who beguiled our first parents, who transformeth himself nigh unto an angel of light" (2 Nephi 9:9) appeared unto them. Adam and Eve prevailed because they knew Christ and were righteous before Him, as if to say, "O thou child of hell, why tempt ye me? Knowest thou that the righteous yieldeth to no such temptations?" (Alma 11:23). It is by obedience to the commandments that the righteous are spared, for "because of the righteousness of his people, Satan has no power" (1 Nephi 22:26).

Because of Satan's deceptive lies, many good hearts have been swayed away from God's intended path. Satan still operates that way, leading us along his forbidden paths as the father of all lies, mocking the Father's word in all its truth. Satan readily contradicts truth; In this we could say that Satan is, for all his intents and purposes, *the dark shadow of truth.*

FALSE PROPHETS

Satan is not beyond trickery: "Therefore it is no great thing if his ministers also be transformed as the ministers of righteousness;

whose end shall be according to their works" (2 Corinthians 14,15). While prophets have the authority to lead us unto Christ, and the required ordinances of His church, a false prophet will lead us away from Christ. Like Satan, their implied authority becomes a diversion from Christ's ordained path. "But there were false prophets also among the people, even as there shall be false teachers among you, who privily shall bring in damnable heresies, even denying (see Joseph Smith—History 1:19) the Lord that bought them, and bring upon themselves swift destruction. And many shall follow their pernicious ways; by reason of whom the way of truth shall be evil spoken of" (2 Peter 2:1–2).

King Noah's people were deceived even by the priests whom he chose. "Yea, and they [the people] also became idolatrous, because they were deceived by the vain and flattering words of the king and priests; for they did speak flattering things unto them" (Mosiah 11:7). Being captivated by the popular lies of King Noah and his priests, the people rejected the unveiled truth of God as preached by Abinadi. "O king, behold, we are guiltless, and thou, O king, hast not sinned; therefore, this man has lied concerning you, and he has prophesied in vain" (Mosiah 12:14).

But one of the priests of Noah, Alma, perceived the truth in Abinadi. "And he was a young man, and he believed the words which Abinadi had spoken, for he knew concerning the iniquity which Abinadi had testified against them; therefore he began to plead with the king that he would not be angry with Abinadi, but suffer that he might depart in peace" (Mosiah 17:2). Later, Alma "fled from the servants of King Noah, repented of his sins and iniquities, and went about privately among the people, and began to teach the words of Abinadi" (Mosiah 18:1).

We can use two forms of knowledge to conclude what is true. One is physical knowledge, and the other is spiritual knowledge. Without the Holy Ghost, spiritual truths cannot be known. But Alma, by using physical knowledge, came to a spiritual conclusion. He did as the Lord directs: "You must study it out in your mind; then you must ask me if it be right, and if it is right I will cause that your bosom shall burn within you; therefore, you shall feel that it is right" (D&C 9:8). It is by the Spirit of truth that facts are clarified or disqualified, as the following verses attest:

- "For the word of the Lord is truth, and whatsoever is truth is light, and whatsoever is light is Spirit, even the Spirit of Jesus Christ" (D&C 84:45).
- "By the power of the Holy Ghost ye may know the truth of all things" (Moroni 10:5).

We need the Spirit of truth in all we study and learn. Even seemingly temporal facts become eternally comprehensive when the Spirit of truth is applied. Take math, for instance; we can memorize facts and formulas, but until we receive an enlightened comprehension of how those facts and formulas affect us and our universe, they remain just numbers. Without the Spirit of truth, facts can easily lead us to incorrect conclusions. This happens in science, politics, relationships, and even religion. To receive truth, we must study and ponder the facts until, through the Spirit of truth, they come together in a comprehensive light. We must desire truth beyond the facts. Yet truth does not come without examining the facts. In patient faith, it comes as Isaiah describes: "precept must be upon precept, precept upon precept; line upon line, line upon line; here a little, and there a little" (Isaiah 28:10). In both spiritual education and secular education, we must expend considerable effort to receive truth and knowledge. If our purpose is pure and our study is adequate, we will receive the light of truth.

We are expected to do our homework as we seek guidance from the Spirit (see D&C 9:7–8). Perhaps that is why, on occasion, it takes longer than expected to receive our answer—we have not yet studied it out sufficiently or sincerely enough to receive revelation. We should apply this process in all aspects of importance in our lives: marriage, relationships, work, talents, health, school, religion, politics, and so forth. Through a lack of complete information, facts may lead us astray, but the Spirit of truth will not. In other words, facts are incomplete without the Spirit of truth to confirm their value and application. Note that the Spirit of truth often requires that we search: "Ask of God; ask, and it shall be given you; seek, and ye shall find; knock, and it shall be opened unto you" (JST Matthew 7:12).

Only by knowing truth can we clarify a lie. While Satan's lies contradict truth, truth by comparison sheds light on evil. The act of choosing God's will over Satan's lies allows us to see and comprehend the pure light of Christ in contrast to the lies of Satan. We gain a better understanding of evil as we choose the pure words of Christ. "Then [our] eyes shall be opened, and [we] shall be as gods, knowing good and evil" (Moses 4:11).

Why do I add basic education to the knowledge of truth? Knowledge gained through education can be used to guide us to Christ or away from Christ. "When they are learned they think they are wise, and they hearken not unto the counsel of God, for they set it aside, supposing they know of themselves, wherefore, their wisdom is foolishness and it profiteth them not. And they shall perish" (2 Nephi 9:28). Satan is quick to stir us up, as he did among the Nephites, into "imagining up some vain thing in their hearts . . . and thus did Satan get possession of the hearts of the people . . . and lead them away to believe that the doctrine of Christ was a foolish and a vain thing" (3 Nephi 2:2). If we do not understand that all truth comes from God, then we have been deceived; our education has not led us to truth and our "wisdom is foolishness and it profiteth [us] not" (2 Nephi 9:28). Without the Spirit of truth, therefore, man is "ever learning, and never able to come to the knowledge of the truth" (2 Timothy 3:7).

In our search for truth, we would be wise to remember the words of Nephi: "Cursed is he that putteth his trust in man, or maketh flesh his arm, or shall hearken unto the precepts of men, save their precepts shall be given by the power of the Holy Ghost" (2 Nephi 28:31). "For whatsoever is born of God overcometh the world: and this is the victory that overcometh the world, even our faith. Who is he that overcometh the world, but he that believeth that Jesus is the Son of God?" (1 John 5:4–5).

SCIENCE AND THE HOLY GHOST

President Henry B. Eyring speaks affectionately of his father, Henry Eyring, who was a scientist of considerable degree and accomplishment and followed the Spirit all his days. President Eyring says of his father:

He was a scientist who searched for truth about the physical world throughout his entire adult life. He used the tools of science well enough to be honored by his peers across the world. Much of what he did in chemistry came from seeing in his mind's eye molecules moving about and then confirming his vision by experiments in a laboratory.

But he had followed a different course to discover the truths that mattered most to him and to each of us. *Only through the Holy Ghost can we see people and events as God sees them.*

President Eyring adds:

For example, if you receive a spiritual impression to honor the Sabbath day, especially when it seems difficult, God will send His Spirit to help. That help came to my father years ago when his work took him to Australia. He was alone on a Sunday, and he wanted to take the sacrament. He could find no information about Latter-day Saint meetings. So he started walking. He prayed at each intersection to know which way to turn. After walking and making turns for an hour, he stopped to pray again. He felt an impression to turn down a particular street. Soon he began to hear singing coming from the ground floor of an apartment building close by. He looked in at the window and saw a few people seated near a table covered with a white cloth and sacrament trays.[85]

Jacob taught, "O how great the holiness of our God! For he knoweth all things, and there is not anything save he knows it" (2 Nephi 9:20). Our great father Abraham understood this truth and sought it with all his heart:

Finding there was greater happiness and peace and rest for me, I sought for the blessings of the fathers, and the right whereunto I should be ordained to administer the same; having been myself a follower of righteousness, desiring also to be one who possessed great knowledge, and to be a greater follower of righteousness, and to possess a greater knowledge, and to be a father of many nations, a prince of peace, and desiring to receive instructions, and to keep the commandments of God, I became a rightful heir, a High Priest, holding the right belonging to the fathers. (Abraham 1:2)

Abraham's faith and works became pure knowledge:

Thus I, Abraham, talked with the Lord, face to face, as one man talketh with another; and he told me of the works which his hands had made; And he said unto me: My son, my son (and his hand was stretched out), behold I will show you all these. And he put his hand upon mine eyes, and I saw those things which his hands had made, which were many; and they multiplied before mine eyes, and I could not see the end thereof. (Abraham 3:11–12)

For Abraham, it seems that knowledge is limited only by our lack of faith, works, and deep desire to know and embrace truth. "Abraham believed God, and it was imputed unto him for righteousness: and he was called the Friend of God" (James 2:23).

CHAPTER 11
WHERE ART THOU? (GENESIS 3:9)

"I was naked; and I hid myself"

—*Moses 4:16*

After partaking of the fruit, "the Lord God called unto Adam, and said unto him: Where art thou?" (Genesis 3:9). When asked to acknowledge their new state of physical and spiritual existence, Adam said, "I heard thy voice in the garden, and I was afraid, *because I beheld that I was naked*, and I hid myself" (Moses 4:16; emphasis added). While yet in the garden, and finding himself in a new physical and spiritual state, Adam expressed his emotions simply by saying, "I was naked; and I hid myself" (Genesis 3:10).

This nakedness Adam spoke of is also a powerful metaphor for how they felt in being sent out of God's presence. It is also symbolic of the power which God allocates to man. "Erik Peterson observes that, according to the early Christian tradition, 'Adam and Eve were stripped by the Fall, in such a way that they saw that they were naked. This means that formerly they were clothed.' Adam and Eve wore the 'robe of light' or the 'robe of sanctity' before their fall; thereafter, they assumed a 'garment of humility.'"[86] In the words of Hugh Nibley, "Adam lost his garment of light at the Fall and had to clothe himself in a garment of skin. . . . His new leather garment was nonetheless a glorious one, a sign of authority,' and 'A garment of protection."[87] Being clothed in this garment of humility is significant to their new mortal surroundings. Not only as a physical protection against the elements but also against an aggressive adversary, who is Satan.

Because Adam and Eve had been stripped of their immortal robes, physical and spiritual feelings of shame came upon them, as the lack of their immortal refinement set in. The impurities of blood would now run through their veins. Mortality had created Adam and Eve's fragile state of being and feeling. Their bodies would certainly decline to the dust of the earth. In addition, they were also to be cast out of the Garden of Eden and God's presence.

"WHO TOLD THEE THAT THOU WAST NAKED?"

As Adam and Eve stepped from the shadows of the trees with fig leaves sewn together to cover their nakedness, God said, "Who told thee thou wast naked?" (Moses 4:17). The question seems odd. Did Adam and Eve need to be told they were naked? Naked is more than being unclothed. In Eden, it became a spiritual withdrawal as they lost immortality as their covering. Jacob described our state when we stand before God after this life, "Wherefore, we shall have a perfect knowledge of all our guilt, and our uncleanness, and our nakedness" (2 Nephi 9:14).

Who was so bold as to tell Adam and Eve they must now hide? It wasn't the Father, for He poses the question from the evidence of their withdrawal. The Father knew they were now under the influence of Satan, not because of the forbidden fruit but because they now shamefully withdrew themselves from the light. It seems that Satan, even from the beginning, is always ready and willing to remind us of our unworthiness—our nakedness—before God. Thus, guile begins to set in as we seek to hide ourselves and our shame from God.

Dale G. Renlund said,

> Just as Satan is our prosecutor and our accuser, he tells us;
>> We are not adequate, the one who tells us we are not good enough, the one who tells us there is no recovery from a mistake. He is the ultimate bully, the one who kicks us when we are down. He spoke against us in

the premortal existence, and he continues to denounce us is this life. He seeks to drag us down. He wants us to experience endless woe.

Elder Renlund also reminds us,

> We have an advocate with the Father, (1 John 2:1).
>
> The Savior forgives, heals, and advocates. He is our helper, consoler, and intercessor—attesting to and vouching for our reconciliation with God.[88]

Satan feeds us excuses for our shame while the Savior said "Come, follow me" (Luke 18:22). Only when we step toward the light, pleading for the cleansing love of the Savior, can we again feel His wondrous healing power. Satan, will tell us anything to keep us from that light and love. But we must trust in the light, and we must believe in the love of God. The Lord compassionately gives us the tools of covenants and ordinances so that we may step forward in confidence to defy Satan's excuses not to come unto Christ. "Take my yoke upon you," the Savior says, "and learn of me; for I am meek and lowly in heart: and ye shall find rest unto your souls" (Matthew 11:29). Sin cannot abide the light of Christ. Too often we think we can willfully force sin out but a far better way is to invite Christ into our lives, much like the Lamanites, "their harts had been changed; that they had no more desire to do evil" (Alma 19:33).

SEWING AN APRON OF FIG LEAVES

"And the eyes of them both were opened, and they knew that they were naked; and they sewed fig leaves together, and made themselves aprons" (Genesis 3:7). By sewing fig leaves together while yet in the Garden, Adam and Eve worked desperately to cover their dying spiritual and physical bodies of nakedness. They had lost the innocence of immortality, and they clearly felt it. An infinite Atonement would be required to recover their immortal souls. They needed a Savior.

The act of sewing fig leaves together to cover their nakedness was a humble expression of innocence lost and a desperate attempt to recover that loss. By offering their humble part, being clothed in fig leaves, Adam and Eve somehow satisfied the requirements for mercy. With a broken heart and a contrite spirit, they qualified for the grace of God and the pathway back: "Thou shalt offer a sacrifice unto the Lord thy God in righteousness, even that of a broken heart and a contrite spirit" (D&C 59:8). Humility, then, easily transfers into a willingness to obey the demands of the Savior. While the green apron of fig leaves represents mortal man's broken heart and contrite spirit as an effort to humbly seek guidance, the coats of skins become a symbol of the merciful promise of redemption through an infinite Atonement. With humble hearts, Adam and Eve sought the Lord,

> The early Christians saw the fig-leaf aprons as symbols of repentance. Irenaeus put it this way: "For [Adam] showed his repentance in making a girdle, covering himself with fig leaves. . . . Thus this act by Adam and Eve suggests that *their hearts were right*, that *they were not rebellious*. The fig leaves foreshadow their works of obedience, as recorded in the Book of Moses, in their offering the firstlings of the flocks" (Moses 5:5; emphasis added).[89]

Adam and Eve had also gained a new power of procreation in the Fall and sought to protect this power from misuse, "for the natural man is an enemy to God, and has been from the fall of Adam, and will be, forever and ever, unless he yields to the enticing of the Holy Spirit" (Mosiah 3:19). This new power could break them if not done in the love of God for the children of God. They did not hesitate to remember their previous covenants for procreation, "Notwithstanding [they] shall be saved in childbearing, if they continue in faith and charity and holiness with sobriety" (1 Timothy 2:15).

This holy gift and power is noted in Alonzo L. Gaskill's *Lost Language of Symbolism*:

> Anciently, both aprons and figs symbolized fertility and reproduction. . . . It was not until the Fall that Adam and Eve were able to "multiply and replenish" the earth as they had been commanded (Moses 5:11). Upon placing themselves in a position to "be fruitful and multiply," Adam and Eve appropriately donned the very symbols of their newly received power. What are we to make of Adam and Eve's wearing aprons of fig leaves that, at the very least, symbolize "fertility" and "reproduction"?

In light of Elder Richard G. Scott's counsel that we should "learn from the lives of Adam and Eve," the whole episode seems highly significant and applicable.[90]

Gaskill also suggests that "in ancient times aprons also symbolized priesthood and work. Adam was engaged in the 'work' of the Lord, a work requiring that he possess priesthood power. 'It seems clear that the Mosaic priest's apron was symbolically associated with the aprons of Adam and Eve."[91] Holding fast to the redeeming love of Jesus Christ, their submission was to God, that they might course the trials of mortality in righteousness. The aprons were evident of their submission to the will of God, a new power for procreation and sacred covenants within the Priesthood.

A REPORT IS REQUIRED

God asked, "Hast thou eaten of the tree, whereof I commanded thee that thou shouldest not eat?" (Genesis 3:11). A report is always required. The days of the Creation were methodically reported back to the Father, for "by mine Only Begotten I created these things" (Moses 2:1). The scriptures are such a report. Our prayers are a report. Family history work, documents, and records are reports. The book of life kept in the heavens is a report. Confession of sin is a report, and the final Judgment will be a review of that all-inclusive report.

Adam and Eve's answer to the Father's question was a report of the Fall, as He now required it of them—not because He needed to know but because they needed to ponder and understand what just took place. From their own mouths and comprehension of the situation, they took responsibility for their choice and gave their report. By His questioning, God confirmed for them their new reality of mortality. He, by His grace, also taught them their need for a Savior as He set before them commandments and covenants for salvation.

"And the man said, The woman whom thou gavest *to be with me*, she gave me of the tree, and I did eat" (Genesis 3:12; emphasis added). This was a true report without guile or excuse. Adam's report on his decision to travel with "the mother of all living" (Genesis 3:20) into mortality, that man might be, was proper, for he was commanded that the woman was "to be with [him]" (Genesis 3:12). Adam was called to cleave unto his wife and to protect and provide for her. Both he and Eve strictly followed the plan. If Adam had partaken of the fruit first, he might have gone into mortality without Eve and all would have been lost (see chapter 30; Walking Through the Scriptures). Thus, they both finished their report to the Father with the words "I did eat," meaning "I did obey"—I kept my covenants.

COATS OF SKIN

Rest and peace came to Adam and Eve as coats of skins were placed upon them to redeem them from the Fall. "Unto Adam and also unto his wife, did I, the Lord God, make coats of skins, and clothed them" (Moses 4:27; see also Genesis 3:21). Isaiah tells us to "put on thy beautiful garments, O Jerusalem, the holy city" (Isaiah 52:1 [1–2]). Joseph Smith wrote, *"and to put on her strength is to put on the authority of the priesthood, which she, Zion, has a right to by lineage."*[92]

Because Adam and Eve trespassed the law of immortality, a new covering, appropriate for mortality, had to be made for them. They must now look to Christ to clothe them in the robes of salvation. Becoming mortal meant that their bodies became pulsed by blood rather than by spirit.[93] These changes led to vulnerability and corruptibility. Their spiritual consciousness declined as they were sent from the Father's presence, just as their physical bodies would decline with age. Yet, because of spiritual and mortal decline, our spiritual awareness may heighten in new ways as we desperately seek the protective powers of Christ in faith. In this way, the eyes of Adam and Eve were opened as they became acutely aware of their need for the Savior.

In a mortal world, salvation became an eminent requirement. Adam and Eve could see and understand the Atonement as they saw their nakedness and understood their need.

> Seeing then that we have a great high priest, that is passed into the heavens, Jesus the Son of God, let us hold fast our profession.
>
> For we have not an high priest which cannot be touched with the feeling of our infirmities; but was in all points tempted like as we are, yet without sin.

Let us therefore come boldly unto the throne of grace, that we
may obtain mercy, and find grace to help in time of need [nakedness]."
(Hebrews 4:14–16)

Clothed in coats of skins, Adam and Eve wait upon a promised
Messiah, who has promised, "I will not leave you comfortless: I will
come to you" (John 14:18). The infinite Atonement is represented
in the clothing given to Adam and Eve to cover their nakedness.
"The Hebrew word for cover is atonement."[94] The words *naked* and
cover are metaphors, expressing a spiritual reality through a physical
symbol for the Lord's Atonement: "And let these, thine anointed
ones, be clothed with salvation, and thy saints shout aloud for joy"
(D&C 109:80).

NAKED BEFORE THE FALL

While being clothed in the raiment of salvation after the Fall,
being naked before the Fall had its own set of covenants. Before the
Fall, "Adam called his wife's name Eve" (Genesis 3:20). The eternal
marriage of Adam and Eve was sealed in Eden. Hugh Nibley said,
"In connection with this ceremony Adam and Eve were told to
'put on your garments of glory.'"[95] Beverly Campbell continues,
"If indeed Adam and Eve were clothed in robes of unparalleled
magnificence, as referenced in other Hebrew texts, we must search
for the symbolic richness in the next verse: 'And they were both
naked, *the man and his wife*, and were not ashamed'" (Genesis
2:25).[96] Adam and Eve were carefully prepared for the Fall. In a
marital promise of procreation, they were sent forth together to be
tried in a mortal world where redemption was the promise.

Before the Fall, "they were both naked, the man and his wife,
and were not ashamed" (Genesis 2:25). Though having robes before
the Fall, they were still considered *naked,* meaning *without* the robes
of salvation. To be *covered* refers to those priestly robes of salvation.
Isaiah said, "He hath clothed me with the garments of salvation,
he hath covered me with the robe of righteousness" (Isaiah 61:10).
Only after the Fall could they receive this specified garment.

All things point to Christ. Before the Fall, Adam and Eve were
naked (without salvation) but not ashamed (without impurities).

After the Fall, naked *and* ashamed, thus they were clothed with salvation. "Unto Adam, and also unto his wife, did I, the Lord God, make coats of skins and clothed them" (Moses 4:27). *Adam and Eve fell that they might be clothed in the power of salvation unto exaltation.* They were clothed in the promise of eventual godhood, which could only be fulfilled through the tree of knowledge of good and evil— by the *mortal* blood of Christ.

Because naked or *clothed* refers to saving ordinances. When we do not keep our covenants, we feel more vulnerable (naked) before God. This spiritual nakedness can lead to an uncanny feeling of physical nakedness as we feel afraid and hide ourselves from God. When we keep our covenants in faith, we feel protected and at peace before God. "And under this head ye are made free, and there is no other head whereby ye can be made free. There is no other name given whereby salvation cometh; therefore, I would that ye should take upon you the name of Christ" (Mosiah 5:8). "Then shall thy confidence wax strong in the presence of God; and the doctrine of the priesthood shall distil upon thy soul as the dews from heaven" (D&C 121:45). This was the ultimate purpose of the tree of knowledge of good and evil, to be clothed in the salvation of Christ—to know good from evil and to become as He is. It was only by partaking of the fruit that the eyes of Adam and Eve were opened and they recognized their critical need for a Savior. Only by a physical and spiritual separation from God can we see, feel, and need the infinite light of our Savior, Jesus Christ.

Being forbidden from entering into the presence of the Lord brings foreboding and a feeling of nakedness, such as with the partaking of the forbidden fruit. The commandments and covenants became Adam and Eve's sure path back to the Father. In like manner, obedience to temple covenants today is key to that eternal destination. "And I will give unto thee the keys of the kingdom of heaven: and whatsoever thou shalt bind on earth shall be bound in heaven: and whatsoever thou shalt loose on earth shall be loosed in heaven" (Matthew 16:19).

"He that overcometh, the same shall be clothed in white raiment; and I will not blot out his name out of the book of life, but I will confess his name before my Father, and before his angels" (Revelation 3:5). 'For as many of you as have been baptized into Christ have put on Christ'—represent the garment worn by Adam before his fall, a return to that pre-transgression state of glory and grace."[97]

After the Fall but before they were cast out of the garden, all other doors were closed. Only through Christ could they find an open door back into the presence of God; there was no other way. The coats of skins were key to that salvation because they wore them in the name of Christ, through His sanctifying grace. In doing so, they are no longer naked but are clothed, "Therefore *clothe yourselves with the Lord Jesus Christ*" (Romans 13:14, New International Version Bible).[98]

Through temple ordinances, we, like Adam and Eve, can be fully clothed in the saving grace of our Savior in preparation for that day when we "shall have a perfect knowledge of [our] enjoyment, and [our] righteousness, being clothed with purity, yea, even with the robe of righteousness" (2 Nephi 9:14). These are the advancing ordinances of salvation that are granted to us on earth.

CHAPTER 12

WHERE GOEST THOU? (MOSES 4:15)

After receiving covenants of salvation, Adam and Eve must now travel the course of mortality. What are they to look for in that harsh terrain?

The account of God's query in the book of Genesis, "Adam . . . where art thou?" changes to "Adam . . . Where goest thou?" in the book of Moses (Genesis 3:9; Moses 4:15). We would do well to ponder these questions in our own hearts from time to time. There are many who believe that this life, in the body, is all there is, but I would challenge that concept. Just being in mortality is not, in itself, an appropriate destination; our life here is merely a bridge to greater inheritances. We must in all wisdom choose today where we will be in the next life. Can we remember who we are, where we came from, and where we are expected to go? Are we not all seekers of truth and light in the presence of God? The confirming knowledge that we are the children of a loving Heavenly Father helps us to realize that our value and worth reach far beyond that of our physical circumstances here in mortality. Believing this, we are unstoppable under the direction of Christ.

If salvation and eternal life are the goal, where then must we find them? As we seek a place in God's presence, we must first find Him here in mortality. According to LDS accounts, the earth is the promised land—though it fell—and will again become a celestial and exalted glory. "For after it hath filled the measure of its creation, it shall be *crowned with glory*, even with the presence of God the Father" (D&C 88:19; emphasis added). It's on this earth that we will find our celestial inheritance in the resurrection (D&C 88:17–18).

Brigham Young explains that:

> "When the earth was framed and brought into existence and man was placed upon it, it was near the throne of our Father in heaven. . . . But when man fell, the earth fell into space, and took up its abode in this planetary system. . . . This is the glory the earth came from, and when it is glorified it will return again unto the presence of the Father, and it will dwell there, and these intelligent beings that I am looking at [congregation], if they live worthy of it, will dwell upon this earth."[99]

Lehi speaks to his son Joseph, "May the Lord consecrate also unto thee this land, which is a most precious land, for thine inheritance and the inheritance of thy seed with thy brethren, for thy security forever" (2 Nephi 3:2). Nephi is told that his people shall be numbered among the house of Israel and "shall be a blessed people upon the promised land forever" (1 Nephi 14:2). All have since died, but their promised inheritance is made sure through covenants between God and man and man's obedience to law.

Who are the seekers of this promised land? Do Adam and Eve fit into this category of seekers of the promised land? The Garden of Eden was a comfortable place. What more could they want? Were they after agency, experience, or maybe just a chance to make it on their own? What they wanted was to be like the Father, to have a mortal body "raised to immortality, corruption to incorruption—raised to endless happiness to inherit the kingdom of God" (Alma 41:4). Certainly, the kingdom of God is a tangible promised land.

Mortality may not have been the promised land, but it was the only way to get to the land of eternal promise. Only through mortality, and the mortal mission of the Savior, could we receive the promise for all that God has. What promised land do we seek? I believe Adam and Eve knew exactly what they were looking for. By their actions, they seem to have concluded that it was not Eden.

Adam and Eve were willing to travel through the wilderness of mortality for a purpose, as stated by Adam: "Because of my transgression my eyes are opened, and in this life I shall have joy, and again in the flesh I shall see God" (Moses 5:10). Mortality is the gauntlet of sorrow that leads "to endless happiness to inherit the kingdom of God" (Alma 41:4). Adam and Eve were the noblest of spirits—always obedient, thus always progressing. They knew why they were in the garden and what they needed to do. It was their choice (Moses 3:17). By agency it becomes man's propensity to climb, for he is the son of God.

Adam and Eve were not the only ones interested in obtaining the promised land. They set the pace for the rest of humanity to travel the course of becoming like the Father. Adam and Eve set the standard for righteous use of agency and would stand firm as witnesses of Christ—that He lives and is the Savior of mankind.

Receiving the promised land of eternal life requires a common experience for all of us: we must first travel through the wilderness of mortality. To do so successfully requires an immense desire to find and follow Christ through faith, hope, sacrifice, righteousness, obedience, and a broken heart and contrite spirit. Traveling through the wilderness allows us to come to know Christ and all His mercies. We find Him in the wilderness as we seek Him in diligence. His Atonement becomes the promised land, the tree of life, where we become eternal creators with God and obtain all that He has (see D&C 84:38).

There are multiple examples of Adam's posterity searching for a better land, even a promised land. Immigrants, migrants, and refugees have been a part of life since Adam and Eve. Man has spread to all ends of the earth looking for land and freedom. It is by faith and revelation that many have traveled to specified lands of promise by the word of God:

By faith, Adam and Eve took their journey toward the promised Savior, eastward in Eden (Genesis 2:8) and then to Adam-ondi-Ahman where Adam worshiped and will again return before the second coming of Christ (D&C 116:1; Daniel 7:9–14) to receive his children.

Let's not forget Abraham who received his inheritance with a magnificent posterity.

> By faith Abraham, when he was called to go out into a place which he should . . . receive for an inheritance, obeyed; and he went out, not knowing whither he went.
>
> *By faith he sojourned* in the land of promise, as in a strange country, dwelling in tabernacles with Isaac and Jacob, the heirs with him of the same promise:
>
> For he looked for a city which hath foundations, whose builder and maker is God. . . .
>
> These all died in faith, not having received the promises, but having seen them afar off, and were persuaded of them, and embraced them, and confessed that they were strangers and pilgrims on the earth.
>
> For they that say such things declare plainly that they seek a country.
>
> And truly, if they had been mindful of that country from whence they came out, they might have had opportunity to have returned.
>
> But now they *desire a better country,* that is, an heavenly: wherefore God is not ashamed to be called their God: for he hath prepared for them a city. (Hebrews 11:8–10, 13–16; emphasis added)

"For we know that if our earthly house of this tabernacle were dissolved, we have a building of God, an house not made with hands, eternal in the heavens" (2 Corinthians 5:1).

When Moses led the children of Israel out of Egypt, he led them "unto the land which the Lord thy God giveth thee, a land that floweth with milk and honey; as the Lord God of thy fathers hath promised thee" (Deuteronomy 27:3). The Israelite nation, led by Jehovah, was given a land of promise, promised covenants of salvation, and even a new name. "For thou art an holy people unto the Lord thy God: the Lord thy God hath chosen thee to be a special people unto himself, above all people that are upon the face of the earth" (Deuteronomy 7:6).

After Lehi and his family "had sailed for the space of many days [they] did arrive at the promised land; and . . . went forth upon the land, and did pitch [their] tents; and . . . did call it the promised land" (1 Nephi 18:23). When the pilgrims were called out of the world, they left England to find religious freedom. The spirit of faith and religion brought them out of distress to the Americas, a promised land, "And it came to pass that I beheld many multitudes of the Gentiles upon the land of promise" (1 Nephi 13:14). In time and after much struggle, they became a city on a hill, a chosen people under God (see 3 Nephi 12:14).

It was the enduring faith of the pioneers that brought them out of the world and through the wilderness to a promised inheritance. The pioneers of the latter days did not create a new movement but rather fulfilled a prophetic promise made to our ancient fathers: It was Joseph of Egypt who professed a restoration in the promised land where his seed would flourish (2 Nephi 3:14–15). Out of captivity and persecution they came. Through their struggles, they became the covenant people of God. This pattern of sanctification has been repeated throughout history. Whether it is Adam and Eve, the pilgrims, the pioneers, or the children of Israel, they seek a promised land with Christ as their guide.

Multitudes have sacrificed for a promised inheritance. The father of the country is George Washington. The father of nations is Abraham of the Old Testament. The father of mankind is Adam. The father of us all is God the Eternal Father. For these patriarchs, love and sacrifice was the cost by which all good works were and are accomplished. In making comparisons, let us remember our Lord's reluctance before the altar of sacrifice. "And he went a little further, and fell on his face, and prayed, saying, O my Father, if it be possible, let this cup pass from me: nevertheless not as I will, but as thou wilt" (Matthew 26:39). He stayed the course and paid the price, He is our Redeemer.

For Adam and Eve, and for the Son of God, the heart knows "there is no other way or means whereby man can be saved, only in and through Christ" (Alma 38:9). All who sacrificed subsequent comforts did so that "men . . . might have [eternal] joy" (2 Nephi 2:25).

CHAPTER 13

I WILL GREATLY MULTIPLY THY SORROW (MOSES 4:22)

"For all those who will not endure chastening, but deny me, cannot be sanctified."

— *D&C 101:5*

Unto the woman [God] said, I will greatly multiply thy sorrow and thy conception; in sorrow thou shalt bring forth children" (Genesis 3:16). As a woman, do I take this scripture as a curse, a warning, or a blessing for motherhood? In what way does sorrow bring forth blessings in this life?

Hugh Nibley wrote:

> To multiply does not mean to add or increase but to repeat over and over again; the word in the Septuagint is *plethynomai*, as in the multiplying of words in the repetitious prayers of the ancients. Both the conception and the labor of Eve will be multiple; she will have many children. . . . It means not to be sorry, but to have a hard time. If Eve must labor to bring forth, so too must Adam labor (Genesis 3:17; Moses 4:23) to quicken the earth so it shall bring forth. Both of them bring forth life with sweat and tears, and Adam is not the favored party.[100]

In the travail of childbirth, it seems that pain is an important tool. Eve knew she would suffer and even die by partaking of the fruit, but she chose the fruit—not for sorrow, pain, and death, but

111

for its proposed gain. Jesus Christ chose to atone for us, not for sorrow, but for love. Only by His sacrificial act of love are we able to overcome the challenges of sorrow in this life. From this perspective, sacrifice is a significant part of learning to love. John declared, "There is no fear in love; but perfect love casteth out fear: because fear hath torment. He that feareth is not made perfect in love" (1 John 4:18). To be made perfect in love requires one's selfless sacrifice on another's behalf.

How many women choose childbirth for the promise of joy? It is the love and sacrifice of self that wins over pain and becomes our sanctifying joy. As Paul says, "Notwithstanding she [they JST] shall be saved in childbearing, if they continue in faith and charity and holiness with sobriety" (1 Timothy 2:15). Perhaps faith, charity, holiness, and sobriety become our lifting tool out of sorrow into the joy of the Lord. It is good to remember that we are not alone in our sorrow. By the Spirit, the burdens of this life can become empowering, rather than overpowering, as we witness the guiding hand of the Lord for our sakes.

John has said, "Ye are of God, little children, and have overcome them: because greater is he [Christ] that is in you, than he that is in the world" (1 John 4:4). And the Savior has added, "Look unto me in every thought; doubt not, fear not" (D&C 6:36). In the bitterness of sorrow, we are not only lifted and comforted but also sanctified through the sweet Atonement of Jesus Christ.

The hymn "How Firm a Foundation" expresses the foundational support the Savior offers us when we sorrow:

When through the deep waters I call thee to go,
The rivers of sorrow shall not thee o'erflow,
For I will be with thee, thy troubles to bless,
And sanctify to thee . . . thy deepest distress.[101]

President Heber J. Grant observed:

When I think of the distress of the Latter-day Saints, the dangers and persecutions through which they went in New York, Ohio, Missouri and Illinois; when I think of the trouble and difficulties of the great pioneer journey from the Missouri river to these valleys; when I think of the reign almost of terror at different times from my childhood until now—the coming of an army against our people; when I think how near they came to starving because of the crickets; when I think of the confiscation of all the Church's property, and the many trials and tribulations through which the people have passed—I say when I think of these things I realize that the Lord has sanctified all their trials to the good of the Latter-day Saints, for these afflictions and tribulations have fitted and qualified them more perfectly to live the gospel of the Lord Jesus Christ.[102]

Paul understood, "But we have this treasure in earthen vessels, that the excellency of the power may be of God, and not of us. We are troubled on every side, yet not distressed; we are perplexed, but not in despair; Persecuted, but not forsaken; cast down, but not destroyed" (2 Corinthians 4:7–9). "And I was with you in weakness, and in fear, and in much trembling" (1 Corinthians 2:3).

In our troubles and even persecution, we must look to Christ for the healing of our hearts. Allowing the Lord to assist becomes our peace. Many who have been wounded stubbornly hold on to tragic events, supposing that the unjust will then pay full price. The miracle of healing does not occur under these divisive and manipulative circumstances. Miracles are made on faith in Jesus Christ, love of others, compassion, mercy, and even unconditional forgiveness. "I, the Lord, will forgive whom I will forgive, but of you it is required to forgive all men" (D&C 64:10). We forgive because He forgives. Our forgiveness then becomes our acceptance of the Atonement of Jesus Christ for all God's children.

Don't allow offenders to steal one more day of your precious life. Believe the Lord when he tells you, "But I say unto you, Love your enemies, bless them that curse you, do good to them that hate you, and pray for them which despitefully use you, and persecute you" (Matthew 5:44). Let's not empower that thief called misery. I don't mean to disregard anyone's tragedy, but we can steal away our own happiness by not moving past those unjust circumstances.

"Endure to the end" (Mark 13:13) is a common scriptural quote. It is also my least favorite, making the burden seem endless, I would rather, it just be taken away. Having said that, it makes no sense to stop in front of the door that we have traveled so far to enter. Only the devil would suggest that. Trials become tutorial experiences that empower us and sanctify us as we continue to endure in Christ. Even the Savior learned "obedience by the things which he suffered; And being made perfect, he became the author of eternal salvation unto all them that obey him" (Hebrews 5:8–9). "But let patience have her perfect work, that ye may be perfect and entire, wanting nothing" (James 1:4). Moroni said, "If ye by the grace of God are perfect in Christ, and deny not his power, then are ye sanctified in Christ by the grace of God, through the shedding of the blood of Christ, which is in the covenant of the Father unto the remission of your sins, that ye become holy, without spot" (Moroni 10:33).

Pain and sorrow are not just found in physical trials. Eve suffered pain and sorrow because of her children's choices. Eve rejoices, "I have gotten a man from the Lord; wherefore he may not reject his words. But behold, Cain hearkened not, saying: Who is the Lord that I should know him? . . . And Adam and his wife mourned before the Lord, because of Cain and his brethren" (Moses 5:16, 27). Loving includes both rejoicing and sorrowing. Like the contrast between light and dark, good and evil, we need to experience both joy and sorrow for love. These are the compatible feelings by which we learn to love one another.

When we lose a loved one, physically of spiritually, it is a time of sorrow. In consoling one with a broken heart, Elder Holland tenderly states, "It's okay to be sad. A piece of your heart is missing. It's missing because it belongs to your son, and he holds it until you are reunited with him."[103] Sorrowing for others is charitable, as it is also evidence of our love. In this we take upon ourselves a portion of Christ's Gethsemane—bringing on our own broken heart and contrite spirit.

Alma taught, "as ye are desirous . . . to be called his people, and are willing to bear one another's burdens, that they may be light: Yea, and are willing to mourn with those that mourn; yea, and comfort those that stand in need of comfort, and to stand as witnesses of God at all times and in all things" (Mosiah 18:8–9). It is by this love for one another that we might know Christ and love as He loved.

As parents, spouses, and friends, our hope rests upon Christ for all that He sacrificed: "And he cometh into the world that he may *save all men* if they will hearken unto his voice; for behold, he suffereth the pains of all men, yea, the pains of every living creature, both men, women, and children, who belong to the family of Adam" (2 Nephi 9:21; emphasis added). Because of His suffering for us, we too learn to have faith, hope and charity for all the children of God. "But charity is the pure love of Christ, and it endureth forever; and whoso is found possessed of it at the last day, it shall be well with him" (Moroni 7:47).

Eve's children brought her pain and sorrow, but they also brought her joy and delight as she learned to love each in trial, error, and salvation. Eve also felt the blessings of her children as her son Seth lived to pass down the keys of the priesthood to the ongoing generations of Adam and Eve (see D&C 107:42–43; Moses 6:10).[104]

Joy comes by knowing Christ. Because of the choice Adam and Eve made in the Garden of Eden—in partaking of the tree of knowledge of good and evil—the Savior said:

> I, the Lord, have suffered the affliction to come upon them, wherewith they have been afflicted, in consequence of their transgressions;
>
> Yet I will own them, and they shall be mine in that day when I shall come to make up my jewels.
>
> Therefore, they must needs be chastened and tried, even as Abraham, who was commanded to offer up his only son.
>
> For all those who will not endure chastening, but deny me, cannot be sanctified. (D&C 101:2–5)

Abraham, when asked to sacrifice his only son, realized that it was not a physical sacrifice but came by the Holy Spirit. Abraham knew as did Nephi, "I know that he loveth his children; nevertheless, I do not know the meaning of all things" (1 Nephi 11:17). With this knowledge, Abraham was able to comply without murmuring. Like Adam, Abraham obeyed, seemingly without knowing, "save the Lord commanded [him]" (Moses 5:6). "By faith Abraham, when he was tried, offered up Isaac: and he that had received the promises offered up his only begotten son, Of whom it was said, That in Isaac shall thy seed be called: Accounting that

God was able to raise him up, even from the dead; from whence also he received him in a *figure* [simile of the ram]" (Hebrews 11:17–19; emphasis added.). Abraham's faith in the Lord was not only unblemished, but it was also raised to a perfect knowledge of the love of God for all men, in that He sacrificed His Only Begotten who "is and shall be the Savior, for he is full of grace and truth" (Moses 1:6).

"All things unto me are spiritual, and not at any time have I given unto you a law which was temporal; neither any man, nor the children of men; neither Adam, your father, whom I created" (D&C 29:34). If we could all come to believe that our physical needs do not supersede our spiritual needs, we would be able to make correct choices, as did Abraham and Adam and Eve. As we turn our hearts to the spiritual aspects of a trial, the trials subside and become our victory over adversity. That is a sweet experience and becomes the prized knowledge of sweet over bitter. Our vision of a trial changes our resolve to endure and becomes our joy in the end. The pioneers crossed the plains because of spiritual reasons, not physical. We pay tithing because of faith, not because of financial gain.

In the distress of physical persecution, Paul teaches, "For our light affliction, which is but for a moment, worketh for us a far more exceeding and eternal weight of glory" (2 Corinthians 4:17).

C. S. Lewis wrote, "The travail of all creation . . . at its most intense may be necessary in the process of turning finite creatures (with free wills) into . . . well, Gods."[105]

In the *Lectures on Faith,* we read:

> A religion that does not require the sacrifice of all things *never has power sufficient to produce the faith necessary unto life and salvation;* for, from the first existence of man, the faith necessary unto the enjoyment of life and salvation never could be obtained without the sacrifice of all earthly things. It was through this sacrifice, and this only, that God has ordained that men should enjoy eternal life; and it is through the medium of the sacrifice of all earthly things that men do actually know that they are doing the things that are well pleasing in the sight of God.[106]

CHANGE DOES NOT COME EASILY

The pains of giving birth remind us not only of the Fall but also of impending joy. Just as pain brings forth a child, which the parents rejoice in, our trials can bring forth change and redemption, which will be the source of eternal joy for all who endure the "labor pains" of their mortal test.[107] "Change does not come easily. If we are to overcome sinful desires or habits, we must experience significant travail preceding our being 'born again.'"[108] Augustine wrote: "Carnal desire . . . does not [cause] pain in the beginning, until [a] habit is bent toward improvement. . . . In order that this [good] habit might be born, there was a painful struggle with [the] bad habit."[109]

"Now I rejoice," Paul says, "not that ye were made sorry, but that ye sorrowed to repentance: for ye were made sorry after a godly manner, that ye might receive damage by us in nothing" (2 Corinthians 7:9–10). He adds: "For as the sufferings of Christ abound in us, so our consolation also aboundeth by Christ. . . . While we look not at the things which are seen, but at the things which are not seen: for the things which are seen are temporal; but the things which are not seen are eternal" (2 Corinthians 1:5; 4:17–18). President Howard W. Hunter wisely said, "If our lives and our faith are centered upon Jesus Christ and his restored gospel, nothing can ever go permanently wrong."[110]

Finally, the Savior assures us, "All these things shall give thee experience, and shall be for thy good" (D&C 122:7). Without trials, "they would have remained in a state of innocence, having no joy, for they knew no misery; doing no good, for they knew no sin. But behold, all things have been done in the wisdom of him who knoweth all things" (2 Nephi 2:23–24).

CHAPTER 14

THY DESIRE SHALL BE TO THY HUSBAND

This does not in any way lessen or diminish Eve's power but ultimately increases 'their power.'

The statement "Thy desire shall be to thy husband" (Moses 4:22; Genesis 3:16) is not meant to play favorites or to submit Eve to her husband's will; it is a tool to humbly bond them together in one purpose, creating a godly order. But it was Adam who, by the keys of the everlasting priesthood and through the covenant of marriage, then called Eve to be the mother of all living (see Genesis 3:20; Moses 4:26). Thus, she shared the partaking of the fruit with Adam, (Moses 4:12), knowing that they were to enter into mortality together "that men might be" (2 Nephi 2:25).

Eve, having been the first to step forward and partake of the fruit, was cautioned to look to her husband for continued priesthood guidance. God commanded Eve, "Thy desire shall be to thy husband" (Moses 4:22). I believe this is to more perfectly merge them *as one*, bringing their act together for their destined mortal trials. In humility and purpose, *Eve was commanded to be 'one' with Adam.* She was also to lean on him for protection and provision both physically and spiritually, so that she might more easily *bear the burdens of her calling* as the mother of all living. They worked together, as a united partnership, so it is not surprising to learn that when Adam was commanded to "eat his bread by the sweat of his brow, as I the Lord had commanded him," that "Eve, also, his wife, did labor with him" (Moses 5:1). Together they willingly lightened one another's burdens, creating a bond of love and service within the family.

The partaking of the fruit brought new directives. Adam was commanded to cleave unto his wife (Matthew 19:5). In contrast, Eve was told her "desire shall be to her husband" (Genesis 3:16). It seems that both were directed to merge as one for an eternal and glorious marriage. To accomplish this, both Adam and Eve had to *first obey God*. This relationship between man, woman, and God brought them into a tri-level perfection in the marriage.

As Eve was asked to look to or desire her husband in righteousness, a type of priesthood veil was placed between her and God so that a more perfect union could occur between Adam and Eve (see chapter 31; Priesthood Veil), thus strengthening them both in power and faith as they leaned to one another in the knowledge of Christ. This did not in any way lessen or diminish Eve's power but ultimately increased 'their power,' in the Lord. Thus, in the priesthood they twain shall be one, under *one* priesthood umbrella, *not two*.

It is this commandment, "Thy desire shall be to thy husband" (Moses 4:22), that put Adam and Eve on the same page. By allowing Adam to project their priesthood in their relationship, Eve was promoting their oneness with the Father and the Son, knitting their purpose together in Christ while unifying the everlasting covenant of marriage in God. The Lord was not asking Eve to obey her husband, but that they *twain shall be one*. They are then magnified as *'one in Christ.'* We also recognize that God is not commanding Adam and Eve to have the same roles but that their specific roles or callings help them in the same purpose and power.

And what was Eve to look to her husband for? Adam, having the keys of the holy order of the priesthood for the family, was then called to protect, feed, shelter, and bestow the patriarchal ordinances that would return them to the Father and Mother. So why, then, was Eve told that her husband "shall rule over thee"? (Genesis 3:16) "Inherent within the Hebrew word translated here as 'rule' are the concepts of a provider, a protector, one who will honorably and righteously preside."[111] Spencer W. Kimball says, "I have a question about the word 'rule.' It gives the wrong impression. I would prefer to use the word 'preside' because that's what he does. A righteous husband presides over his wife and family.[112] In "The Family: A Proclamation to the World," the First Presidency reaffirmed this idea, reminding us that "by divine design, fathers are to preside over their families in love and righteousness."[113]

"God also provided that Adam and Eve would rule together, as Elder Bruce C. Hafen, formerly of the Seventy, and his wife, Marie, explained: 'Genesis 3:16 states that, Adam is to 'rule over' Eve, but this doesn't make Adam a dictator. . . . 'Over' in 'rule over' uses the *Hebrew bet*, which means ruling 'with,' not ruling 'over'. . . . The concept of interdependent, equal partners is well-grounded in the doctrine of the restored gospel."[114]

"God's intent in this post-fall world in which we live is that men preside in righteousness over their homes, *counseling with their wives in all things."* President Kimball added: "The wife follows the husband as he follows Christ. No woman has ever been asked by the Church authorities to follow her husband into an evil pit. She is to follow him as he follows and obeys the Savior of the world, but in deciding this, she should be sure she is fair."[115] "Tragically, in many families and in many cultures, Genesis 3:16 has been seen as an authorization for unrighteous dominion on the part of man."[116]

In all of this, it's wise to remember that Abraham was also told to hearken unto Sarah. "In all that Sarah hath said unto thee, *hearken unto her voice*" (Genesis 21:12; emphasis added). In looking up the word *hearken* in the scriptures, it mostly refers to God or the spirit of revelation. Therefore, each is to hearken to the other for the spirit of revelation.

In a marriage relationship, the spirit of revelation can originate through either the husband or the wife. That revelation should then be confirmed by one's companion. If a couple is not in tune with each other, they miss being in tune to the spirit of revelation as a family.

COMPARING HIS AND HER CALLINGS

Equality does not mean having the same callings in a relationship. Instead, it's about being unified in the same voice, purpose, reward, and joy of the eternal blessings in marriage. This is noted as a blessing is placed upon Emma's head by Joseph Smith, her husband and Prophet. D&C 25:1, 13–16 (emphasis added) says:

> Hearken unto the voice of the Lord your God, while I speak unto you, Emma Smith, my daughter; for verily I say unto you, all those who receive my gospel are *sons and daughters* in my kingdom.
>
> Lift up thy heart and rejoice, and cleave unto the covenants which *thou* hast made.
>
> Continue in the spirit of meekness, and beware of pride. Let thy soul delight in thy husband and the glory which shall come upon him.
>
> Keep my commandments continually, and a crown of righteousness thou shalt receive. And except thou do this, where I am you cannot come.
>
> And verily, verily, I say unto you, that this is my voice unto all. Amen.

Emma is not counseled to obey her husband but to obey the Lord and be one with her husband, as he is one with the Lord.

Like Emma, we too often compare ourselves to our husband's callings. Sister Tarasevich related her feelings of conflict in the *Ensign*: she desired to be a missionary like Ammon. She, however, felt the contrast as she considered her husband's leadership opportunities in their mission, in which she comparatively felt unequal, inadequate, and isolated:

> An inner voice began to question her gently. "What was Ammon's first assignment?" "To be a servant, to tend the flocks, and to gather the scattered sheep," she responded. "Well then be as Ammon." . . . "I began to see what I could do to tend the flock and gather the scattered sheep." . . . It wasn't long before she felt the words of Ammon sing in her heart, "Behold my joy is full, yea, my heart is brim with joy, and I will rejoice in my God" (Alma 26:11).[117]

It is not always men who create a subjugation of women. Women (or men), with eyes of comparison, can easily subjugate their own self-worth (or that of their companion) as a lesser party, blocking their own inherent power of influence and love. The eyes of comparison become the eyes of separation, rather than the eyes of unity, love, and growth.

HARDENED CRUST OF SOCIETY

Historically, it is more often man's pride that causes a subjugation of women, creating a hardened crust in society. The closer we get to making women and men equal, the closer we get to the exalted thrones of God (1 Corinthians 11:11; emphasis added). There are no lesser callings in the gospel, just less faithful responses to callings. As taught in D&C: "Behold, there are many called, but few are chosen" (D&C 121:34). It is not *what* we are called to do but *how* we choose to view those callings. To be clear, having the keys of the priesthood is not a *higher* calling than that of Eve. It is, however, Adam's divine portion of that godly partnership which he has with Eve. Nor does "authority" make one higher than another but simply creates a directive for that which is required by divine appointment. Being equal partners means they are on the same divine level.

Too often in a freer society, many women are trying to balance the act of injustice by declaring to the world that women are equal to, if not better than men. Trying to turn the tables in this manner is no more beneficial when women profess *equality with separation* or even *independence from men*. This competitiveness is not a joining of powers but a division of power. That plan is no better than men's pernicious "rule," for God commanded that they should be one; equal as in "one."

Rodney Turner, professor of religious studies at BYU puts it beautifully:

> While women are fully justified in denouncing male exploitation, to insist upon being accepted as neuter persons rather than female persons is to expose themselves to even more pernicious forms of male exploitation in the future. They forget that woman's nature was meant to have a mollifying effect on man. For it was from her that he was to first learn the ways of tenderness and compassion, of sacrifice and devotion. Only by magnifying their roles as mothers can women effectively temper their sons. When women reject their divine

appointment and strike out in pursuit of some quasi-liberty patterned after the behavior of men, there is no one left to gentle their sons and prepare them to love and honor woman as she was meant to be loved and honored. Thus, an emotional vacuum is created in the hearts of men and women alike. Life for everyone becomes unbalanced, skewed in favor of the material and the rational as opposed to the spiritual and the emotional. Hearts become hardened. Lives are blighted. Minds destroyed. Bodies corrupted. Souls lost.[118]

We are all the sons and daughters of God. When Jesus said, "Let your light so shine before men, that they may see your good works, and glorify your Father which is in heaven" (Matthew 5:16), He did not specify this just for the man or women; it is a command for all his disciples.

"Before the Fall, Adam and Eve were one. Similarly, we could extrapolate from this passage that in the highest degree of the celestial kingdom men and women will once again be perfectly one."[119] That is not to say that we cannot also be one now; for better or worse, Jesus commanded, "they twain shall be one flesh, and all this that the earth might answer the end of its creation" (D&C 49:16). It is in the order of God that we come together as a whole. First the keys of the priesthood by Adam, then his ordained marriage to Eve and the godly powers of procreation by them. Only through these ordinances can we proclaim, "Families are Forever."

CHAPTER 15

AN HELP MEET FOR HIM

Who, me?

Eve was the catalyst for making Adam's life truly productive. She would take him forward into a forbidden realm, which was vital to their progression and even the progression of every Adam and Eve that would follow them into this mortal world (Moses 4:26). Thus, "she was the mother of all living" (Genesis 3:20). Eve's job in being a help meet to Adam would complete him, and together they would fulfill their divine destiny and find eternal joy in the presence of God and godhood. We are told that Eve, "by endowment and preparation, corresponded in all things to Michael, *She was his completion.*"[120] Thus, in all that man may become in the presence of God, there also stands a woman, equally as great, for they are commanded to be one "in the Lord."

As Elder Earl C. Tingey, formerly of the Presidency of the Seventy, has said:

> You must not misunderstand what the Lord meant when Adam was told he was to have a helpmeet. A helpmeet is a companion suited to or equal to [the other]. [They] walk side by side ... not one before or behind the other. A help meet results in an *absolute equal partnership* between a husband and a wife. Eve was to be equal to Adam as a husband and wife are to be equal to each other.[121]

Equal does not mean the same; it means they are compatible in a unifying relationship. Thus, love and appreciation for the gifts of each is required.

"'I will make,' God said, 'an *help meet* for him' (Moses 3:18) . . . not one word, but two, meaning the Lord would bring forth 'a helper, aid, or partner' who was 'suited to, worthy of, or corresponding to' Adam (Genesis 2:18, footnote a)." "Eve was the prepared companion who was suited to Adam, *a 'full partner... in both temporal and spiritual things,'* as Elder McConkie expressed it."[122] "She was to be, in the Hebrew, the indispensable help, aid, succor, and protection, which strengthens, girds, or *saves the onward course*."[123]

The ultimate purpose for the words "I will make him a help meet for him" (Genesis 2:18) comes together in D&C 132. Regarding those who do not marry in the everlasting covenant of marriage, "therefore, when they are out of the world they neither marry nor are given in marriage. . . . For these angels did not abide my law; therefore, they cannot be enlarged, but remain separately and singly, without exaltation, in their saved condition, to all eternity; and from henceforth are not gods, but are angels of God forever and ever" (D&C 132:16–17). That is the finishing law of the eternities; man and woman together as one in Christ. United, they bring forth life, which extends into the eternities. Russell M. Nelson reminds us, "In God's eternal plan, salvation is an individual matter; [but] exaltation is a family matter."[124]

EXAMPLES OF HELP MEET IN THE SCRIPTURES

Starting in Genesis, we can acknowledge the help of many women throughout the scriptures as well as in latter-day history. Abraham calls upon Sarah as his help meet:

SARAH: "Therefore it shall come to pass, when the Egyptians shall see thee, that they shall say, this is his wife: and they will kill me, but they will save thee alive. Say, I pray thee, thou art my sister: that it may be well with me for thy sake; and *my soul shall live because of thee*" (Genesis 12:12–13; emphasis added).

It was in faith that Abraham and Sarah, by the hand of the Lord, allowed Sarah to fall into the hands of Pharaoh in Egypt. In following the command of the Lord, to go into Egypt, Abraham was promised to become a great nation; his seed would bless all the families of the earth.

REBEKAH: When Isaac was blind to the foreordained birthright of his son Jacob over Esau, Rebekah stepped in. Because of her prophetic understanding, wisdom, and stealth, it was Jacob, rather than Esau, that received the rightful blessings of the priesthood lineage. This was accepted of the Lord as Isaac also became resigned to the Lord's will (see Genesis 27). As one flesh with Isaac, Rebekah rightfully perceived her place to be his help meet, and the Lord accepted Isaac's priesthood ordination and blessing on Jacob. Jacob wisely listened to his mother's insight, in contrast to his father's desires and was blessed for that wisdom. Rebekah did not step in as prophet of the Lord but very prophetically as Isaac's help meet, and Jacob and Esau's mother, when it was needed.

ZIPPORAH: The wife of Moses is also an example: "And it came to pass, that the Lord appeared unto him [Moses] as he was in the way, by the inn. The Lord was angry with Moses, and his hand was about to fall upon him, to kill him; for he had not circumcised his son" (JST Exodus 4:24). If Moses was unable to keep the commandments of the Lord, as he also taught them, his words would be of little value to the Israelite people in leading them out of Egypt. "Then Zipporah took a sharp stone and circumcised her son, and cast the stone at his feet. . . . And the Lord spared Moses and let him go, because Zipporah, his wife, circumcised the child." (JST Exodus 4:25–26).

Why did the Lord accept Moses as having circumcised the child, a priesthood ordinance? It was because Zipporah was his wife; she was his equal. They are eternally *one* under God's covenant. Elder M. Russell Ballard said: "When men and women go to the temple, they are both endowed with the *same* power, which by definition is priesthood power. . . . The endowment is literally a gift of power."[125]

Man is not singular in the priesthood when he enters into the highest ordinance of marriage. In the bond of marriage, Zipporah performed her right as his wife when Moses was not able. She reigned with him under the priesthood umbrella of the family. When the patriarch is not present in the home, the matriarch becomes the first line of authority in that home. That in no way means that a wife can conduct the ward business of her bishop husband, that being *his* calling or his individual line of authority. But perhaps she can step in to save him as her companion and wife when it is a personal or family matter. This being her specified calling as help meet and mother of all living. This however, is done most effectively *when and how the Spirit inspires.*

DEBORAH: "And Deborah, a prophetess, the wife of Lapidoth, she judged Israel at that time" (Judges 4:4). When faced with imminent war, "Barak said unto her, if thou wilt go with me, then I will go: but if thou wilt not go with me, then I will not go" (Judges 4:8).

Adam also waited upon Eve to open the doors of mortality. In the attitude that, "If thou wilt go with me, then I will go" (see chapter 30; Walking Through the Scriptures).

In speaking of Deborah as a prophetess, James E. Talmage submitted that the gift of prophecy may be possessed by women: "The ministrations of Miriam and Deborah show that this gift may be possessed by women also."[126]

ABIGAIL: "And David said to Abigail, Blessed be the Lord God of Israel, which sent thee this day to meet me: And blessed be thy advice, and blessed be thou, which hast kept me this day from coming to shed blood, and from avenging myself with mine own hand" (1 Samuel 25:32–33). Abigail, the wife of Nabal, a woman in the Old Testament, became one of David's wives after the death of Nabal (1 Samuel 25:39) and is worth reading about. Her wisdom and courage to do what was right, in spite of traditional rule, is inspired and blessed by the Lord's hand.

HULDAH:

> And the king [Josiah] commanded . . . saying,
>
> Go ye, inquire of the Lord for me, and for the people, and for all Judah, concerning the words of this book that is found: for great is the wrath of the Lord. . . .
>
> So Hilkiah the priest, and Ahikam, and Achbor, and Shaphan, and Asahiah, *went unto Huldah the prophetess*, the wife of Shallum the

son of Tikvah, the son of Harhas, keeper of the wardrobe; (now she dwelt in Jerusalem in the college;) and they communed with her.

And she said unto them, Thus saith the Lord God of Israel, Tell the man that sent you to me, *Thus saith the Lord,* Behold, I will bring evil upon this place, and upon the inhabitants thereof, even all the words of the book which the king of Judah hath read. (2 Kings 22:12–16; emphasis added)

Huldah's prophetic announcement to the king of Judah was—without question—sent forth as the voice of the Lord.

ESTHER: "Go, gather together all the Jews that are present in Shushan, and fast ye for me, and neither eat nor drink three days, night or day: I also and my maidens will fast likewise; and so will I go in unto the king, which is not according to the law: and if I perish, I perish" (Esther 4:16). Esther's eyes were opened as Mordecai made her aware of her saving role in the lives of her captive nation. As a righteous queen, she opened the eyes of King Ahasuerus to save her people from the king's dreaded decree.

IN THE NEW TESTAMENT

Peter reminds us that, "On my servants and on my handmaidens I will pour out in those days of my Spirit; and they shall prophesy" (Acts 2:18). This moves us into the New Testament, where remarkable and faithful women knew Christ in the meridian of time.

MARY: "And the angel came in unto her, and said, Hail, thou that art highly favoured, the Lord is with thee: blessed art thou among women" (Luke 1:28). "And Mary said, Behold the handmaid of the Lord; be it unto me according to thy word" (Luke 1:38).

Joseph received revelation in relation to his betrothed wife, "The angel of the Lord appeared unto him in a dream, saying, Joseph, thou son of David, fear not to take unto thee Mary thy wife: for that which is conceived in her is of the Holy Ghost" (Matthew 1:20).

ELIZABETH: In the days of Herod, Elizabeth was the wife of priest Zacharias, "And they were *both* righteous before God, walking in all the commandments and ordinances of the Lord blameless" (Luke 1:6; emphasis added).

And it came to pass, that, when Elizabeth heard the salutation of Mary, the babe leaped in her womb; and Elizabeth was filled with the Holy Ghost:

And she spake out with a loud voice, and said, Blessed art thou among women, and blessed is the fruit of thy womb.

And whence is this to me, that the mother of my Lord should come to me?

For, lo, as soon as the voice of thy salutation sounded in mine ears, the babe leaped in my womb for joy.

And blessed is she that believed: for there shall be a performance of those things which were told her from the Lord. (Luke 1:41–45)

It was also Elizabeth on John's eighth day who spoke, "Not so; but he shall be called John" (Luke 1:60). Zacharias then confirmed her words in writing, "His name is John" (Luke 1:63).

MARY: "(It was that Mary which *anointed* the Lord with ointment, and wiped his feet with her hair, whose brother Lazarus was sick)" (John 11:2; emphasis added). "There came unto him a woman having an alabaster box of very precious ointment, and poured it on his head, as he sat at meat" (Matthew 26:7). Jesus said, "For in that she hath poured this ointment on my body, *she did it for my burial. Verily I say unto you, Wheresoever this gospel shall be preached in the whole world, there shall also this, that this woman hath done, be told for a memorial of her*" (Matthew 26:12–13; emphasis added).

Mary consecrated the Savior's body for His burial; Jesus qualified her anointing not only as acceptable but as significant. Her act implies that she understood His burial and perhaps even His promised resurrection. Jesus is the "Anointed One" (Luke 4:18–21). According to President Nelson, "the Christ or the Messiah, both signifies an *anointing by God* for that supernal responsibility."[127]

LATTER-DAY WOMEN

The women of today are no less engaged in the gospel of Jesus Christ. The restored gospel is flooded with the courageous and merciful act of everyday women.

LUCY MACK SMITH: Even in the latter days women are justified in their testimonies. "Although Lucy was a loving and amiable woman, she could chastise with fire when the occasion demanded. Her great devotion to the cause of the Lord and her fine sense of justice made her an authoritative figure."[128] Because of her zeal and consecration to the gospel, the mother of the prophet of the restoration should be a wise example to all covenant women.

EMMA SMITH: This was Lucy Mack Smith's tribute to Emma: "I have never seen a woman in my life, who would endure every species of fatigue and hardship, from month to month, and from year to year, with that unflinching courage, zeal, and patience, which she has ever done; for I know that which she has had to endure—she has been tossed upon the ocean of uncertainty—she has breasted the storms of persecution, and buffeted the rage of men and devils, which would have borne down almost any other woman."[129] Oh, how Joseph loved Emma!

ELIZA R. SNOW: Eliza R. Snow, president of the Relief Society in 1884, stated:

> Is it necessary for sisters to be set apart to officiate in the sacred ordinances of washing, anointing, and laying on of hands in administering to the sick? It certainly is not. Any and all sisters who honor their holy endowments, not only have right, but should feel it a duty, whenever called upon to administer to our sisters in these ordinances, which god has graciously *committed to His daughters as well as to His sons; and we testify that when administered and received in faith and humility they are accompanied with almighty power.*[130]

In the latter-day restoration Joseph explained, "I will organize the women under the priesthood, after the pattern of the priesthood," Joseph said. "I now have the key by which I can do it."[131] "On September 28, 1843. Soon after Emma had washed and anointed Jane Law, Rosannah Marks, Elizabeth Durfee, and Mary Fielding Smith. It was the first time a woman had officiated in a temple ordinance in the latter days."[132] Brigham Young said, "A righteous woman has a quiet, yet powerful, influence among the children of men; she is an help meet, ordained by God. She is the mother of all living, for now and into the eternities." Brigham Young rightly states that "Mother Eve" has "a splendid influence" over Adam.[133]

We might ask how Christ would respond to the everyday miracles of faithful women. Perhaps He would respond much the same as He did with John: "And John answered and said, Master, we saw one casting out devils in thy name; and we forbade him, because he followeth not with us. And Jesus said unto him, *Forbid him not: for he that is not against us is for us*" (Luke 9:49–50; emphasis added). Could it also be said of woman, Forbid her not; for she that is not against us is also for us? Like Eve, each of these courageous women crossed over some traditional law to more perfectly keep the command of the Lord. The list is endless because womanhood and motherhood are endless and eternal.

CHAPTER 16

ADAM'S RIB

A covenant of marriage

We have all been bewildered at some point at the story of Adam's rib being taken out of him and used to create Eve. We tend to project our own personal explanations for this interesting story. But what is the truth? Was the rib literal or metaphoric, and what could it possibly mean? By going back through the scriptures, as well as forward into latter-day revelations, we learn that Adam's rib was a priesthood ordinance performed in Eden in which Adam and Eve received their marriage covenants. The rib is a metaphor for the eternal marriage of Adam and Eve.

Hyrum L. Andrus, a prolific LDS author and scholar, wrote,

> In light of Latter-day Saint theology, a study of the context in which the account of Eve's creation is related suggests that the rib story is symbolic of the New and Everlasting Covenant of Marriage. God gave Eve to Adam to be his wife before death entered into the world. She was organized for the express purpose that she might be his companion and that she might be one with him, bone of his bone and flesh of his flesh.[134]

The priesthood was taken out of man, symbolically as the rib, to combine man and woman as one in the everlasting covenant of marriage. This power was equally shared with the woman for eternal creations. This covenant cannot be had by man alone or by woman alone; only together can they obtain this exalted glory. Together they are divinely authorized to procreate as the gods. Adam to Eve is the *key* to their creative powers; Eve to Adam is the magnification of that creative power, being the literal *life* of that power.

John A Widtsoe clarifies, "The 'rib' story is clearly a figure of speech. . . . Every child born on earth is begotten by an earthly father."[135] Though the rib story is where, in name, the woman Eve first appears on the scene of Adam's immortal life in the scriptures, it is not about her birth as many suppose. The birth of both Adam and Eve is written before the rib story as God created "them," "male and female" (Genesis 1:27). This also indicates the order in which they must abide in marriage—male and female—which is also in God's image.

The rib, often projected as a birthing process for Eve, is much like the symbolism of baptism, or being born of Christ. Eve, in her new priesthood order, through marriage, was given a new name, a new calling, and a new empowerment for procreation. In this similitude, Eve was born of Adam, or of his priesthood, through the ordained key of the new and everlasting covenant of marriage.

Hugh Nibley sheds further light on the use of this word in the scriptures: "The word *rib* expresses the ultimate in proximity, intimacy, and identity. When Jeremiah speaks of 'keepers of my tsela' [Hebrew word for rib], he meant bosom friends, inseparable companions. Such things are to be taken figuratively, as in Moses 3:22."[136] However, in Genesis 2:22, "The rib . . . made I a woman, and brought her unto the man," Hugh Nibley explained, "when we are told not that the woman was made out of the rib or from the rib, but that she *was* the rib, a powerful metaphor."[137]

Joseph Fielding Smith and Bruce R. McConkie wrote:

The *imagery used to veil* the account of Eve's birth is most beautiful, particularly so in a day when there is so much confusion about the role of women. Symbolically, she was not taken from the bones of Adam's head, not from the bones of his heel, for it is not the place of woman to be either above the man or beneath him. Her place is at his side, and so she is taken, *in the figurative sense*, from his rib . . . the *bone that girds the side and rests closest to the heart.* Thus we find Adam declaring; she shall be called Woman, because she was taken out of man (Moses 3:23). Eve, unlike the rest of God's creations, was of Adam's bone and his flesh, meaning that she was *equal to him in powers, faculties, and rights.*[138]

Even in Hebrew, the word *helpmeet* is in two words *'ezer knegdo.* "*Biblical Archeology Review* proposed that *ezer knegdo* be translated 'a power equal to him.'"[139]

There is a mutual covenant of marriage between Adam and Eve:

> The phrase, 'bone of my bones, and flesh of my flesh,' refers to a mutual covenant the two parties have made with each other. *Bone* in Hebrew symbolizes *power*, and flesh, *weakness.* Bone of my bones and flesh of my flesh' thus becomes a ritual pledge to be bound in the best of circumstances as well as the worst. The man's use of this phrase here implies a covenant similar to the marriage agreement today and is reminiscent of the phrase 'for better or for worse' used in marriage vows.[140]

The account of the rib, as the marriage, is performed and repeated in Genesis 2:23, Abraham 5:17, and Moses 3:23. In *The Words of Joseph Smith*, "Marriage was an institution of heaven; instituted in the Garden of Eden . . . it was necessary it should be solemnized by the authority of the everlasting Priesthood."[141]

"So the Gods went down to *organize man* in their own image" (Abraham 4:27; emphasis added). God organized man to become married, to become mortal, to be fruitful and replenish the earth, to become gods. "For behold, this is my work and my glory—to bring to pass the immortality and eternal life of man" (Moses 1:39). Satan knows very well that when you destroy eternal marriage, and procreation in that marriage, you destroy the power to create eternally. Thus, marriage became Satan's most vital target, it being the very heart of eternity, "wherefore he sought to destroy the world" (Moses 4:6).

When speaking of the image of Heavenly Father, we can assume that includes Heavenly Mother as well, for they are male and female. The highest order of the everlasting priesthood is not singular, it is not twain; it is *one* or *they.* The highest ordinance of godhood is eternal marriage, being "in the image of [God's] own body, male and female" (Moses 6:9; emphasis added), "bone of my bone and flesh of my flesh" (Genesis 2:23; Moses 3:23; Abraham 5:17).

In the Garden of Eden, this most significant covenant of marriage must precede procreation according to God's laws and covenants. "In the image of his own body, male and female, created he them" (Moses 6:9); and they covenanted to be *one with Him*, becoming as He is. Therefore, being in the image of God, we are also commanded to create in our image. This brings us to the eternal command to be fruitful and replenish the earth, thus creating eternal families as do the Father and the Mother under the ordinance of marriage. Elder Oaks confirms, "The power to create mortal life is the most exalted power God has given his children. Its use was mandated in the first commandment (Genesis 1:28)."[142] "Therefore shall a man leave his father and his mother, and shall cleave unto his wife; and they shall be one flesh" (Moses 3:24). The unity of marriage under the new and everlasting covenant, and procreation under that covenant, is of God the Father and is therefore eternal. It is the basis of all creation in which, by the powers of heaven, it brings to pass the immortality and eternal life of man.

"While speaking of Eve we cannot separate her from Adam. They are not to be separated. To do so would deprive Eve of her rightful place. This we must learn: Adam and Eve are one, bone of bone and flesh of flesh. Their journey is the pattern of faith."[143]

CHAPTER 17

WE MAY ULTIMATELY QUALIFY

In the New and Everlasting Covenant

Entering into this new and everlasting covenant of marriage, as did Adam and Eve, procures great power for both male and female. Howard W. Hunter said, "Whatever Jesus lays his hands upon lives. If Jesus lays his hands upon a marriage, it lives. If he is allowed to lay his hands on the family, it lives."[144]

"When Joseph married Emma, he had believed that their union would end at death. But the Lord had since revealed to him that marriages and families could endure beyond the grave through the power of the Priesthood. Recently, while visiting church branches in the eastern states with Parley Pratt, Joseph had told him that righteous Saints could cultivate family relationships forever, allowing them to grow and increase in affection. No matter how much distance separated faithful families on earth, they could trust in the promise that one day they would be united in the world to come."[145]

Before the resurrection is upon us, if we have not received perfection—and I'm pretty sure we won't—we will be able to continue our spiritual progress until we, as married couples, finally reach the same level of righteousness as God our Father, eventually becoming like Him and receiving all that He has, including the fullness of the power of the priesthood. Are we not all commanded to "be ye therefore perfect, even as your Father which is in heaven is perfect" (Matthew 5:48)? This perfection that Christ speaks of is a process, not a self-acclamation. Yet we often feel like we have to be perfect before we are accepted of God. Do we even know what being perfect means?

The word *perfect* in the English language can feel unattainable. But the word *perfect* in Christ's time, and in different languages, means something entirely different from what we often perceive it to be in the English language today. "In Hebrew the word 'tam' or 'tamim', does not carry that same meaning of 'without flaw' in an absolute sense as does the term 'perfect' in English. 'Tamim' basically means to be complete, mature or healthy. We need only to seek to be one in Christ, and through Him we might then be made perfect."[146]

Even in French, the word *parfait* is translated as *perfect*. However, *parfait*, when speaking of the common word used in English, is a pudding or yogurt dessert that is layered with different confections. It often involves adding fruit, granola, cake, and other delectable sweets to create a delightful combination of flavors and textures in one dish: thus creating our own confection of perfection.

Like the dessert, "So we, being many, are one body in Christ, and every one members one of another" (Romans 12:5); "One Lord, one faith, one baptism" (Ephesians 4:5). In marriage and family, in learning to love one another, we might become one desirable whole in the spirit of Christ—our own "confection of perfection." We are, therefore, commanded to "love one another: for love is of God; and every one that loveth is born of God, and knoweth God" (1 John 4:7).

How do we learn to love perfectly? It does not happen automatically but rather "precept upon precept; line upon line, line upon line; here a little, and there a little" (Isaiah 28:10). We are allowed a process, or probation, in which we can learn to love perfectly. Surely this perfect love needs to start in the home, with family. Only when love for others is first established in the home can the love in our hearts become universal. We can't have charity, the pure love of Christ (see Moroni 7:47), if the core of our family has been forgotten. "Therefore if thou bring thy gift to the altar, and there rememberest that thy brother hath ought against thee; Leave there thy gift before the altar, and go thy way; first be reconciled to thy brother, and then come and offer thy gift" (Matthew 5:23–24). Even if our family members are contrary to that effort, we can still love them; even if they never change—it is our heart that we must change. As husband and wife, this love for one another is developed through Christlike attributes.

As charity is the pure love of Christ, charity must also be perfected. What is charity? It is not just the ability to love and be kind to those we are comfortable with but is the ability to love and be kind to all who are under the Atonement of Christ. This becomes a full acceptance of Christ's Atonement for all persons under the lineage of Adam and Eve, even ourselves. With steady progress, we too can learn of Christ, and love as He loves.

Remember, however, we do not believe in a perfectionism that translates into *without error*. We are all able to reach a level of perfection, but not because we are without flaw, for "I give unto men weakness that they may be humble; and my grace is sufficient for all men that humble themselves before me; for if they humble themselves before me, and have faith in me, then will I make weak things become strong unto them" (Ether 12:27). Therefore, humility and repentance are the first virtues of perfection; "And it came to pass that they did repent, and inasmuch as they did repent they did begin to prosper" (Helaman 4:15).

We don't love our neighbor or spouse because our neighbor or spouse is perfect but because we are made perfect in Christ. Only through humility can we obtain what He has obtained, and only by His perfect grace. "Behold, he offereth himself a sacrifice for sin, to answer the ends of the law, unto all those who have a broken heart and a contrite spirit; and unto none else can the ends of the law be answered" (2 Nephi 2:7). In *finding ourselves flawed before Christ, we become perfectly teachable.* "The meek will he guide in judgment: and the meek will he teach his way" (Psalm 25:9).

A perfect marriage, then, is man and woman seeking Christ in humility, patience, and love towards one another. This is how the twain makes one. Because there are two halves to the body of marriage, "so ought men to love their wives as their own bodies. He that loveth his wife loveth himself" (Ephesians 5:28). The body of marriage cannot prevail until it is properly fitted together as one through Christ. Both halves must be considered equal or the balance is skewed. Until both halves are united equally, it is not yet whole. Only through Christ can the covenant of marriage be properly aligned, healed, and made whole.

It takes time to perfect a marriage for eternity. It takes positive action to build trust. When one chooses to *react* to their partner, they are choosing a defensive pose, such as not listening, causing contention, and being self-centered. This separates us from those we should love, causing jealousy, hurt, pain, and sorrow; this is Satan's *favorite vice* in the holy ordinance of marriage.

Responding (listening, being patient) to those around us, on the other hand, comes from the love of Christ; it binds us to another's needs. When we direct our attention to another's situation and need, it provides a conduit of compassion, love, and charity as the Spirit attends us, and we become partners with Deity in building a marriage. The instructions are simple and laid in comprehensive order when Jesus said, "Thou shalt love the Lord thy God with all thy heart, and with all thy soul, and with all thy mind. This is the first and great commandment. And the second is like unto it, Thou shalt love thy neighbor as thyself. On these two commandments hang all the law and the prophets" (Matthew 22:37–40). And on such hangs the everlasting covenant of marriage.

However, in this same regard, man and woman cannot become eternal partners by love alone. Love is not complete without the ordinances of God. It takes the godly ordinance of marriage and the spirit of love combined to become a complete marriage in the eternities. "In order to obtain the highest, a man must enter into this order of the priesthood [meaning the new and everlasting covenant of marriage]" (D&C 131:2; brackets in original).

Unfortunately, man and woman don't always match in their desire to be one in Christ. Prayer is needed to bring the two together. Sometimes those prayers are left to only one of the partners. Many have saved a marriage through mighty prayer for a partner.

Remember, however, that praying for a partner's perfection is insufficient unless we are also praying for our own love, understanding, patience, and responsibility to that partner.

In spite of this, we need to understand that we cannot change our spouse; we must simply love them. Though change may occur by our example and faith, others must take responsibility for their own willingness to make the necessary changes. We cannot keep our partner's covenants for them. Putting the burden on our spouse or family to fix us or make us happy is not how a great marriage is created; this can only end in misery for both. We must take responsibility for our own choices. Even King David "[fell] from his exaltation, and received his portion; and he shall not inherit them [wives] out of the world, for I gave them unto another, saith the Lord" (D&C 132:39; emphasis added).

The command to be one is found throughout the scriptures. But it came first unto Adam and Eve. There is only one way to become *one*, and that is through Christ our Savior. Man and woman can be eternally united through Christlike attributes as well as through priesthood ordinances. Like baptism: "Except a man be born of water *and* of the Spirit, he cannot enter into the kingdom of God" (John 3:5; emphasis added). So also a perfect marriage is both by the new and everlasting covenant of marriage, as well as through a Christlike spirit of love for one another.

CHAPTER 18

MOTHER EVE

"Because she was the mother of all living"
—*Moses 4:26*

Though parenting is required of both Adam and Eve, it was Adam who "called his wife's name Eve." Her name did not appear in the scriptures till she was named the mother of all living by Adam. Up until then she was referred to as female, woman, or more collectively as Adam. The name Eve then distinguishes her person from that of Adam as it also personalizes her individual traits, "Adam called his wife's name Eve; because she was the mother of all living" (Genesis 3:20). "In announcing her name, Adam revealed his understanding of her call and acknowledged his responsibility to protect and provide for Eve in her role."[147] Therefore, Adam did as commanded; he left Father and Mother to cleave unto his wife, to provide for and protect the family.

Eve truly is the mother of all living; it is the integrity of her purpose, her body, and her heart—it is her name, and it is her *calling*. Adam, being instructed of God, recognized and understood early on Eve's role to somehow advance them toward mortality. Even now, it is often a mother's inherent instinct to bring children into the family. That propensity is born of Eve. It is her gift and her joy. It seems Adam refrained from the command to replenish the earth, while Eve carefully reminded him of their responsibility to that first command.

Because a man does not naturally understand the complexity of a woman's maternal desires, he may easily assume that she does not know what she is doing when she instinctively craves children. Such is related in the story of Hannah who was barren: "Then said Elkanah her husband to her, Hannah, why weepest thou? and why eatest thou not? and why is thy heart grieved? am not I better to thee than ten sons?" (1 Samuel 1:8). Though Elkanah tried to comfort Hannah in her sorrowing, he did not comprehend her hunger for childbearing. She was inconsolable as she went to the temple of God for answers. It was through her personal plea and covenant to God that she was able to bear the child prophet Samuel (1 Samuel 1:17) while offering him to God that he might serve the Israelite nation (1 Samuel 1). In this same respect, we often give our children to serve God as missionaries and then in marriage. In this, mother-hood becomes intimately connected to godhood.

Across the continent and over the vast sea, Lehi lead his family toward the promised land. It was in this new land that the gospel of Jesus Christ was established. And it was there that the Lamanite women of the church flourished in their faith, bringing us an unforgettable story of faithful mothers in the gospel and their 2,000 obedient sons. As women of great faith, they set the standard before their young sons. Helaman proclaims, "Now they [the two thousand warriors] never had fought, yet they did not fear death; and they did think more upon the liberty of their fathers than they did upon their lives; yea, they had been taught by their mothers, that if they did not doubt, God would deliver them. And they rehearsed unto me the words of their mothers, saying: We do not doubt *our mothers knew it*" (Alma 56:47–48; emphasis added). Because of the teachings and faith of their mothers, the young warriors were able to withstand their enemies. "But behold, to my great joy, there had not one soul of them fallen to the earth; yea, and they had fought as if with the strength of God; yea, never were men known to have fought with such miraculous strength; and with such mighty power did they fall upon the Lamanites, that they did frighten them; and for this cause did the Lamanites deliver themselves up as prisoners of war" (Alma 56:56). Whether in war or peace, mother (and fathers) can have a saving influence upon their sons and daughters.

Brigham Young states: "The mothers are the moving instruments in the hands of Providence to guide the destinies of nations. . . . Consequently, you see at once what I wish to impress upon your mind is, that the mothers are the machinery that give zest to the whole man, and guide the destinies and lives of men upon the earth."[148] Bruce C. Hafen confirms Young's statement, "Good and virtuous women establish stable families as the basic unit of society more quickly than any other—the woman's touch, which nurtures those habits of the heart without which no civil society can exist."[149]

What does it take to be a great mother? "A true mother . . . is a kind of love that," in *The Words of Joseph F. Smith*, "comes nearer being like the love of God than any other kind."[150] The Prophet Joseph Smith said "the time would come when none but the women of the Latter-day Saints would be willing to bear children."[151] It takes a comprehensive spiritual perspective to sacrifice "that men might be" (2 Nephi 2:25) in such a confused world. It is the righteous, though misunderstood, woman who takes this mantle upon herself, as did Eve. He also stated, "While Adam came to govern and provide, Eve came to bear and nurture children. The gift of children was the burden Eve carried in her heart and brought to Eden."[152]

Eve is the essence of womanhood and motherhood, but that is not to say that mothering was easy for Eve. She too had her untold trials, "And Adam and his wife mourned before the Lord, because of Cain and his brethren" (Moses 5:27). Most mothers feel like failures at some point in their monotonous, lonely, and often daunting task. Even comparing themselves to examples of such greatness as set forth in this chapter can bring on a depressive mood as they feel they are unqualified for the job. It's okay. If it weren't hard, it wouldn't be great. We as mothers, or even those who bear the heart of a mother, are all needed. Sometimes the only consolation we have is to love our children beyond the task at hand. And remember, "You are never alone, because you are doing the Lord's most important work, and He is right there at your side at every moment. When children are being the most unlovable is when they need love the most. That's why God made mothers."[153] Just know, whenever you have the heart of a mother, the Spirit of God will attend you.

David O. McKay understood this:

> The sweetness, as well as the greatness, of motherhood lies in the overcoming of self-love by mother for her children. By nature, the true mother is self-sacrificing. She is ever giving something of her life to make another happier or better. Motherhood is the one thing in all the world which most truly exemplifies the God-given virtues of creating and sacrificing. Though it carries the woman close to the brink of death, motherhood also leads her into the very realm of the fountains of life, and makes her co-partner with the Creator in bestowing upon eternal spirits mortal life.[154]

If I am a successful mother, it is not because I am perfect, or because I have always made the right choice, or even because I have given birth or have not, but because I loved my children and have offered thousands of silent prayers in their behalf—and always will. Successful parenting is not just getting your child to do what you think is right, but in loving them even when they don't.

There are many righteous women in the scriptures who have received revelation from God, particularly in behalf of their offspring: Hannah, Naomi, Ruth, Mary, Elizabeth, Sampson's mother, Rebekah, Sarah, and many others. Mothers and wives have a *direct* relationship with God when conducting the affairs of their family in righteousness. If you are not married or have not given birth, do not be dismayed. It's not just married women and mothers that have this power; it is accounted unto all covenant women. We have all been given that same promise. We are all under the same eternal gifts and promises.

It's true that "Adam was the first patriarch, and he was responsible for blessing his posterity and helping them live righteously,"[155] but he could not have done so without Eve at his side. Adam and Eve, together, became one in purpose. As father and mother of all mankind, they might have taken on a different perspective in parenting, but not a different purpose. Joseph Smith stated, "Eve, we might say, is the wellspring of life. *All creation was dependent upon her motherhood.* God breathed into Adam his spirit or breath of life; but to Eve he gave the breath of lives."[156] Elder Boyd K. Packer taught, "The limitation of priesthood responsibilities to men is a tribute to the incomparable place of women in the plan of salvation. . . . Men and women have complementary, not competing, responsibilities. There is difference but not inequity. . . . In the woman's part, she is not just equal to man; she is superior! She can do that which he can never do; not in all eternity can he do it."[157] However, just because Eve is superior in childbearing does not translate as her being superior in companionship with Adam. This is not meant to reduce Adam's qualifications, especially in parenting, but to bring a needed spotlight to Eve's gifted powers. My point is that while being different, they still remained one in purpose through Christ. Adam supported Eve's calling while Eve enhanced Adam's. They are Father Adam and Mother Eve. Together, they are Adam.

CHAPTER 19

EVE AND THE PRIESTHOOD

That they might be one in Christ

Though the keys of the priesthood are through Adam, he is not alone in that priesthood. Priesthood is a companionship between Adam and Eve; that is why Eve completes Adam. Though Eve has a part in the priesthood, it is connected to Adam, and Adam's priesthood is perfected through Eve. They, together, are a whole functioning priesthood. They must, therefore, be united as a whole for that priesthood to stand eternal.

"The name of Adam and Eve as a united partnership is 'Adam.'"[158] "But I would have you know, that the head of every man is Christ; and the head of the woman is the man; and the head of Christ is God" (1 Corinthians 11:3). We take upon us the *name of the Lord*, that we might be one with him. Woman takes upon herself the *name of her husband* that she might be one with him as he takes upon himself the priesthood to preside over the family, that *they might be one in Christ*. "In the image of his own body, male and female, created he them, and blessed them, and called *their* name Adam" (Moses 6:9; emphasis added). This family name through man is indicative of the priesthood keys that he presides under and shares with Eve, just as it was in Eden. This patriarchal order has to be shared with a matriarch, and their posterity under priesthood ordinances and covenants. There is no sealing power without this specified order.

This explains the prevalent tradition in which the woman takes on the name of the man in marriage, making the plural singular. They are one—they are Adam. "They are no more twain, but one flesh" (Mark 10:8). Both halves of the priesthood are required to make a whole; otherwise the priesthood remains dysfunctional. Because eternal marriage and family is the *last great ordinance* of the priesthood, that also makes it the *first order of the Priesthood*. It all points to family. God's purpose and our purpose is the family. "For behold, this is my work and my glory—to bring to pass the immortality and eternal life of man" (Moses 1:39). To be sure, God's work and His glory are His family.

Because women's authority comes by way of the keys of the priesthood, her need is to look to those keys for her desired callings, as does a man. This does not mean that man is more functional than woman, or that she is less intelligent or less in tune to the spirit of revelation and comprehension than man. It does not mean that a woman's voice should not be heard or considered; it means that they are united in one voice and one purpose. Man and woman are not singular entities but compound units in godhood. That unified power, however, is only functional under the priesthood keys given by God, first to Adam—for both man and woman. "It was more than an outpouring of spiritual gifts and divine power on the elders of the church. As soon as the temple [Kirtland] was was finished, both men and women would be able to receive the ordinance, strengthen their covenant relationship to God, and find greater power and protection in consecrating their lives to the kingdom of God."[159] Both men and women are endowed with power from on high when they take out their individual endowments. But the highest order of the priesthood must be held by both a man and a woman together.

Reason says that two complementing spirits are best suited to fulfill all righteousness. Thus, God's image is man and woman (see Genesis 1:27). "For it must needs be that there is an opposition in all things. If not so, . . . *righteousness could not be brought to pass*"

(2 Nephi 2:11; emphasis added). Man and woman are not perfect without each other. Only through Christ do they come to a perfect knowledge of truth. The key here is "through Christ." The focus is not man, nor woman, but Christ; otherwise there is no power in the twain.

Both are endowed with priesthood power. Men and women are both children of a loving Heavenly Father, both made in his image. They have the same baptism, the same sacramental covenant, the same gift of the Holy Ghost, the same gift of the spirit for personal or relevant revelation, according to responsibility and stewardship, and according to Elder Oaks, both have the authority to act under the keys of the priesthood.[160] Both men and women have the same baptismal covenants and responsibilities, as well as the same temple ordinances with the same priesthood promises and blessings for eternity. These priesthood ordinances and blessings are equally available to both men and women. The only powers that are distinctly different to gender are priesthood keys and ordained priesthood position, is that of womanhood or motherhood. But even those are not completely functional if not shared with the opposite gender. This difference appropriately promotes a unified partnership. Clearly, one gender gift is not more important than the other but a means of uniting men and women, even becoming a means of great power when shared with equality. Elder M. Russell Ballard has taught, "Men and women, though spiritually equal, are entrusted with different but equally significant roles."[161] The only real separation between these gender gifts is personal pride, "because of the hardness of your hearts" (Matthew 19:8).

In the marriage, Elder Boyd K. Packer said, "The priesthood does not have the strength that it should have and will not have until the *power* of the priesthood is firmly fixed in the families."[162] If we try to individualize priesthood for the personal power of men or women, it will not stand. Gender need not be competitive in their responsibilities; rather, they are meant to be a powerhouse of strength for one and the other.

President James E. Faust taught, "Every father is to his family a patriarch and every mother a matriarch as coequals in their distinctive parental roles."[163] Fathers and mothers, sons and daughters, as a family, are considered a plural unit, as one, in marriage, under a patriarchal order. Men and women's order and plurality before they take on their own family are under their parents' patriarch covenants (or the presiding patriarchal order). Eventually, however, man is told to leave his father and mother and cleave unto his wife in marriage (see Genesis 2:24). That becomes their new order of plurality or patriarchal and matriarchal strength, becoming as gods, becoming themselves mother and father. This is similar to how the Aaronic and Melchizedek Priesthoods are set up: going from a parented Aaronic priesthood to becoming the parenting Melchizedek priesthood. There is no singular unit in godhood or in the priesthood order: *family is the priesthood order*. We cannot become one with God if we are not one with each other in the family.

That does not, however, diminish in any way that the priesthood was first given to Adam:

> He (Adam) obtained the First Presidency, and held the keys of it from generation to generation. He obtained it in the Creation, before the world was formed (Genesis 1:26–28). He had dominion given him over every living creature. He is Michael the Archangel, spoken of in the Scriptures. Then to Noah, who is Gabriel: he stands next in authority to Adam in the Priesthood; he was called of God to this office, and was the father of all living in this day, and to him was given the dominion. These men held keys first on earth, and then in heaven.[164]

How did Adam hold his high calling to the priesthood? It was not by himself; it was in the holy ordinance of the new and everlasting covenant of marriage that he ultimately qualified. Elder Talmage wrote, "It is a precept of the church that women of the church share the authority of the Priesthood with their husbands, actual or prospective, and therefore women . . . taking the endowment . . . are not ordained to specific rank in the Priesthood. Nevertheless there is no grade, rank, or phase of the temple endowment to which women are not eligible on equality with men."[165]

Elder M. Russell Ballard says,

> Our Father in Heaven is generous with His power. All men and *all women* have access to this power for help in their lives. All who have

made sacred covenants with the Lord and who honor those covenants are *eligible to receive personal revelation, to be blessed by the ministering of angels, to commune with God, to receive the fullness of the gospel, and, ultimately, to become heirs alongside Jesus Christ of all our Father has.*[166]

Elder Ballard also explained, "In the Church there is a distinct line of authority. We serve where called by those who preside over us. In the home it is a partnership with husband and wife equally yoked together, sharing in decisions, always working together."[167]

President Joseph Fielding Smith said:

I think we all know that the blessings of the priesthood are not confined to men alone. These blessings are also poured out upon our wives and daughters and upon all the faithful women of the Church. These good sisters can prepare themselves, by keeping the commandments and by serving in the Church, for the blessings of the house of the Lord. The Lord offers to his daughters *every spiritual gift and blessing that can be obtained by his sons,* for neither is the man without the woman, nor the woman without the man in the Lord [see 1 Corinthians 11:11].[168]

These gifts are not lost today. On the contrary, more than ever we need women of all nations to step forward in faith and proclaim the Lord Jesus Christ. The restoration of the gospel of Jesus Christ becomes a font of great power for both men and women.

Dallin H. Oaks further explains, "Priesthood power blesses all of us. Priesthood keys direct women as well as men, and priesthood ordinances and priesthood authority pertain to women as well as men."[169] To truly be one as commanded, we as members of the Lord's church must keep in mind that, as Elder Widtsoe states: "Men have no greater claim than women upon the blessings that issue from the priesthood and accompany its possession."[170]

When Adam arrived in the Garden without Eve, God said "It is *not good* that the man should be alone; I will make him an help meet for him" (Genesis 2:18). It wasn't until after Eve appeared on the scene that "God saw every thing that he had made, and, behold, it was *very good*" (Genesis 1:31). Eve was his crowning finish and it was very good.

CHAPTER 20

ADAM AND THE PRIESTHOOD

The priesthood is meant to exalt families

Abraham speaks of the priesthood lineage from Adam: "It was conferred upon me from the fathers; it came down from the fathers, from the beginning of time, yea, even from the beginning, or before the foundation of the earth, down to the present time, even the right of the firstborn, or the first man, who is Adam, or first father, through the fathers unto me. I sought for mine appointment unto the Priesthood according to the appointment of God unto the fathers concerning the seed" (Abraham 1:3–4).

The seed spoken of here is in reference to families. In this President Russell M. Nelson explains the responsibility that husbands have to love their wives. He says that of all priesthood duties, a husband's *primary responsibility* is to his wife. "Priesthood offices, keys, callings, and quorums are meant to exalt families. . . . Priesthood authority has been restored so that families can be *sealed* eternally (D&C 2:1). So brethren, your foremost priesthood duty is to nurture your marriage—to care for, respect, honor, and love your wife. Be a blessing to her and your children."[171] "Govern your house in meekness, and be steadfast" (D&C 31:9).

In the scriptures we are told, "And Adam knew Eve his wife; and she conceived" (Genesis 4:1). "And she bare unto him sons and daughters, and they began to multiply and to replenish the earth" (Moses 5:2). I had always assumed that when it says Adam *knew* his wife, it meant that they had physical relations, and then had children, because that is how it seems to be categorized in the scriptures. That is our basic understanding of the magnificent relationship of Father Adam and Mother Eve. But I believe I have been wrong in that assumption. I now believe that *Adam knew Eve*, not only as his wife and the mother of all living, but he also understood that Eve was indeed the heart of Eden. She was the motivating force behind all life. She also undoubtedly is the heart of Adam. A husband does not truly know his wife until he entirely loves her. Thus, when we look into the foundation of Adam and Eve's life and the heart that permeates within, we can easily identify their story as perhaps the greatest love story ever known.

If a man, holding the authority and keys of the priesthood, does not understand that his first responsibility is to his wife and family in nurturing his marriage—to care for, respect, honor, and love his wife, and be a blessing to their children—then he simply does not understand those keys and authority. He has lost the entire focus of it. For Adam, the priesthood can be defined in the words "cleave unto thy wife." "Therefore shall a man leave his father and his mother, and cleave unto his wife: and they shall be one flesh," is repeated almost exactly in three books of scripture: Genesis 2:24, Abraham 5:18, and Moses 3:24. And again in D&C 42:22, it says, "Thou shalt love thy wife with all thy heart, and shalt cleave unto her and *none* else" (emphasis added). The scriptural repetition of this commandment stands without contest.

Adam was perfectly obedient to these commandments, as was Eve; not every man carries that same note of perfection. In an attitude of superiority, "We have learned by sad experience that it is the nature and disposition of almost all men, as soon as they get a little authority, as they suppose, they will immediately begin to exercise unrighteous dominion" (D&C 121:39). I think man mistakenly feels that if he loves his wife and listens to her and abides by her council, he is not a man and his priesthood is somehow diminished by her advice, thus perceiving himself to be weak. This is unfortunate because it shows he knows little about *his own* (their) priesthood. Admittedly, it is difficult to submit to the laws of eternity when our hearts are stubbornly fixed upon our own self-worth and not that of our spouse. Some have not yet connected all the dots when it comes to the priesthood. Perhaps that is why we are still here, struggling through a chaotic life.

We may read further in D&C 121 to study and comprehend to a greater extent what the priesthood of God is and should be:

> Hence many are called, but few are chosen.
>
> No power or influence can or ought to be maintained *by virtue of the priesthood*, only by persuasion, by long-suffering, by gentleness and meekness, and by love unfeigned;
>
> By kindness, and pure knowledge, which shall greatly enlarge the soul without hypocrisy, and without guile—
>
> Reproving betimes with sharpness, when moved upon by the Holy Ghost; and then showing forth afterwards an *increase of love* toward him whom thou hast reproved, lest he esteem thee to be his enemy;
>
> That he may know that thy faithfulness is stronger than the cords of death.
>
> Let thy bowels also be full of charity towards all men, and to the household of faith, and let virtue garnish thy thoughts unceasingly; then shall thy confidence wax strong in the presence of God; and the *doctrine of the priesthood* shall distil upon thy soul as the dews from heaven.
>
> The Holy Ghost shall be thy constant companion, and thy scepter an unchanging scepter of righteousness and truth; and thy dominion shall be an everlasting dominion, and without compulsory means it shall flow unto thee forever and ever. (D&C 121:40–46; emphasis added)

I think we can conclude that this counsel is for women as well as for men. If both parties of the same priesthood would adhere to these words, we would be able to jointly experience heaven as did Enoch: "And the Lord called his people Zion, because they were of *one heart and one mind, and dwelt in righteousness*" (Moses 7:18 [17–20]; emphasis added).

Men and women do not need to be opposite; they instead need to be interlocking companions to a bigger picture. Only together as man and wife can they make a whole, functioning priesthood. By becoming of *one heart and one mind* in all things, as the Lord God commanded, only then can *they* unlock the keys of the priesthood and reign forevermore in the creative powers of truth and light.

In considering the equal partnership between husband and wife, Elder L. Tom Perry eloquently said, "*There is not a president or a vice president in a family.* The couple works together eternally for the good of the family. . . . They are on equal footing. They plan and organize the affairs of the family jointly and unanimously as they move forward. . . . Both husband and wife have a sacred obligation to refrain from thoughts and actions that might undermine that equal partnership."[172]

Because men and women carry different roles in life, misunderstandings can abound if our hearts are not turned toward God and each other. Much of men's and women's misunderstanding of each other can perhaps be illustrated in Alma 42:24: "For behold, justice exerciseth all *his* demands, and also mercy claimeth all which is *her* own" (emphasis added). This scriptural example appropriately illustrates a common temperamental difference between men and women. Men tend to view right and wrong (justice) as more black and white; women, on the other hand, tend to be more comprehensive in their emotional, spiritual, and compassionate views (mercy). Men and women would do well to blend these valued traits into a whole truth. The intricate linkage between man and woman and the connective truth between justice and mercy can be finely tuned and perfected only by the love and power of our Lord and Savior, Jesus Christ.

In the woman's part, while she is naturally given a compassion and understanding of the emotional and spiritual basis of the family, she also carries with her an openness of heart. With this openness of heart comes a lot of joy, love, nurturing, and caring, as well as an abundance of impulsiveness, emotion, guilt, sorrow, and pain. This, however, also becomes the experiential knowledge which gives her a greater capacity for mercy. This spirit of charity comes naturally to her, in which she is given a closer bond to the love of Christ.

In the women's organization of the Church of Jesus Christ of

Latter-day Saints, the Relief Society, the name itself reflects the spirit of women, as does the motto, "Charity Never Faileth."

> *Wherefore, cleave unto charity, which is the greatest of all,* for all things must fail—
>
> But *charity is the pure love of Christ, and it endureth forever*; and whoso is found possessed of it at the last day, it shall be well with him.
>
> *Wherefore, my beloved brethren, pray unto the Father with all the energy of heart, that ye may be filled with this love,* which he hath bestowed upon all who are true followers of his Son, Jesus Christ; that ye may become the sons of God; that when he shall appear we shall be like him, for we shall see him as he is; that we may have this hope; that we may be purified even as he is pure. (Moroni 7:46–48; emphasis added)

We can perhaps relate "cleave unto charity" back to the command for Adam to "cleave unto his wife," for she naturally possesses this Christlike gift of charity, which is the greatest of all. Protect her, guard her, and know her, for she is Eve and, as such, she is charity. Therefore, man cannot receive the highest order of the priesthood without a woman by his side.

The highest order of the priesthood is man and woman in eternal marriage.

> Abraham received all things, whatsoever he received, by revelation and commandment, by my word, saith the Lord, and hath entered into his exaltation and sitteth upon his throne.
>
> Abraham received promises concerning his seed, and of the fruit of his loins . . . which were to continue so long as they were in the world; and as touching Abraham and his seed, out of the world *they* should continue; both in the world and out of the world should *they* continue as innumerable as the stars; or, if ye were to count the sand upon the seashore ye could not number them. (D&C 132:29–30; emphasis added)

This promise is yours also, because ye are of Abraham, and the promise was made unto Abraham; and by this law is the continuation of the works of my Father, wherein he glorifieth himself. "Go ye, therefore, and do the works of Abraham; *enter ye into my law and ye shall be saved*" (D&C 132:32; emphasis added).

> Except a man and his wife enter into an everlasting covenant and

be married for eternity, *while in this probation . . ,* by the power and authority of the Holy Priesthood, they will cease to increase when they die; that is, they will not have any children after the resurrection. But those who are married by the power and authority of the priesthood in this life, and continue without committing the sin against the Holy Ghost, will continue to increase and have children in celestial glory.[173]

Only together "shall *they* be gods, because *they* have no end; therefore shall *they* be from everlasting to everlasting, because *they* continue; then shall *they* be above all, because all things are subject unto *them*. Then shall *they* be gods, because *they* have all power, and the angels are subject unto *them*" (D&C 132:20 [19–20]; emphasis added).

When a decision is made in the home, if it is not unanimous with both husband and wife, the process of decision-making needs to start over until they are one in that decision. This may take some humbling prayer to acquire that oneness with the Spirit, but *only then is the priesthood properly magnified in the home.* It is the same in the councils of the prophet and the Apostles; when unanimity is reached, the spirit of all is one in Christ. Though the prophet presides under Christ, he cannot lead properly except he and his apostles become completely united in that same knowledge of truth, without which there is dissension and apostasy. So it is in marriage. Elder Tom Perry said, "The couple works together eternally. . . . They are on equal footing. They plan and organize the affairs of the family *jointly and unanimously* as they move forward."[174]

The common mistake we make in determining what the priesthood is or should be is the practice of *categorizing men and women separately in the priesthood; this gives us only half of that divine priesthood order.*

CHAPTER 21

WHO IS ADAM?

To know Eve, we must know Adam, for they are one.

I have not spoken much of Father Adam as an individual, because my devotion has been to Eve's story that I might advocate on her behalf. But we cannot speak highly of Eve without also speaking of her beloved companion, Adam. Without Adam, there is no story for Eve to tell. Many latter-day prophets, however, have covered this mighty forefather's legacy in abundance. From beginning to end, he is the mighty Michael who fought for us long before we came to this earth and stood among his posterity for over 900 years as their patriarch. It is Adam, the Ancient of Days, who will finish this mortal existence in victory, for he will come to call his posterity (D&C 29:26) at the end of man's probationary time. There is no way to describe the glory and power he now illuminates on high as he has, and always will, stand next to Christ.

The little that I will present to you of the mighty Michael is covered by the prophets of today and will suffice for this script, for we know him as Father Adam: "Latter-day Saints know our noble patriarch as the great archangel, Michael, who not only helped create the earth but will yet lead the Lord's armies in casting out Satan and his followers."[175]

As a leader, Adam/Michael lead the war against Satan before we came here and caused that Satan should be cast out of the heavens. A beautiful rendition can be related by taking excerpts from *The Man Adam* by Robert L. Millet:

> Adam's role in the eternal plan of God began in our premortal first estate. There he was known as Michael, literally one "who is like God." Indeed, by his diligence and obedience there, as one of the spirit sons of God, he attained a stature and power second only to that of Christ, the Firstborn. None of all our Father's children equaled him in intelligence and might, save Jesus only. He was "called and prepared from the foundation of the world according to the foreknowledge of God" (Alma 13:3) to perform his labors on earth. Michael stood with Jehovah in defense of the plan of the Father, the plan of salvation, this in opposition to the amendatory offering of Lucifer, a "son of the morning." (2 Nephi 24:12; D&C 76:25–27)

Robert L. Millet continues, "'The contention in heaven was,' Joseph Smith explained, that 'Jesus said there would be certain souls that would not be saved; and the devil said he could save them all, and laid his plans before the grand council, who gave their vote in favor of Jesus Christ. So the devil rose up in rebellion against God, and was cast down, with all who put up their heads for him.'"[176] Or, as the Revelator saw in vision: "There was war in heaven; Michael and his angels fought against the dragon; and the dragon and his angels fought against Michael; And the dragon prevailed not against Michael. . . . Neither was there place found in heaven for the great dragon, who was cast out; that old serpent called the devil, and also called Satan, which deceiveth the whole world; he was cast out into the earth; and his angels were cast out with him (JST Revelation 12:6–8)." So we see that Michael the archangel, Adam, led the forces of God against the armies of Lucifer in the War in Heaven.

Michael's power and authority was well established as, "Under the direction of Elohim and Jehovah, he assisted in the creation of the earth. . . . Adam and Eve brought mortality into being through partaking of the fruit of the tree of knowledge of good and evil. With the fall of our first parents came blood and posterity and probation and death, as well as the need for redemption through a Savior, a 'last Adam.'"[177] This connection between Adam and the

Savior is significant, "And so it is written, the first man Adam was made a living soul; the last Adam was made a quickening spirit. . . . The first man is of the earth, earthy: the second man is the Lord from heaven" (1 Cor. 15:45, 47).

Being chosen as the patriarch of all mankind, Adam would establish the gospel of Jesus Christ on the earth for all time:

> To Adam, the gospel was first preached, and upon him the priesthood was first bestowed. From Adam and Eve the message of the gospel of salvation went forth to all the world. Following his death, which occurred almost a millennium after he entered mortality, Adam's watch-care over his posterity continued. Revelations have come and angels have ministered under his direction. Priesthood has been conferred and keys delivered at his behest.[178]

As Latter-day Saints understand it, alongside Christ, "Michael was directly involved in the preparation of the physical world in which he and his posterity would undergo a mortal probation."[179] Adam was not the only one to participate in the creation of the earth; there were many others. Elder Bruce R. McConkie wrote,

> Christ and Mary, Adam and Eve, Abraham and Sarah, and a host of mighty men and *equally glorious women* comprised that group of "the noble and great ones," to whom the Lord Jesus said: "We will go down, for there is space there, and we will take of these materials, and we will make an earth whereon these may dwell" [Abraham 3:22–24; emphasis added]. This we know: Christ, under the Father, is the Creator; Michael, His companion and associate, presided over much of the creative work; and with them, as Abraham saw, were many of the noble and great ones.[180]

The keys of the priesthood were first established under the stewardship of Adam: "The Prophet Joseph Smith taught that 'the Priesthood was first given to Adam; he obtained the First Presidency, and held the keys of it from generation to generation. He obtained it in the Creation, before the world was formed, as in Genesis 1:26, 27 and 28.'"[181]

Adam's ministry encompasses all time. From the creation of the earth, till the end of time, his ministry reaches into the eternities. Adam's direct service to the Savior is without end:

Few persons have been more directly involved in the plan of salvation . . . than *the Man Adam.* His ministry among the sons and daughters of earth stretches from the distant past of premortality to the distant future of resurrection, judgment, and beyond. . . .

At the end of the earth—meaning at the end of the Millennium . . . the final great battle between good and evil, known as "the battle of the great God" (D&C 88:114), or the battle of Gog and Magog will take place. And once again, the mighty Michael, the eternal captain of Jehovah's army, will come face to face with his foe, Satan. "The devil and his armies shall be cast away into their own place, that they shall not have power over the saints any more at all."[182]

GARDEN OF EDEN TO GARDEN OF GETHSEMANE

To further illustrate the dedicated companionship between Adam and Christ, we even find evidence of Adam's possible role in Gethsemane. The relationship between Adam and Christ is illustrated in this powerful precept that Elder McConkie puts forth:

There is one other occasion in which Michael as a disembodied spirit may have played a particularly significant role in the plan of our Father. Luke records that on the night of Atonement, following the Last Supper, Jesus bowed in awful alienation and grief in the Garden of Gethsemane beneath the load of the world's sins. He uttered his soul-cry: "Father, if thou be willing, remove this cup from me: nevertheless not my will, but thine, be done. And there appeared an angel unto him from heaven, strengthening him" (Luke 22:42–43). An angel sent from the courts of glory. An angel sent to assist, to support, to sustain the sinless Son of Man in the depths of his greatest agony. The angelic ministrant is not named, if we might indulge in speculation, we would suggest that the angel who came into this second Eden was the same person who dwelt in the first Eden. At least Adam, who is Michael, the archangel—the head of the whole heavenly hierarchy of angelic ministrants—seems the logical one to give aid and comfort to his Lord on such a solemn occasion. Adam fell, and Christ redeemed men from the fall; theirs was a joint enterprise, both parts of which were essential for the salvation of the Father's children.[183]

ADAM IS THE ANCIENT OF DAYS

Doctrine and Covenants carries an array of prophetic script on Adam, such as: "And also with Michael, or Adam, the father of all, the prince of all, the ancient of days" (D&C 27:11). "And the Lord appeared unto them, and they rose up and blessed Adam, and called him Michael, the prince, the archangel" (D&C 107:54). In companionship, "Among the great and mighty ones who were assembled in this vast congregation of the righteous were Father Adam, the Ancient of Days and father of all, And our glorious Mother Eve, with many of her faithful daughters who had lived through the ages and worshiped the true and living God" (D&C 138:38–39).

Adam's legacy is not yet finished, though it will be written in time, "But, behold, verily I say unto you, before the earth shall pass away, Michael, mine archangel, shall sound his trump, and then shall all the dead awake, for their graves shall be opened, and they shall come forth—yea, even all" (D&C 29:26).

How appropriate it is that Adam, who brought death into the world through the Fall, should be the one to call forth his posterity from the grave, to herald the resurrection with the sound of his trumpet. "Michael, the seventh angel, even the archangel, shall gather together his armies, even the hosts of heaven. And the devil shall gather together his armies; even the hosts of hell, and shall come up to battle against Michael and his armies. . . . For Michael shall fight their battles, and shall overcome him who seeketh the throne of him who sitteth upon the throne, even the Lamb" (D&C 88:112–13,15).

Alonzo Gaskill said, "Significantly, Adam . . . then known as mighty Michael . . . headed the force that cast Lucifer out of the premortal world. Here we see that he also caused Satan's removal from Eden. Finally, near the conclusion of the Millennium, it will once again be Adam who will defeat the devil and his hosts, casting them permanently from this earth into outer darkness."[184]

Words alone cannot express what this father did and continues to do for his posterity. He stands as guardian and teacher to us all. His example and priesthood becomes our pathway home to God the

Father. The power and majesty of this forefather has also brought us our inheritance through the Atonement of Jesus Christ. In awe and great humility, we know him simply as Father Adam as he stands resolutely next to Christ.

CHAPTER 22

ELOHEIM/ELOHIM

God in Hebrew, Elohim, is not singular but plural.

I always thought Eloheim was a singular name for God the Father. I soon discovered that there was more to learn about this all-inclusive name. Adam and Eve, Christ, you and I are inherently linked to this name. Understanding God's name gives us a more accurate concept of godhood. Though the personage of God is single in body, godhood is not singular. This is conclusive as we look at the plurality of the name of God; just as there is a Father in Heaven there must also be a Mother and child in heaven.

The encompassing of others in love, light, and truth is basic to all godly power. A righteous family, linked in the heavens with our Father in Heaven, also indelibly links us to the powers of heaven. Studying the name Eloheim gives us a pattern for our own potential growth through family and the required ordinances, It is in these terms that we see and know who God really is: a caring and loving father.

The term *one* in regards to Adam is not singular, for "they twain shall be one" (Mark 10:8). In the eternal ordinance of the temple, we are sealed to our fathers as one family. He is the one and only God but not because He is singular. The title "Father in Heaven" indicates multiplicity but also "one" in family.

"According to Joseph Smith he is God but is there more?

Eloheim . . . signifies to bring forth; Eloheim is from the word *Eloi*, God ... reads—*'Berosheit baurau Eloheim ait aashamayeen vehau auraits*—power of refutation. The head one of the Gods said, Let *us* make a man in *our* own image. The word Eloheim ought to be in the plural.'"[185] According to Talmage, however, "In form the word is a Hebrew plural noun; but it connotes the plurality of excellence or intensity, rather than distinctively of number. It is expressive of supreme or absolute exaltation and power."[186] Plurality of intensity as Talmage states would certainly include posterity: "For behold, *this is my work and my glory*—to bring to pass the immortality and eternal life of man" (Moses 1:39). The Lord said to Adam, "thus may all become my sons" (Moses 6:68).

The inclusion of others in the image of God the Father is evident in the use of El from the name Eloheim. According to the Bible Dictionary, "many biblical names employ El with other words, such as Bethel ('the house of God'), Eleazar ('God has helped'), Michael ('who is like God'), Daniel ('a judge is God'), Ezekiel ('God will strengthen'), and Israel ('to prevail with God' or perhaps 'let God prevail')" (See Bible Dictionary, "El").

The plurality of power as Father and Son is also indicated in an *Old Testament Student Manual*:

> Because Jesus is one with God and is also God, the Old Testament prophets sometimes referred to Him as "Jehovah Elohim," which the King James translators rendered "lord god." To avoid awkward repetition, "lord god" was used to translate the Hebrew phrase "Adonai Jehovah," which otherwise would translate as "lord lord" (see Genesis 15:2, 8; Deuteronomy 3:24). Thus, in the King James Version of the Old Testament, the Hebrew word for Jehovah is almost always translated just this way: lord or god.[187]

The relationship of Father and Son as one in name, power, and godhood is often evident in Bible studies, "And *they* are one God, yea, the very Eternal Father of heaven and of earth (Mosiah 15:4). Even to the Apostles, Jesus, in praying for them, speaks of His oneness with the Father, "And the glory which thou gavest me I have given them; that they may be one, even as we are one: I in them, and thou in me, that they may be made perfect in one" (John

17:22–23). Jesus also includes His Apostles in this glorious oneness. In our world, we think of one not as a whole but rather separate, but in scriptural terms *one* is not singular but whole. We are also one as a covenant family in God, being grouped together in one heart, mind, and purpose, under one eternal Father.

> From . . . the scripture [Genesis 1:26–7], we know that "[God] created man, male and female, after his own image and in his own likeness." . . . The use of the words *us* and *our* in this scripture also teaches us about the relationship between the Father and the Son. God further taught, "By mine Only Begotten [Son] I created these things." The Father and the Son are separate and distinct individuals—as any father and son always are. This may be one reason the name of God in Hebrew, *Elohim, is not singular but plural.*[188]

We are, however, taught to distinguish between the Father and the Son. From Talmage we learn, "Elohim, as understood and used in the restored Church of Jesus Christ, is the name-title of God the Eternal Father, whose firstborn Son in the spirit is Jehovah—the Only Begotten in the flesh, Jesus Christ."[189] Eloi is singular and becomes Elohim in the plural, in relation to the Son of God, or the *Gods.* Would Elohim then become relevant as a family name in that the Son takes on the Father's name? As stated in a previous paragraph, the Old Testament prophets sometimes referred to [the Son] as 'Jehovah Elohim,'" indicating perhaps a first and last name. For example, Tom becomes Thomson in the plural by lineage, or Fredric becomes Frederickson as the family takes on Fredric's given name. Would Eloi (see Mark 15:34) then become Eloheim in the plurality of a family name? If that is the case, could we go so far as to include Mother in Heaven in reference to the name "Elohim" as plural? (see Genesis 5:2; Moses 6:9). Just as Adam and Eve are named Adam.

Of the same necessity we also take on the name of Christ (see Alma 46:18). When we are baptized (adopted) into His church? It was the Savior Himself who said, "For thus shall my church be called in the last days, even The Church of Jesus Christ of Latter-day Saints." (D&C 115:4). Even the Bride (Church of Christ) takes on the bridegroom's name, which is "The Church of Jesus Christ" (See

Chapter 5, Enmity). President Russell M. Nelson ask, "So, what's in a name? When it comes to the name of the Lord's Church, the answer is "Everything!"[190] King Benjamin exhorts, "Hear and know the voice by which ye shall be called, and also, the name by which he shall call you, That Christ, the Lord God Omnipotent, may seal you his" (Mosiah 5:12,15). This may be one reason that in the millennium Isaiah speaks of "And in that day seven women shall take hold of one man, saying, We will eat our own bread, and wear our own apparel: only let us be called by thy name, to take away our reproach" (Isaiah 4:1); perhaps, that they might also be linked back to the Father under patriarchal ordinances.

The name Eloheim was not just an inclusion of Father to Son. According to Robert D. Hales, "From these testimonies, recorded in Holy Scripture, we know that, [God] created man, male and female, after his own image and in his own likeness (D&C 20:18). Some people may be surprised to learn that we look like God. One prominent religious scholar has even taught that imaging God in the form of man is creating a graven image and is idolatrous and blasphemous."[191] But God Himself said, "Let us make man in our image, after our likeness: . . . So God created man in his own image, in the image of God created he him; male and female created he them" (Genesis 1:26–27). From this scripture, we know the image of God is male and female, or I would purport, Father and Mother in Heaven.

THE CHARACTER OF THE FATHER AND THE SON

The character of the Father and the Son is not uncharacteristic to that of earthly father and son relationships. The King Follett sermon, noted as a funeral sermon for King Follett, was given by Joseph Smith in 1844, in Nauvoo, Illinois. In this inspired sermon, Joseph related the intimate relationship between Father and Son, and how kingdoms are empowered by eternal lineage.

Taking excerpts from his sermon, Joseph Smith taught:

> The scriptures inform us that Jesus said, as the Father hath power in himself, even so hath the Son power—to do what? Why, what the Father did. The answer is obvious—in a manner to lay down his body and take

it up again . . . and you have got to learn how to be gods yourselves, and to be kings and priests to God, the same as all gods have done before you, namely, by going from one small degree to another, and from a small capacity to a great one; from grace to grace, from exaltation to exaltation. . . . To inherit the same power, the same glory and the same exaltation, until you arrive at the station of a god, and ascend the throne of eternal power, the same as those who have gone before. . . . My Father worked out His kingdom with fear and trembling, and I must do the same; and when I get my kingdom, I shall present it to My Father, so that He may obtain kingdom upon kingdom, and it will exalt Him in glory. He will then take a higher exaltation, and I will take His place, and thereby become exalted myself. . . . Jesus treads in the tracks of His Father, and inherits what God did before; and *God is thus glorified and exalted in the salvation and exaltation of all His children.* . . . You thus learn some of the first principles of the gospel, about which so much hath been said.[192]

Boyd K. Packer confirmed the knowledge that "'the spirit itself beareth witness with our spirit, that we are the children of God: And if children, then heirs; heirs of God, and joint-heirs with Christ' (Rom. 8:16–17). 'What is man that thou art mindful of him?' Christ, our Redeemer, our *Elder Brother*, asked, 'What manner of men ought ye to be?' And then He answered, 'Verily I say unto you, even as I am'" (3 Nephi 27:27).[193]

Since that sermon, known as the King Follett discourse, the doctrine that humans can progress to exaltation and godliness has been taught within the Church. Lorenzo Snow, the Church's fifth President, coined a well-known couplet: "As man now is, God once was: As God now is, man may be."[194] Little has been revealed about the first half of this couplet, and consequently little is taught. When asked about this topic, President Gordon B. Hinckley told a reporter in 1997, "That gets into some pretty deep theology that we don't know very much about." When asked about the belief in human's divine potential, President Hinckley responded, "Well, as God is, man may become. We believe in eternal progression. Very strongly."[195]

IS THERE A MOTHER IN HEAVEN?

If there is a Father in Heaven there must also be a Mother in Heaven. King equates Queen, male equates female; and so in that perfect image of man and woman, Adam equates Eve. Lest we forget, in the image of Christ as the bridegroom, we must also equate the need for a bride, or the church of God. Marriage covenants are a predominant factor in all of eternity. "Therefore shall a man leave *his father and his mother*, and shall cleave unto his wife: and they shall be one flesh" (Genesis 2:24; emphasis added). The simplicity of this statement not only indicates that both Father and Mother were present in Eden, but the requirement for Adam to follow after his wife in mortality was exemplary of that godly relationship. Elder Rudger Clawson wrote, "We honor woman when we *acknowledge Godhood in her eternal Prototype*."[196]

Christ speaks of being one with the Father; so is woman also one with her husband, or God with his Goddess. Our Heavenly Mother might say as did the Son, "He that hath seen me hath seen the Father; and how sayest thou then, Shew us the Father?" (John 14:9). Or perhaps more to the point, "and how sayest thou then, Shew us the Mother?" Heavenly Father and Mother are one heart, mind, love, intelligence, and purpose. They *are Elohim just as God called* their *name Adam,* "What therefore God hath joined together, let not man put asunder" (Mark 10:9). If man should separate himself from woman he would be singular and without the love, glory, life, and intelligence which she could afford him. The creative and eternal powers to procreate would also be separated from the man and, as a result, man would no longer be crowned as one of the gods.

Elder M. Russell Ballard taught, "Prophets have taught that our heavenly parents work together for the salvation of the human family. We are part of a divine plan designed by Heavenly Parents who love us."[197] President Harold B. Lee stated, "We forget that we have a *Heavenly Father and a Heavenly Mother* who are even more concerned, probably, than our earthly father and mother, and that influences from beyond are constantly working to try to help us when we do all we can."[198]

The Church of Jesus Christ of Latter-day Saints teaches that all human beings, male and female, are beloved spirit children of Heavenly Parents, a Heavenly Father and a Heavenly Mother.[199] This understanding is rooted in scriptural and prophetic teachings about the nature of God, our relationship to Deity, and the godly potential of men and women. The doctrine of a Heavenly Mother is a cherished and distinct belief among Latter-day Saints.[200]

Subsequent Church leaders have affirmed the existence of a Mother in Heaven. In 1909, the First Presidency taught that "all men and women are in the similitude of the universal Father and Mother, and are literally the sons and daughters of Deity."[201] Susa Young Gates (daughter of Brigham Young) wrote in 1920 that Joseph Smith's visions and teachings revealed the truth that *the divine Mother [is] side by side with the divine Father.*[202] Zina Huntington overcome by grief at her mother's passing asked Joseph Smith, "will I know my mother as my mother when I get over on the other side?" "More than that," he said, "you will meet and become acquainted with your eternal Mother, the wife of your Father in Heaven." "Have I then a Mother in Heaven?" Zina asked, "You assuredly have," said Joseph." "How could a Father claim His title unless there were also a Mother to share that parenthood?"[203] In "The Family: A Proclamation to the World," issued in 1995, the First Presidency and Quorum of the Twelve Apostles declared, "Each [person] is a beloved spirit son or daughter of heavenly parents, and, as such, each has a divine nature and destiny."[204]

Regarding our Mother in Heaven, President Spencer W. Kimball shared this thought regarding the song "O My Father": "We get a sense of the ultimate in maternal modesty, of the restrained, queenly elegance of our Heavenly Mother, and knowing how profoundly our mortal mothers have shaped us here, do we suppose her influence on us as individuals to be less if we live so as to return there?"[205]

DO WE PRAY TO HEAVENLY MOTHER?

In lieu of Heavenly Mother, "Latter-day Saints direct their worship to Heavenly Father, in the name of Christ, and do not pray to Heavenly Mother. In this, they follow the pattern set by Jesus Christ, who taught His disciples to 'always pray unto the Father in my name' (3 Nephi 18:19).[206] Latter-day Saints are taught to pray to Heavenly Father, but as President Gordon B. Hinckley said, 'The fact that we do not pray to our Mother in Heaven in no way belittles or denigrates her.'"[207] In praying to the Father, we are appropriately addressing the keys of heaven and earth. Praying directly to Mother in Heaven would not acknowledge that uniting patriarchal power, the keys of the priesthood, which was passed down through Adam. The name Adam, and thus the keys of the priesthood which he held, signify that their marriage was ordained and sealed by God. They hold that power jointly, as man and woman, under the keys of the priesthood, in his name. "For Adam was first formed [in the priesthood], then Eve' (1 Timothy 2:13). When we address our Father in Heaven, are we not also equally addressing our Mother in Heaven, who shares that parental title?

LDS Topics informs us:

> As with many other truths of the gospel, our present knowledge about a Mother in Heaven is limited. Nevertheless, we have been given sufficient knowledge to appreciate the sacredness of this doctrine and to comprehend the divine pattern established for us as children of heavenly parents. Latter-day Saints believe that this pattern is reflected in Paul's statement that "neither is the man without the woman, neither the woman without the man, in the Lord" (1 Corinthians 11:11). Men and women cannot be exalted without each other. . . . As Elder Dallin H. Oaks of the Quorum of the Twelve Apostles has said, *"Our theology begins with heavenly parents. Our highest aspiration is to be like them."*[208] We could perhaps even say that the priesthood is *man and woman* in its proper and final ordination.

CHAPTER 23
TRANSGRESSION

Transgression is an eternal law in and of itself.

Because the transgression was necessary, God forgave the original transgression by Adam and Eve. This was done through the Atonement of Jesus Christ, bringing them back into the presence of the Father; "Behold I have forgiven thee thy transgression in the Garden of Eden. Hence came the saying abroad among the people, that the Son of God hath atoned for original guilt, wherein the sins of the parents cannot be answered upon the heads of the children, for they are whole from the foundation of the world" (Moses 6:53–54). "We might have reasoned from other scriptures that Adam did not have to repent of his transgression committed in the garden but this scripture categorically says it in one sentence. The atonement unconditionally covers Adam's original sin."[209] In the Church of Jesus Christ of Latter-day Saints, we concur with that scriptures in the second article of faith, "We believe that men will be punished for their own sins and not for Adam's transgression" (Article of Faith 2).

To Adam, the Lord said, "I am the Only Begotten of the Father from the beginning, henceforth and forever, that as thou hast fallen thou mayest be redeemed, and all mankind, even as many as will" (Moses 5:9). This was a reassurance that the Fall was not a plan of failure but a well-orchestrated plan for redemption. This transgression of Adam and Eve into mortality was a necessary, and even planned step towards godhood.

"The word transgress means to 'pass over, step across, or go beyond' a boundary."[210] God set boundaries in Eden, and then Adam and Eve intentionally 'crossed over' those into mortality . . . *not because our first parents were sinful* or rebellious in their nature . . . but again, because they needed to formally, or technically transgress God's law in order to introduce the conditions requisite for their growth and exaltation. *There was no other way!*"[211]

In the time of Adam and Eve in Eden, transgression was the only way to progress. Jacob, in the Book of Mormon, speaks of Adam and Eve as "having no joy, for they knew no misery; doing no good, for they knew no sin" (2 Nephi 2:23). Godhood does not stand still but is in a constant mode of creation, always progressing from eternity to eternity. We needed a transgression, without which we would all stand still, being unable to obtain a far greater objective. Transgression in these terms becomes eternal progression.

Elder Oaks goes on to say,

> This transition, or fall, could not happen without a transgression . . . an exercise of moral agency amounting to a willful breaking of a law (see Moses 6:59). This would be a planned offense; a formality to serve an eternal purpose. ... It was Eve who first transgressed the limits of Eden in order to initiate the conditions of mortality. Her act ... was formally a transgression but eternally a glorious necessity to open the doorway toward eternal life. Adam showed his wisdom by doing the same. And thus Eve and Adam fell that men might be (2 Nephi 2:25). Eve's choice was momentous: because of her choice, sin and death afflicted her and Adam and their posterity. However, by entering mortality, she and Adam gained the opportunity to have children and to strive toward exaltation.[212]

Admittedly, 1 John 3:4 informs us that "sin is the transgression of the law," but that does not necessarily mean that all transgressions are sins. The transgression from immortality to mortality was necessary and even commanded (Genesis 1:28; Jacob 4:9). *This transgression was, in fact, an eternal law in and of itself,* by which

Adam and Eve are then able to become "as the gods" by way of the Atonement. Otherwise, God would not have planted both trees in the midst of the garden to give them that all important choice. In that choice, he also promised, "But, behold, I say unto you that I, the Lord God, gave unto Adam and unto his seed, that they should not die as to the temporal death, until I, the Lord God, should send forth angels to declare unto them repentance and redemption, through faith on the name of mine Only Begotten Son" (D&C 29:40–42).

Without a transgression into mortality, we would not have bodies, even according to the promised resurrection. We would not have a continuation of family under the Father who is in heaven. We would not have a knowledge and understanding of eternal values. Without a transgression, all life and intelligence would be dormant. Transgressing from the tree of life to the tree of knowledge of good and evil is the full package that Adam and Eve understood and willingly partook of in the Fall of man. The Lord promised "that *as thou hast fallen thou mayest be redeemed*, and all mankind, even as many as will [believe]" (Moses 5:4–12; emphasis added).

Bruce R. McConkie poetically expresses the fall this way:

Be fruitful, and multiply. Provide bodies for my spirit progeny. Thus saith thy God, eternity hangs in the balance. The plans of deity are at the crossroads. There is only one course to follow; the course of conformity and obedience. Adam… our father, and Eve, our mother, must obey. They must become mortal. Death must enter the world. There is no other way. They must fall that man may be. Such is the reality. Such is the rational. Such is the divine will. Fall thou must, O mighty Michael. Fall? Yes, plunge down from thy immortal state of peace, perfection, and glory to a lower existence; leave the presence of thy God in the garden and enter the lone and dreary world…. Yes, Adam, fall; fall for thine own good; fall for the good of all mankind; fall that many may be; bring death into the world; do that which will cause an atonement to be made, with all the infinite and eternal blessings which flow there from. And so Adam fell as fall he must.[213]

CHAPTER 24

SACRIFICE REQUIRED

"I know not, save the Lord commanded me"
—Moses 5:6

There is no evidence of truth or redemption without sacrifice. All of us must give of ourselves, whether it be God the Father, His Son Jesus Christ, Adam and Eve, or you and I. There is no reward without some kind of selfless act on our part. There is no life, love, or joy except by the priceless gift of sacrifice. Sacrifice becomes a needed tutorial for godhood. Only by sorrow can we better understand compassion. We must die before we are resurrected unto life. We must know the evil to know the good. It is in sacrifice for others that we learn to know and love one another. Love determines our convictions. We are defined by trial. We are made in sacrifice.

Sacrifice is an act coupled with an intense desire to obtain salvation which, by the Fall, has now become a treasure to our hearts. Sacrifice is obedience as we submit our will to the will of God. Without obedience, we continue in misery, for we have yet to learn by the commandments the good from the evil.

Godhood must be learned, experienced, and tested. Like Adam and Eve, each one of us chose to come to earth with full knowledge of the personal trial we would face. We need to trust in that personal pre-earth decision. We need to believe in what we knew then, that through our Elder Brother Jesus Christ, we could be saved by the probationary laws given to us in mortality. Being schooled in this way would give us a full comprehension of the love of God as it also offered new realms of progression and salvation for our hungry souls.

Sacrifice is the fulfilling of the law, "Wherefore the law was our schoolmaster to bring us unto Christ, that we might be justified by faith. But after that faith is come, we are no longer under a schoolmaster" (Galatians 3:24–25). In sacrifice and after strict obedience to God's word, comes salvation. Adam, obediently sacrificed according to the Lord's every word.

> And Adam and Eve, his wife, called upon the name of the Lord, and they heard the voice of the Lord from the way toward the Garden of Eden, speaking unto them, and they saw him not; for they were shut out from his presence.
>
> And *after many days* [trial of faith] an angel of the Lord appeared unto Adam, saying: Why dost thou offer sacrifices unto the Lord? And Adam said unto him: I know not, save the Lord commanded me.
>
> And in that day the Holy Ghost fell upon Adam, which beareth record of the Father and the Son, saying: I am the Only Begotten of the Father from the beginning, henceforth and forever, that *as thou hast fallen thou mayest be redeemed*, and all mankind, even as many as will. And Adam and Eve blessed the name of God, and they made all things known unto their sons and their daughters. (Moses 5:4, 6, 9, 12; emphasis added)

In sacrifice and after strict obedience to God's word, comes salvation. "Unto Adam also and to his wife did the Lord God make coats of skins, and clothed them" (Genesis 3:21). They, being clothed in robes of salvation now understood, experientially, that the *Fall was not a plan of damnation but a plan of redemption*.

How then, should we be redeemed? It is done in faith, on His name, "Surely the shedding of the blood of animals cannot remit man's sin except it be done in imitation of something such as the shedding of the blood of Jesus Christ."[214] He is the law, as he assumes the pure will of the Father: "not my will, but thine, be done" (Luke 22:42). "For it is expedient that there should be a great and last sacrifice; yea, not a sacrifice of man, neither of beast, neither of any manner of fowl; for it shall not be a human sacrifice; but it must be an infinite and eternal sacrifice" (Alma 34:10). "In this was manifested the love of God toward us, because that God sent his only begotten Son into the world, that we might live through him" (1 John 4:9). The meat and blood sacrifice of animals was a reminder of Christ's required mortal sacrifice for the fall of man. In finishing that requirement, the blood sacrifice was done away. We now covenant by the bread and wine (water) to remember His flesh and blood which He gave for our salvation.

Redemption comes through Christ; as James E. Talmage believed, the physiological cause of Christ's death was a broken heart:

> This element in our Lord's sacrifice suggests two differences between animal sacrifices and the sacrifices of a broken heart. First is the difference between offering one of our possessions, such as an animal, and offering our own hearts. Second, one who offers an unblemished animal, the firstling of a flock, acts in similitude of the Father's sacrifice of his unblemished, firstborn son.
>
> By contrast, one who offers his own broken heart acts in similitude of the Son's terrible personal sacrifice of Himself. Thus, the figurative breaking of our own hearts, represented by our repentance and our faithful endurance of the mortal crucible... our own taste of a bitter cup . . . is a self sacrifice that mirrors the Savior's own self-sacrifice.[215]

His was a sacrifice of all that he had, because of love. "And the world, because of their iniquity, shall judge him to be a thing of naught; wherefore they scourge him, and he suffereth it; and they smite him, and he suffereth it. Yea, they spit upon him, and he suffereth it, because of his loving kindness and his long-suffering towards the children of men" (1 Nephi 19:9). We too become as He is when we also apply our own broken heart and contrite spirit for the remission of our sins.

To His disciples He said, 'Learn of me; for I am meek and lowly in heart' (Matthew 11:29). . . . Christ's example teaches us that a broken heart is an eternal attribute of godliness. When our hearts are broken, we are completely open to the Spirit of God and recognize our dependence on Him for all that we have and all that we are."[216] It is also through this broken heart that we find healing and joy that comes only through the pure love of Jesus Christ.

The resurrection is already available to all God's children that have chosen mortality. But the plan of salvation comes only through obedience to God's laws. Why then, in the plan of redemption, if the Lord loves us as He says He does, do we have to work so hard to receive His promised salvation? To begin with, if salvation were free it would have no value. We would have no apparent purpose in being saved, because there would be no condemnation. We would then cease to exist. Elder Bruce R. McConkie has written: "Lucifer wanted to . . . impose salvation upon all men without effort on their part . . . an impossible thing since *there can be no progression except by the upward pull of obedience to law.*"[217]

Salvation or damnation is based on whether or not we apply the principle of sacrifice with the principle of obedience. It is by obedience to God's laws that chaos and destruction are removed. Within the laws of obedience "faith and repentance bringeth a change of heart unto [us]—wherewith [we] have been made free" (Helaman 15:7, 8). Only in Christ atonement, do we become eternal creators.

Robert J. Matthews teaches:

> Jesus cried aloud, and he said, "Abba, Father, all things are possible unto thee; take away this cup from me: nevertheless not what I will, but what thou wilt" (Mark 14:36). This was the Father's Chosen and Beloved Son, his Only Begotten, pleading for an escape from the experiences that resulted in his blood coming through the pores of his skin. Yet the Father did not excuse him nor devise another way. If there were another way, this would have been the time to put it into operation. The fact that no other system was used, even at the Son's pleading, suggests in the strongest terms that *no other way* was possible. Surely, if there had been any other way, the Father would have hearkened when his Son thus plead.
>
> In blood are the seeds of mortal life and death. The scripture says: "As in Adam all die, even so in Christ shall all be made alive" (1 Corinthians 15:22). In other words, as by Adam . . . came blood which brings death, so by Christ's blood came redemption from sin and

death. . . . Each [Adam and Jesus] had fulfilled his foreordained part, and now the two principles were together as Jesus triumphed over sin and mortality.[218]

Because of His obedience and sacrifice, we can also triumph over sin and mortality, through faith and an enduring hope in Christ. "And moreover, I say unto you, that salvation doth not come by the law alone; and were it not for the atonement, which God himself shall make for the sins and iniquities of his people, that they must unavoidably perish, notwithstanding the law of Moses" (Mosiah 13:28). "Know ye not that . . . ye are not your own? For ye are bought with a price" (1 Corinthians 6:19–20). Furthermore, "Ye know that ye were not redeemed with corruptible things, as silver and gold . . . but with the precious blood of Christ" (1 Peter 1:18–19).

KEYS OF SALVATION ARE GIVEN

By sacrifice we then obtain all that God has and thus receive the crowning ordinance of the Holy Priesthood, which is after the order of the Son of God, which "administereth the gospel and holdeth the key of the mysteries of the kingdom, even the key of the knowledge of God" (D&C 84:19).

Hence, unto Adam, the great progenitor of the human family, were given the "keys of salvation." Then, "who hath appointed Michael [Adam] your prince, and established his feet, and set him upon high, and given unto him the keys of salvation under the counsel and direction of the Holy One, who is without beginning of days or end of life" (D&C 78:16). Where did Adam get the keys of redemption? It was by the power of the Redeemer that he was authorized.

Adam and Eve knew that while faith and obedience bring peace and joy, all else brings pain and anguish. We can overcome weakness by compliance to our covenants. "Freedom comes not by resisting it [the law], but by applying it."[219] That is what covenants are for, to overcome all deceit, to be given knowledge, receiving all truth and the joy it provides. Strengthened in faith by covenants, gives us the literal *power* to overcome evil and receive all that God has.

"*O how great the goodness of our God, who prepareth a way for our escape from . . . death and hell*, which I call the death of the body, and also the death of the spirit" (2 Nephi 9:10; emphasis added). "Therefore God conversed with men, and made known unto them the plan of redemption, which had been prepared from the foundation of the world; and this he made known unto them according to their faith and repentance and their holy works" (Alma 12:30). Jesus Christ, by sacrifice, is the hope and the eternal joy of all who believe.

CHAPTER 25
COATS OF SKIN AND SACRAMENTS

"And let these ... anointed ones . . . be clothed with salvation"
—D&C 109:80

Joseph Fielding wrote: "After Adam and Eve had partaken of the forbidden fruit, but before they were expelled from the garden, the Father taught them the law of sacrifice. Animals were slain that Adam and Eve might be clothed in 'coats of skins.' 'Unto Adam, and also his wife, did I, the Lord God, make coats of skins, and clothed them'" (Moses 4:27).[220] The skins placed upon Adam and Eve's bodies were to be a spiritual protection to them in a fallen world.

Animals sacrificed in the Garden of Eden were not only representative of the sacrifice of the mortal Christ but also of that death which should come upon Adam and Eve because of their transgression. Therefore, covenants were made between Christ and man that we might be redeemed from the Fall. The wearing of those skins was to be a constant reassurance that Christ would perform all that was promised and that man would always remember Him and keep His commandments.

"God made them coats of skins, large, and strong, and durable, and fit for them; such is the righteousness of Christ. Therefore clothe yourselves with the Lord Jesus Christ."[221] "The Hebrew translated 'to cover' is actually the same as the Hebrew word from which we get our English word *atonement*. This suggests that he will provide atonement for them."[222]

These skins covered not only their bodies, but also linked them back to God the Father in covenants. We can see this as "unto Adam also and to his wife did the Lord God make *coats of skins, and clothed them*," then confirmed, "behold, the man is become as *one of us*, to know good and evil" (Genesis 3:22; emphasis added). This puts forth that the coats of skins are directly related to godhood. In this, they would not only be restored to a physical immortality but perhaps to a greater level of godhood, as they proved to be obedient to His commandments, in the wearing of the skins, and in keeping covenants and ordinances. "Wherefore, thou shalt do all that thou doest in the name of the Son, and thou shalt repent and call upon God in the name of the Son forevermore" (Moses 5:8). Adam and Eve were given a promise of redemption in the wearing of the coats of skins. The saving ordinances that were performed in Eden and in their subsequent mortality were then performed in ancient temples and again in the restored Church of Jesus Christ of Latter-day Saints. These ordinances were first established under Adam.

"The prophet [Joseph Smith] introduced an ordinance to the men. Part of it involved washings and anointings, similar to the ordinances given in the Kirtland temple and the ancient Hebrew temple and the ancient Hebrew tabernacle. The men were given a sacred undergarment that covered their bodies and reminded them of their covenants." These ordinances were first established in Eden in similitude of the coats of skins which Adam and Eve wore.[223]

The wearing of clothing to acknowledge Christ's sacrifice continued throughout religious history. The priestly clothing in Moses' day was not the skins of beast, but Aaron was dressed in priestly robes: "he put upon him the *coat*, and girded him with the girdle, and clothed him with the robe" (Leviticus 8:7). The significance of priestly robes worn throughout the Old and New Testament was a symbolic reference to the coats that Adam and Eve wore. Even Christ, who was acknowledged as a Rabbi (John 6:25), did not wear a coat of skins but was nevertheless acknowledged for the coat He wore at His crucifixion. There was also a *coat*, made of one piece, "which was a goodly garment, woven throughout in one piece, without seam." To rend it would be to spoil; so the soldiers cast lots to determine who should have it; and in this circumstance the Gospel writers saw a fulfillment of the psalmist's prevision: "They parted my garments among them, and upon my vesture did they cast lots (Matthew 27:35,36)."[224] The significance of this coat was not specified, nevertheless, it was made a point of in holy writ.

John the Baptist was noted for his humble clothing "with a garment of camel's hair," (Mark 1:6) to set him apart from the proud Pharisees. Other ancient prophets are said to have worn priestly "mantles." The Lord has counseled to "clothe yourselves with the bond of charity, as with a mantle, which is the bond of perfectness and peace" (D&C 88:125).

> A mantle is a robe or a cloak and the term is often used symbolically to express a covering that characterizes a trait or the authority which an individual possesses. For example, when Elijah cast his mantle upon Elisha, this was symbolic of the authority being transferred from the one to the other (1 Kings 19:19). Elisha later used both the mantle of cloth and the mantle of authority to perform miracles. (2 Kings 2:13–14)[225]

Joseph of Egypt wore a coat of many colors, showing forth his priestly birthright as the favored son of Israel, and his brothers despised him. "And they took Joseph's coat, and killed a kid of the goats, and dipped the coat in the blood" (Genesis 37:31). There is some obvious scriptural significance in the priestly coats of those chosen by God. In the words of Hugh Nibley, "Adam [and Eve's] new leather garment was nonetheless a glorious one, a sign of authority,' and 'a garment of protection.'"[226]

As Christ spoke to the Apostles, by the will of the Father, they were told "stand at my right hand at the day of my coming in a pillar of fire, being clothed with robes of righteousness, with crowns upon their heads, in glory even as I am, . . . even as many as have loved me and kept my commandments, and none else" (D&C 29:12).

Along with wearing the coats of skins, the meat portion of the sacrificial animals was not just a nutritional need, but the spiritual implications found in the sacrifice were far more adhesive to the law than were the physical implications. "And the wave breast and heave shoulder shall ye *eat* in a clean place; *thou, and thy sons, and thy daughters with thee*: for they be thy due, and thy sons' due, which are given out of the sacrifices of peace offerings of the children of Israel" (Leviticus 10:14; emphasis added).

Another sacrificial offering by the people was done during the Passover. In Exodus 12:3, Moses and Aaron were commanded to "speak ye unto *all the congregation* of Israel, saying, In the tenth day of this month they shall take to them every man a lamb, according to the house of their fathers, a lamb for an house."

> And they shall *eat* the flesh in that night, roast with fire, and unleavened bread; and with bitter herbs *they shall eat it.* . . .
>
> I will pass over you, and the plague shall not be upon you to destroy you, when I smite the land of Egypt.
>
> And this day shall be unto you for a memorial; and ye shall keep it a feast to the Lord throughout your generations; ye shall keep it a . . . *feast by an ordinance* for ever. (Exodus 12:8, 13–14; emphasis added).

The Passover was performed yearly by the congregation of Israel before Christ's resurrection, and traditionally to this day.

Having fulfilled the Mosaic promise through His atoning blood, the meat offering, after the resurrection, was embodied in the new sacrament offering of bread and wine. As the Lord required the Apostles to "take, eat: this is my body" (Mark 14:22), such laws were given as *"divine laws given of heaven, prescribing rules on spiritual concerns, for faith and worship, both to be answered by man to his Maker"* (D&C 134:6; emphasis added). All sensory, tactical, and spiritual elements, even the wonder of miracles were manifest and given for their remembrance, learning and consecration. But few were truly converted as they often fell into self-indulgent idolatry. Even He, Himself, came among them and was rejected of them.

In the same similitude of the coats of skins, and the sacramental partaking of *His flesh*, in Hebrews we are told that the veil of the temple is the *flesh of Christ* (see Hebrews 10:20 [19–22]); "Christ who stands between the patron and the Father" (see 1 Timothy 2:5; 2 Nephi 2:27) and becomes our advocate for salvation.

Like the coats of skins given to Adam and Eve in the garden, the vestitures and ordinances performed in the temple, ancient and latter-day, are required for full salvation and exaltation. They, like baptism, are extended acts of obedience to the laws of God. "For he hath clothed me with the garments of salvation, he hath covered me with the robe of righteousness" (Isaiah 61:10). Whether we speak of coats of skins, meat sacrifice, sacramental bread and wine, temple ordinances, or baptism, all are covenants by obedience. They are performed according to the laws which God prescribed for our salvation as they continue to point us to the atoning power of Christ. Many today do not acknowledge these temple symbols and fall away. "But blessed are they who have kept the covenant and observed the commandment, for they shall obtain mercy" (D&C 54;6).

Metaphorically, to be clothed means to be given a covenant or garment of oath, covered not only in body but also in the spirit of promise. *Naked* in the scriptures often refers to losing or being without a covenant unto salvation. God would not send us forth into a trying world without a hope of salvation. Being clothed in the garment of promised salvation by the power and authority of God, was a powerful reassurance that they were not alone. "I will not leave you comfortless: I will come to you" (John 14:18; see also Chapter 12).

Along with the commandments and being clothed, covenants are made between God and man. It cannot, however, be a two-way covenant without prescribed laws to keep. Though God does not break his covenants with us—for He is perfect—we easily break our covenants with God; in which case, we may then feel naked before God without His overshadowing promise of salvation in those covenants. We are told, "I, the Lord, am bound when ye do what I say; but when ye do not what I say, ye have no promise" (D&C 82:10). Those who do not keep God's commandments often question, "What is truth?" However, within the covenants we are promised, "He that keepeth his commandments receiveth truth and light, until he is glorified in truth and knoweth all things" (D&C 93:28).

It was in anticipation of the Atonement that we came to earth; *it is what we seek.* To find those blessings, we need agency, which is only plausible if we have been given laws to guide us in that agency. Thus God clothed us and gave us commandments, or directives, to obtain all that He has: this because of His love for His children.

Paul spoke to the Corinthians on being clothed from heaven,

> For we know that if our earthly house of this tabernacle were dissolved, we have a building of God, an house not made with hands, eternal in the heavens.
>
> For in this we groan, earnestly desiring to be clothed upon with our house which is from heaven:
>
> If so be that being clothed we shall not be found naked.
>
> For we that are in this tabernacle do groan, being burdened: not for that we would be unclothed, but clothed upon, that mortality might be swallowed up of life. . . .
>
> For we must all appear before the judgment seat of Christ; that every one may receive the things done in his body, according to that he hath done, whether it be good or bad. (2 Corinthians 5:1–4, 10)

Like Adam and Eve, being clothed in the holy garments of the temple becomes a power to "become one of [the gods]" (Genesis 3:21). Due to persecution, Brigham Young turned to leaving the Nauvoo temple behind, but was met with anxious faces. He understood the saints need for the endowments. Turning around, Brigham followed them back inside the newly built edifice. "They knew they needed to endure the hardship ahead, overcome the sting of death, and return to the presence of God."[227]

When we break the law (and we all do), all is not lost, because God is merciful and will again apply those laws of salvation through sincere repentance on our part. "Thou shalt repent and call upon God in the name of the Son forevermore" (Moses 5:8). That is the grace, the forgiveness, which He offers us, in which we may once again set our course to be cleansed and attain all that God has by a renewed commitment to obey His commandments in faith.

I WAS NAKED AND YE CLOTHED ME

Remembering the words in Matthew, I was "naked and ye clothed me" (Matthew 25:36), bring us to acknowledge that "we love him, because he first loved us" (1 John 4:19). In His example of clothing the naked, He sets the way for us to care for those in need. Being converted unto Christ makes King Benjamin's admonition pertinent. In compliance to the command to love our neighbor as ourselves, we are admonished, "And also, ye yourselves will succor those that stand in need of your succor: ye will administer of your substance unto him that standeth in need; and ye will not suffer that the beggar putteth up his petition to you in vain, and turn him out to perish" (Mosiah 4:16). Thus, in our acts of compassion towards others, we acknowledge His compassion towards all, and in those acts of kindness we become as one with Him, as He made His ultimate sacrifice for us.

Adam and Eve subsequently learned that the shedding of animal's blood as a sacrifice was in similitude of the atoning blood of Christ (see Moses 5:7). Thus, the garments given them in Eden were to serve as a reminder that, through the atoning blood of Christ, they could be protected and redeemed from a fallen world. Through His blood, they could obtain a remission of sins, be born again, and return to His divine presence. All this was to be done in remembrance of Jesus Christ, in whom salvation comes. "And moreover, I say unto you, that there shall be no other name given nor any other way nor means whereby salvation can come unto the children of men, only in and through the name of Christ, the Lord Omnipotent" (Mosiah 3:17).

CHAPTER 26
BLOOD

"Blood is the badge of mortality"[228]

Blood is not something I will miss after the resurrection. As a corrupt substitute for immortality, it carries with it a vast array of pain, disease, degeneration, inconvenience, death, and trials through a temporal probation. However, I am grateful to have been privileged to experience mortality, to give birth, and to receive the covenants of salvation through the atoning blood of Christ. "There is no other way or means whereby man can be saved, only in and through the blood of Christ. Behold, he is the life and the light of the world. Behold, he is the word of truth and righteousness" (Alma 38:9). Because of mortality, my eyes are open and I shall be redeemed through the *mortal blood* of Christ.

Blood, or mortality, is a necessary tool in which we can become independent and responsible for our own choices and growth. The tree of knowledge of good and evil gives us a full scope of choice-making as experienced in a mortal world, "that every man may act . . . according to the moral agency which I have given unto him, that every man may be accountable for his own sins in the day of judgment" (D&C 101:78).

Because blood is impure, it is also temporal; that makes it a probationary step, a perfecting tool, towards eternal life. Blood reminds us that we have been given time to learn and grow as we choose. I think that when we lose blood, fear sometimes grips our heart as a reminder that "time" is running out.

I have included some blood facts that give me greater understanding and peace about my short, but required, time here in mortality. The Prophet Joseph Smith taught us that resurrected beings do not have blood, but possess bodies of flesh and bones, "having spirit in their bodies, and not blood." The Prophet also said, "When our flesh is quickened by the Spirit, there will be no blood in this tabernacle." In speaking of the place where God dwells, the Prophet said, "Flesh and blood cannot go there; but flesh and bones, quickened by the Spirit of God, can"[229] (see also 1 Corinthians 15:50). "This much we know about blood: (a) it is a vital part of our mortal lives and is basic to the reproductive process of mortals; (b) it was the agent of redemption in the atonement of Jesus Christ, he shed his blood to redeem all people from the effects of the Fall and, upon the condition of repentance, from their personal sins; and (c) blood will not exist in the bodies of resurrected beings."[230] It seems that after the resurrection, spirit flows through our veins in place of blood. The spirit is a pure substance that can enter God's presence as it also purifies our body.

"With these known facts it becomes evident that blood is the badge of mortality, and since it will not exist in the deathless bodies of Adam and Eve and their posterity in the resurrection, it is therefore reasonable to conclude that blood did not exist in the deathless, premortal bodies of Adam and Eve prior to the Fall."[231]

"When God created the earth, man, and all things in the earth, there was no death and all of these things would have remained forever and had no end if death had not entered by the transgression of Adam." This brings to mind the declaration in the Doctrine and Covenants that to God all things are spiritual. "Wherefore, verily I say unto you that all things unto me are spiritual, and not at any time have I given unto you a law which was temporal" (D&C 29:34). That is, God is everlasting and endless; He is a spiritual (immortal) being, and that which He does is spiritual, not temporal."[232]

God and His words are everlasting, but Satan's words will perish; they hold no promise.

"According to the scriptures *it was Adam, not God that brought death. Death was not part of the Lord's original creation of this earth or anything in the earth.*"[233] "Were it not for *our* transgression we never should have had seed" (Moses 5:11). "Because that Adam fell, we are; and by *his* fall came death" (Moses 6:48). Blood is the mortal life of the body (see Genesis 9:4–6; Leviticus 17:10–14). Thus, blood becomes the seed of mortality, of life and death.

Blood came by way of the transgression (causing blood to flow into the body instead of Spirit), which brought on a physical death. "Death literally means 'separation' or to be 'separated from.' Thus the physical death is the separation of the body from the spirit. Spiritual death means to be out of the presence of, alienated or separated from, God or righteousness."[234] Our bodies are considered corrupt because of a physical and spiritual separation from God. In *The Man Adam*, we are also taught: *"If God had created man mortal,* then death, sin, and all the circumstances of mortality would be God's doing and would be eternal and permanent in their nature. *Whereas if man brings the Fall upon himself, he is the responsible mortal agent, and God is able to rescue and redeem him from his fallen state."*[235]

"All things have been done in the wisdom of him who knoweth all things" (2 Nephi 2:24). Remember, Elder Orson F. Whitney said, "The fall had a twofold direction . . . downward, yet forward."[236] The Prophet Joseph Smith said: *"Adam was made to open the way of the world."*[237] Robert J. Matthews adds, "Adam and Eve had the privilege of getting things under way by their own actions. This is far *better than their being created mortal and sinful."*[238]

We learn in Doctrine and Covenants that God does not create temporal or mortal conditions and does not function on a mortal level: "Behold, I gave unto him that he should be an agent unto himself; and I gave unto him commandment, but no temporal commandment gave I unto him, for my commandments are spiritual; they are not natural nor temporal, neither carnal nor sensual" (D&C 29:34–35). All God's commandments are *eternal laws; they live.* We may therefore choose to act on eternal law and life or on that which is merely *temporal.*

GREAT DROPS OF BLOOD

"We know that He lay prostrate upon the ground as the pains and agonies of an infinite burden caused Him to tremble and would that He might not drink the bitter cup."[239] Luke recorded: "And being in an agony, he prayed more earnestly; and he sweat as it were *great drops of blood* falling down to the ground" (JST Luke 22:44). King Benjamin taught his people: "And lo, he shall suffer temptations, and pain of body, hunger, thirst, and fatigue, even more than man can suffer, except it be unto death; for behold, blood cometh from every pore, so great shall be his anguish for the wickedness and the abominations of his people" (Mosiah 3:7). While blood is the badge of mortality, it is also the means by which salvation comes in the name of Jesus Christ.

CHAPTER 27

DUST

Adam "became of dust a living soul"
—Moses 6:59

I found the word *dust* to be fascinating in definition as a metaphor and, at the same time, as a literal term. The word itself is simple, but it metaphorically and physically connects both heaven and earth in profound ways. The study of this term has given me a broad understanding of all aspects of life: spirit, immortal, mortal, millennial, resurrected, and even in the partaking of the tree of life in God's presence. These all became connected for me through the word *dust*. Thus, the word *dust* became surprisingly comprehensive since it also becomes a basic component of creation for all of God's work.

In the scriptures, the word *dust* is recognized as it pertains to Adam, "Thou shalt return unto the ground—for thou shalt surely *die*—for out of it wast thou taken: for dust thou wast, and unto dust shalt thou return" (Moses 4:25; emphasis added). Because of the figurative expression in the scriptures of Adam being created from the "dust of the earth" as it pertains to himself and all his posterity, the theological view generally holds it as a literal term for man's creation. Adam was not created *from* the dust of the earth any more than he had been created mortal. Only after the Fall did Adam's body and the earth fall to become mortal in its corrupt form;

therefore, the elements—as a corrupt form—are often referred to as dust. However, dust has a multitude of metaphoric references in the scriptures, most of which refer to mortal earth, life, body, death, or the natural man. All will be considered in this chapter.

DUST OF THE GROUND

Adam was *not* literally made of dust as we might think. As President Brigham Young remarked, "When you tell me that father Adam was made . . . from the earth, you tell me what I deem an idle tale. . . . and if he had been made in such a manner he would be nothing but a brick in the resurrection. He was made . . . as you and I are made, and no person was ever made upon any other principle."[240]

The scriptures tell us, "And the Lord God *formed* man of the dust of the ground, and breathed into his nostrils the breath of life; and man became a living soul" (Genesis 2:7). "In Hebrew, however, the verb *bara* (translated in the Genesis phrase "God *formed* man"): we find one of the possible translations of *bara* as used in the Old Testament is 'to beget.'"[241] We find further evidence to this as, "Elder Parley P. Pratt noted that Moses wished to reveal to mankind the true origin of Adam and Eve, but they could not receive it. So, according to Elder Pratt, Moses veiled the truth."[242] Thus, the word *dust* became metaphoric for man's creation.

ELEMENT IS SELF-EXISTENT

Elder Bruce R. McConkie wrote: "Although Adam's physical body was created only after this earth had been organized, his spirit had been in existence in an organized capacity for millions, if not billions of years prior to the creation. Indeed, even the matter from which Adam's body was made existed prior to his being physically organized."[243] In this spiritual realm, "there stood one among them that was like unto God, and he said . . . We will go down, for there is space there, and we will take of these materials, and we will make an earth whereon these may dwell" (Abraham 3:24).

The Prophet Joseph Smith tells us,

Now, the word create came from the word *baurau*, which does not mean to create out of nothing; it means to organize; the same as a man would organize materials and build a ship. Hence, we infer that God had materials to organize the world out of chaos—chaotic matter, which is *element*, and in which *dwells all the glory* [Spirit]. . . . The pure principles of element are principles which can never be destroyed; they may be organized and re-organized, but not destroyed. They had no beginning and can have no end.[244]

God organized the earth from chaotic matter; this matter became organized as it *obeyed His voice in all things*.

In an official statement from the First Presidency and Council of the Twelve we read: "God created the earth as an organized sphere; . . . 'The elements are eternal.' (D&C 93:33). So also life is eternal, and not created; *but life, or the vital force, may be infused into organized matter* (2 Corinthians 6:16)."[245]

This infusion of spirit into element, dust, or body, is illustrated in Genesis 2:7–8, Moses 3:7–8 and Abraham 5:7–8:

Genesis 2:7–8	Moses 3:7–8	Abraham 5:7–8
And the Lord God *formed man of the dust of the ground,* and *breathed into his nostrils the breath of life*; and man became a living soul. And the Lord God planted a garden eastward in Eden; and there he put the man whom he had formed. (emphasis added)	And I, the Lord God, *formed man from the dust of the ground*, and *breathed into his nostrils the breath of life*; and man became a living soul, the first flesh upon the earth, the first man also; nevertheless, all things were before created; but *spiritually were they created and made according to my word.* And I, the Lord God, planted a garden eastward in Eden, and there I put the man whom I had formed. (emphasis added)	And the *Gods formed man from the dust of the ground*, and *took his spirit (that is, the man's spirit), and put it into him; and breathed into his nostrils the breath of life*, and man became a living soul. And the Gods planted a garden, eastward in Eden, and there they put the *man, whose spirit they had put into the body which they had formed.* (emphasis added)

Man's spirit was in existence before the creation of the earth. Dust (which is also eternal) can be infused with spirit (breath).

With the infusion of spirit, dust or physical element can take on a span of life's variable orders, such as premortal, mortal, and post mortal bodies (see Abraham 3:24–26).

Element, termed as dust, seems to specifically point to us as an organized body, spirit, and *blood* which also carries with it the seeds of death (see Abraham 5:7). Without spirit, mortal elements revert back to the earth (dust) from whence it came. In *Guide to the Scriptures,* we learn that "Adam was created from the dust of the ground *meaning* that the physical body which he received was created from the elements of the earth."[246] "Similarly all men are created from the dust of the earth; that is, the elements organized into a body are assembled together *'through the birth process.'*"[247]

Though dust or elements were not created nor can they be destroyed, they can be organized and reorganized to meet the demands of godly laws. "For behold, the dust of the earth moveth hither and thither, to the dividing asunder, at the command of our great and everlasting God" (Helaman 12:8).

It would seem that this element of dust can be changed, perfected, and even immortalized by the perfecting of one's obedience to the laws of the spirit. Dust responds to the laws of truth and light, also being responsive to our faith in Jesus Christ, who is the Creator. Dust obeys the word of God (priesthood), "For behold, this is my work and my glory—to bring to pass the immortality and eternal life of man" (Moses 1:39). "What? know ye not that your body is the temple of the Holy Ghost which is in you, which ye have of God, and ye are not your own?" (1 Corinthians 6:19).

Thus, by a perfected immortal Father and Mother, Adam and Eve were created to inherit an immortal body of flesh and bone; just as our children, through the Fall, are created to inherit bodies of *flesh, bone, and blood* in mortality.

Dust is an element in different stages of perfection and can be inherited through our progenitors' progressive stages, just as we can inherit DNA through our mortal parentage—just as Jesus inherited both mortal and immortal capabilities through His parentage. It is by these same inherited eternal laws of creation that we are also commanded to pass on our physical, spiritual order, through the command to be fruitful and replenish the earth.[248] Thus, our body is not our own, as we receive it from our parentage and also gift it to our posterity. We are then responsible for our gifted body and are instructed on its care and usage.

It is by obedience to both spirit and body that as individuals we can become perfected in Christ. *It is by the spirit of faith that elements are controlled*, more specifically in the name of the Creator, Jesus Christ. Miraculous healings in the name of Jesus Christ are evidence of this. "I am the light and the life of the world. I am Alpha and Omega, the beginning and the end" (3 Nephi 9:18).

In the spirit world, Lucifer and his followers never received physical bodies; their spirits never developed sufficient faith and obedience to follow Christ, in order to receive a body. "And they who keep not their first estate shall not have glory in the same kingdom with those who keep their first estate" (Abraham 3:26). Nor can they receive salvation through the blood of Christ, for they had not qualified to receive bodies. Because of their open rebellion, even within the realms of pure knowledge, they are left to wander the earth as unembodied spirits, seeking residence in those bodies that apparently risk voids of truth and light. Where the light of Christ does not reside, negative influences bring the body and spirit into physical and emotional chaos. We may, however, seek healing by "the peace of God, which passeth all understanding, [and] shall keep your hearts and minds through Christ Jesus" (Philippians 4:7). "That whosoever believeth in him should not perish, but have eternal life" (St. John 3:15); But "because of the simpleness of the way, or the easiness of it, there were many who perished" (1 Nephi 17:41). To the ruler of the synagogue, Jesus consoled, "Be not afraid, only believe" (Mark 5:36) as He continued in His path to raise the damsel from her deathbed. To the Apostles, Jesus admonished, "Why sleep ye? rise and pray, lest ye enter into temptation" (Luke 22:46). He continued, "The spirit truly is ready, but the flesh is weak" (Mark 14:38). The key to life, progression, knowledge, healing, and salvation is faith in Jesus Christ, the Creator. All power is given unto Him and in Him are we redeemed.

The Holy Ghost is also an unembodied spirit, made available to fill us with a rich testimony of Jesus Christ. *"For ye are the temple of the living God; as God hath said, I will dwell in them, and walk in them; and I will be their God, and they shall be my people"* (2 Corinthians 6:16; emphasis added). By our agency, we can choose which spirit we desire to entertain.

DUST IS OFTEN A DEGENERATIVE TERM FOR ELEMENT

Figuratively, dust is in reference to the Fall, grave, or death, as in the following expression: "thou shalt return unto the ground—for thou shalt surely die—for out of it wast thou taken: for dust thou wast, and unto dust shalt thou return" (Moses 4:25; Gen. 3:19). In this scripture, *dust* and *death* become synonymous terms. As a mortal, spirit can live without a physical body [dust], but the physical body cannot live without the spirit (see James 2:26).[249] It is the spirit that maintains the life of the body.

Element, dust of the earth or mortality, incorporates blood as an impure substance for temporal purposes. Paul stated, *"flesh and blood* cannot inherit the kingdom of God" (1 Corinthians 15:50; emphasis added). When man dies, "the dust return[s] to the earth as it was: and the spirit shall return unto God who gave it" (Ecclesiastes 12:7). But on the day of resurrection, the sleeping dust is restored to its perfect frame as the spirit is inseparably united with a glorified, heavenly body that is no longer quickened by mortal blood, *but by Spirit.*[250]

THE RESURRECTED LORD

Every person born on earth will be resurrected because Jesus Christ overcame death (see 1 Corinthians 15:20–22).[251] "The soul shall be restored to the body, and the body to the soul; yea, and every limb and joint shall be restored to its body; yea, even a hair of the head shall not be lost; but all things shall be restored to their proper and perfect frame" (Alma 40:23). In a resurrected body of flesh and bone, the blood will be purified through Jesus Christ and spirit will flow in its place.

HAVE YE ANY MEAT?

In speaking to the Apostles after the resurrection, Christ identified other differences between body and spirit.

> Behold my hands and my feet, that it is I myself: handle me, and see; *for a spirit hath not flesh and bones, as ye see me have.* And when he had thus spoken, he shewed them his hands and his feet. And while they yet believed not for joy, and wondered, he said unto them, Have ye here any meat? And they gave him a piece of a broiled fish, and of an honeycomb. And he took it, and did eat before them. (Luke 24:39–43; emphasis added)

This signified to them that He was both body and spirit; the spirit does not eat the physical elements of the earth, but the body does.

The resurrection combines two eternal forms: the spirit, which houses truth and light (see D&C 84:45), and physical elements, which are of the earth. "That which is born of the flesh is flesh; and that which is born of the Spirit is spirit" (John 3:6). The resurrection combines these two matters for greater perfection. They can both be refined in the perfect light of Christ's Atonement as one eternal form.

In mortality, the developmental perfecting of a soul (body and spirit) depends on the value of truth and light that is received through the Spirit. How we choose to care for the body (temple of our spirit; see 1 Corinthians 3:16) also greatly affects the outcome of our soul. When the nutritional value of the body is ignored, non-nutritive substance fills the void, which brings on negative physical results. Truth and light nourish the spirit. When a void is present, darkness naturally becomes a replacement for the lack of spiritual light. When we care for the body, we care for the spirit; when we care for the spirit, we care for the soul.

From an immortal body in Eden to the mortal body we have today and well into the Millennium, and even into the resurrection, we are wisely given dietary counsels that are also incorporated in the gospel of Jesus Christ. From the trees in the garden to the tree of life in the resurrection, the dietary laws are also often a spiritual counsel, such as in the partaking of the sacrament or when we are again able to partake of the tree of life in the physical yet immortal presence of our eternal Father. In all these the "spirit and element, inseparably connected, receive a fullness of joy" (D&C 93:33 [33–34]).

Remember, however, that though the body is nourished by food, it cannot be perfected and sustained without the spirit. Much like a car, it must be maintained by an intelligent being or it is not functional and eventually succumbs to decay, returning to the dust from which it came. Also, one who lives in body but not in spirit is unable to function on higher levels of truth and light. Jesus admonishes, "I am the true light that lighteth every man that cometh into the world" (D&C 93:2).

In the scriptures, *dust* refers to any tangible mortal element, particularly the body. But it also refers to the natural man. In this, there are two deaths to consider: one is of the body (temporal), and the second is of the spirit (eternal). Both are used as relevant terms for dust and death. "Many scholars have noted that the name Adam literally means "earth" or "soil."[252] "Philo of Alexandria suggested that when we hear the name Adam in the scriptures, it is to remind us of that which is perishable, earthly, or temporary."[253]

> And so it is with us. We are each appropriately called Adam because we are earthly and perishable. From the dust we were made, and to that dust our mortal bodies will one day return (see Genesis 3:19). In addition, since the earth is a standard symbol for things which are temporal, worldly, or temporary in nature, it is possible that this *figurative description* of the origin of man [dust] serves to highlight both our carnal or worldly nature and also the temporal nature of the mortal experience.[254]

FROM SPIRIT TO IMMORTAL

As spirit children, we expressed our desire for a physical body, and the Lord said, "And they went down at the beginning, and they, that is the Gods, organized and formed the heavens and the earth" (Abraham 4:1). These physical creations of flesh and bone were immortal before the Fall of Adam and Eve. "For *I, the Lord God, created all things, of which I have spoken, spiritually [immortal], before they were naturally [mortal] upon the face of the earth*" (Moses 3:4–5; emphasis added).

Bruce R. McConkie said, "We must keep in mind that the creation is a past event." These statements are thus, as Elder McConkie wrote, "interpolative; they are inserted in the historical account . . . to give us its recitations, but are commentary about what [the Lord] had already set forth in its sequential order."[255] "Parts of these verses can apply to the physical-spiritual creation. As we have said, the spiritual creation—the placement of all things in a physical but spiritual state (tangible but immortal, not subject to death)—preceded the natural or mortal creation, that organization and state of things which came as a result of the Fall."[256]

> And thus the word of the Lord in modern revelation is made clearer "by the power of my Spirit. For by the power of my Spirit created I them; yea, all things both spiritual and temporal—first spiritual [the paradisiacal creation], secondly temporal [after the Fall], which is the beginning of my work; and again, first temporal [reference again to this mortal creation], and secondly spiritual [man and all forms of life in and after the resurrection], which is the last of my work" (D&C 29:30–32).[257]

FROM IMMORTAL TO MORTAL

"Man, when he was first placed upon this earth," Elder Orson Pratt explained, "was an immortal being, capable of eternal endurance; his flesh and bones, as well as his spirit, were immortal and eternal in their nature; and it was just so with all the inferior creation; . . . all were immortal and eternal in their nature; and the earth itself, as a living being, was immortal and eternal in its nature."[258] After Adam partook of the forbidden fruit, blood became "the life-giving fluid in Adam's body, and was inherited by his posterity. Previously the life force in Adam's body, which is likewise the sustaining power in every immortal body, *was the spirit.*"[259]

"Inasmuch as blood did not become a part of the physical organization of animal life until after the Fall, death was held in abeyance. The revelations attest that by reason of transgression came the Fall, and through the Fall came death (Moses 6:59; 2 Nephi 9:6)."[260]

RADICAL CHANGES

Mortality brought on a new physical reality. Elder Bruce R. McConkie wrote, "Radical changes were in the offering for man, the earth and all forms of life when the fall came." He further declared, "When Adam fell, the earth fell also and became a mortal sphere, one upon which worldly and carnal people can live."[261] Previously, Adam's physical body was immortal and in the presence of God.

"Therefore I give unto you a commandment, to teach these things freely unto your children, saying: That *by reason of transgression cometh the fall, which fall bringeth death,* and inasmuch as ye were *born into the world by water, and blood, and the spirit,* which I have made, and *so became of dust a living soul*" (Moses 6:58-59; emphasis added). This reference indicates that we became of the dust only after the Fall. "And it came to pass that after I, the Lord God, had driven them out, that Adam began to till the earth, and to have dominion over all the beasts of the field, and to eat his bread by the sweat of his brow, as I the Lord had commanded him. And Eve, also, his wife, did labor with him" (Moses 5:1).

Mortality also brought a curse upon man and beast. God curses the serpent (referring to Satan): "upon thy belly shalt thou go, and *dust* shalt thou eat all the days of thy life" (Genesis 3:14; emphasis added).

> Is it the earth that we tread underfoot that the devil eats, brethren? No, it is people who are earthly minded, sensual and proud, who love the earth and place all their hopes in it. They labor entirely for carnal advantages . . . and think little or nothing of the salvation of their souls. People like these, then, the devil seeks. . . . They were assigned to him at the beginning of the world when it was said to him, "Dust you shall eat." Therefore let each one look to his own conscience. If he sees that he has greater care for his body than for his soul, let him fear that he will become the food of the serpent.[262]

It is interesting to me that even in the Millennium, Satan will be, as mentioned by Isaiah, consuming the dust: "The wolf and the lamb shall feed together, and the lion shall eat straw like the bullock: and dust shall be the serpent's meat" (Isaiah 65:25). Satan will not hurt or destroy in the millennial reign for he will be cast out with all his followers.

MILLENNIUM

During the Millennium, because Jesus Christ will reign on the earth, both the body and spirit will possess a new countenance. "Old men shall die; but they shall not sleep in the dust, but they shall be changed in the twinkling of an eye" (D&C 63:51). Thus, there will be no graves during this period of time, for those who die shall be instantaneously resurrected (see D&C 101:31). Thus we see that *dust* as a corrupt term will not be utilized in the millennial reign of Christ.

IN HIS OWN IMAGE

If dust is used as a metaphor in the creation of Adam, then what was he made of?

Genesis 1:27	Moses 2:27	Abraham 4:27
So *God created man in his own image*, in the image of God created he him; *male and female* created he them (emphasis added).	And *I, God, created man in mine own image*, in the image of mine Only Begotten created I him; *male and female* created I them (emphasis added).	So the *Gods went down to organize man in their own image*, in the image of the Gods to form they him, *male and female* to form they them (emphasis added).

In 1909, the First Presidency taught that "all men and women are in the similitude of the universal Father and Mother, and are literally the sons and daughters of Deity."[263]

In speaking to Adam, the Lord said, "And thou art after the order of him who was without beginning of days or end of years, from all eternity to all eternity. Behold, thou art one in me, a *son of God*; and thus may all become my sons, Amen" (Moses 6:67–68 [64–68]; emphasis added).

IN THE IMAGE OF MINE ONLY BEGOTTEN?

Adam and Eve were born in the image of God, in the image of their immortal parents, male and female. How are they also born in the image of the only Begotten? "And I, God, created man in mine own image, *in the image of mine only Begotten created I him*; male and female created I them" (Moses 2:27; emphasis added). Adam's image, as it pertains to the Only Begotten, is likened to the words which Paul spoke: "And so it is written, the *first man Adam was made a living soul*; the *last Adam* was made a quickening spirit" (1 Corinthians 15:45; emphasis added). This statement indicates a mirror image, which directly links Adam and the Savior as the beginning and the end of mortality.

Elder Jeffrey R. Holland said that "it was part of His divine plan, which provided for a Savior, the very Son of God Himself— another 'Adam,' the Apostle Paul would call Him. . . . the 'last Adam.' . . . 'For as in Adam all die, even so in Christ shall all be made alive.'"[264] Adam represents the fall of man: blood and dust. Christ represents the resurrected and immortal body of man. Adam born immortal became mortal; Jesus born mortal brought back Adam's immortality.

The physical image of God was pure immortal flesh, bone, and spirit. The physical image of the Only Begotten, however, was the image of being born in infancy and growing in body and spirit *by a mortal mother, as the Son of God*. Thus, Adam and Eve were the first born of *immortal parentage*; they were the literal son and daughter of God. Born to immortal parents, they became mortal parents and rose once again to be immortal parents.

THE ONLY BEGOTTEN

From Elder McConkie we read:

Christ is universally attested in the scriptures to be the Only Begotten. At this point, as we consider the "creation" of Adam, and lest there be any misunderstanding, we must remember that *Adam was created in immortality. But that Christ came to earth as a mortal*; thus our Lord is the Only Begotten in the flesh, meaning into this mortal sphere of existence. *Adam came to earth to dwell in immortality until the fall changed his status to that of mortality.*[265]

Christ came to change our mortal to immortal and—if we are willing—bring us back into the presence of the Father.

ADAM'S LINEAGE TO GOD

Luke, in providing the genealogy of Jesus, spoke of Cainan, who "was the son of Enos, which was the son of Seth, which was the son of Adam, which was the son of God" (Luke 3:38). The Joseph Smith Translation of this passage speaks of *"Adam, who was formed of God, and the first man upon the earth"* (JST Luke 3:45; emphasis added). In another account, we read the line of great patriarchs from Adam to Enoch. "And this is the genealogy, the sacred record affirms, of the sons of Adam, who was the son of God, with whom God, himself, conversed" (Moses 6:22).

ADAM: AN IMMORTAL EMBRYO THAT BECAME A MAN

President Spencer W. Kimball stated on numerous occasions: *"We are gods in embryo.* Indeed, we are God's creations, His children and His offspring. Our resurrected Father in Heaven made us in His image . . . in the image 'of his own body'" (Moses 6:9).[266] "As God's offspring, we have His attributes in us. We are gods in embryo, and thus have an unlimited potential for progress and attainment."[267]

So that there will be no misunderstanding of our original creation, we will look at the plain language of Joseph F. Smith in a written statement by his First Presidency: "For those whose limited spiritual understanding precludes a recitation of all the facts, the revealed account, in figurative language, speaks of Eve being created from Adam's rib (Moses 3:21–25). In a formal doctrinal pronouncement, the First Presidency of the Church (Joseph F. Smith, John R. Winder, and Anthon H. Lund) said that 'all who have inhabited the earth since Adam have taken bodies and become souls in like manner,' and that the first of our race began life as the human germ or embryo that becomes a man."[268]

JEHOVAH, CREATOR OF EARTH AND MAN

Bruce R McConkie explained our creation,

In the ultimate and final sense of the word, the Father is the Creator of all things. That he used the Son and others to perform many of the creative acts, delegating to them his creative powers, does not make these others creators in their own right, independent of him. He is the source of all creative power, and he simply chooses others to act for him in many of his creative enterprises. But there are two creative events that are his and his alone. *First, he is the Father of all spirits*, Christ's included; none were fathered or created by anyone else. *Second, "he is the Creator of the physical body of man."* Though Jehovah and Michael and many of the noble and great ones played their assigned roles in the various creative events, yet when it came time to place man on earth, the *Lord God himself performed the creative acts.* "I, God, created man in mine own image, in the image of mine only Begotten created I him; male and female created I them" (Moses 2:27; emphasis added). Thus we can conclude that scriptural references to Jesus Christ as the creator of man (Isaiah 45:12; Mosiah 26:23; Ether 3:15-16) are illustrations of the Son speaking for the Father by *divine investiture of authority.*[269]

Christ speaks for the Father as our Elder Brother, "the Son being swallowed up by the will of the Father" (Mosiah 15:7). "Giving the Son power to make intercession for the children of men" (Mosiah 15:8). "The Father, being the Father and the Son," the Father, because he was conceived by the power of God; and the Son, because of the flesh; thus becoming the Father and the Son. And they are one God, yea the very Eternal Father of heaven and earth" (Mosiah 15:2, 3). Having been given all authority under heaven, Christ speaks for the Father.

CORRUPTIBLE TO INCORRUPTION

As our Elder Brother, Christ is designated to be our only source of salvation and promised resurrection. "Now this I say, brethren, that *flesh and blood* cannot inherit the kingdom of God; neither doth corruption inherit incorruption. . . . For this corruptible must put on incorruption, and this *mortal must put on immortality.* So when this corruptible shall have put on incorruption, and this mortal shall have put on immortality, then shall be brought to pass the saying that is written, *Death is swallowed up in victory"* (1 Corinthians 15:50, 53–54; emphasis added). Immortality could not have been resumed if Adam and Eve had not been born immortal before the Fall. That was the purpose of *the promised Messiah,* who by the Father, also retained the gift of immortality; he would *return* their corrupted souls to the incorruptible. What is the Fall if they had not fallen from an immortal birth?

SEA OF GLASS OR DUST?

The earth too will be immortalized. Because it fell at the time of the partaking of the forbidden fruit, it will also have a renewed body in the resurrection and will no longer be considered dust. "And the end shall come, and the heaven and the earth shall be consumed and pass away, and there shall be a new heaven and a new earth" (D&C 29:23). We are told that the earth will become a sea of glass in its resurrected immortal state: "The angels do not reside on a planet like this earth; but they reside in the presence of God, *on a globe like a sea of glass and fire, where all things for their glory are manifest, past, present, and future, and are continually before the Lord*. The place where God resides is a great Urim and Thummim" (D&C 130:6–8; emphasis added). About the earth's transfiguration we know that "when the earth shall be transfigured, even according to the pattern which was shown unto mine apostles upon the mount; of which account the fulness ye have not yet received" (D&C 63:21).

As an interesting metaphor for the seed of Abraham, "like a sea of glass and fire," sand becomes glass by fire, just as Abraham's posterity, by faith, will be like the sands of the sea, by the lineage of the priesthood which runs through the covenant seed of Abraham's posterity. These are they who will inherit the earth in all its immortal glory. "Yet the number of the children of Israel shall be as the sand of the sea . . . it shall be said unto them, Ye are the sons of the living God" (Hosea 1:10). It is they who shall inherit the earth in its celestial glory.

In contrast, Satan will consume the dust of the earth. "Dust shalt thou eat" (Genesis 3:14); dust being fallen man, the natural man. Figuratively speaking, the sea of glass seems to declare who will inherit the earth in its exalted immortal estate; these will be the covenanted seed of Abraham as the "sand of the sea" (see Genesis 32:12; see also D&C 130:7).

Not everyone will inherit this glorious earth. In the premortal existence, there were many who never developed sufficient light and truth to obtain a body. Even so, there will be many who will not develop sufficient light and truth to inherit the earth in its celestial glory: "and they who keep not their first estate shall not have glory in the same kingdom with those who keep their first estate; and they who keep their second estate (faith in Christ) shall have glory added upon their heads for ever and ever" (Abraham 3:26).

For man, the resurrected immortal body exchanges the blood of man for spirit, "having spirit in their bodies, and not blood."[270] What is exchanged in a new and immortal earth? I would venture to say that dust is exchanged for what seems to be a crystal-like sea of glass, Urim and Thummim. It makes sense that both blood and dust are dropped as corruptible material in a resurrected sphere for both man and earth.

THE DUST OBEYS

The earth, like Adam, had fallen, not by sin but by obedience. The earth too fell that men might be. See Helaman 12:7–18:

O how great is the nothingness of the children of men; yea, even they are less than the dust of the earth.

For behold, the dust of the earth moveth hither and thither, to the dividing asunder, at the command of our great and everlasting God.

Yea, behold at his voice do the hills and the mountains tremble and quake.

And by the power of his voice they are broken up, and become smooth, yea, even like unto a valley.

Yea, by the power of his voice doth the whole earth shake;

Yea, by the power of his voice, do the foundations rock, even to the very center.

Yea, and if he say unto the earth—Move—it is moved.

Yea, if he say unto the earth—Thou shalt go back, that it lengthen out the day for many hours—it is done;

And thus, according to his word the earth goeth back, and it appeareth unto man that the sun standeth still; yea, and behold, this is so; for surely it is the earth that moveth and not the sun.

And behold, also, if he say unto the waters of the great deep—Be thou dried up—it is done.

Behold, if he say unto this mountain—Be thou raised up, and come over and fall upon that city, that it be buried up—behold it is done.

And behold, if a man hide up a treasure in the earth, and the Lord shall say—Let it be accursed, because of the iniquity of him who hath hid it up—behold, it shall be accursed.

Because of *man's disobedience, he is considered less than the dust of the earth,* for the earth moveth according to the word of God. On the other hand, when we are considered *as* the dust of the earth in obedience, we are told, "And thy seed shall be as the dust of the earth, and thou shalt spread abroad to the west, and to the east, and to the north, and to the south: and in thee and in thy seed shall all the families of the earth be blessed" (Genesis 28:14).

As the children of our eternal Father and Mother in Heaven, it is our proposed inheritance to rise above the dust of the earth as we claim our immortality and eternal life as gods. Eve proclaimed, "Were it not for our transgression we never should have had seed, and never should have known good and evil, and the joy of our redemption, and the eternal life which God giveth unto all the obedient" (Moses 5:11).

CHAPTER 28

CHILD IN EDEN

"In the image of mine Only Begotten created I [Adam]"
—*Moses 2:27*

How the heavens must have cheered at the immortal birth of Adam and Eve! They were the noblest of the noble; they had proven their dedication in the spirit world, as Michael and Eve fought Lucifer for our guarded agencies. Adam and Eve became our vested portal into mortality, receiving bodies like the Father. Our passage had arrived and our hopes soared; confidence in our soon-to-be-mortal parents was without question. They were chosen by the grace of God, as was the infinite Savior of our souls. The plan was perfect; in their roles as the first to obtain bodies like mother and father, we were also guaranteed that we would receive bodies of flesh and bone. Our first mortal parents would be a foundational witness to the coming of our Lord and Savior, Jesus Christ, and his birth as the Son of God. As witness of His coming, Adam would possess a mirror image of the Savior's mortal mission. "And so it is written, The first man Adam was made a living soul; the last Adam was made a quickening spirit [resurrection]" (1 Corinthians 15:45).

Though we do not have a scriptural reference for the growth and development of Adam and Eve in their immortal childhood, in the book of Moses we read, "And I, God, created man in mine own image, *in the image of mine Only Begotten created I him*; male and female created I them" (Moses 2:27; emphasis added). We were "after the order of [Christ] who was without beginning of days or end of years, from all eternity to all eternity. Behold, thou art one in me, a *son of God*; and thus may all become my sons" (Moses 6:67–68 [64–68]).

How is it that man was created in the image of the Only Begotten? J. Rubin Clark tells us, "Think for a moment about the Only Begotten Son of God. He was *Jesus the Christ*—Creator, Redeemer, and Savior. How did he appear to men? Remember that we were made after his image. He was the pattern of our existence. He was our physical prototype as well as our great spiritual example, the model for our lives."[271] With a perfect understanding of our godly attributes Christ said, "Therefore I would that ye should be perfect even as I, or your Father who is in heaven is perfect" (3 Nephi 12:48).

As Adam and Eve were created by God in His image, they were also created in the image of the Only Begotten. The image of the Only Begotten is that of mortal and immortal parentage. We can, therefore, reasonably use Christ as a prime example of Adam's immortal growth and development in Eden. Adam's image, to that of the Only Begotten, also has a direct connection between the first and last Adam; "By Adam came the fall of man. And because of the fall of man came Jesus Christ, . . . and because of Jesus Christ came the redemption of man" (Mormon 9:12). Adam being mirrored with the Savior in purpose and mission is seen as the beginning and end of a mortal probation.

In order to perceive the growth and development of Adam, we will use the likeness of the young Jesus. Therefore, as we follow Jesus in his developing stages of mortal life, we might also have an image or likeness of Adam's physical and spiritual growth. Adam was the beginning of our race, and as Joseph F. Smith stated, "our race began life as the human germ or embryo."[272] So it was with Jesus, as he was seen as a babe, "Ye shall find the babe wrapped in swaddling clothes, lying in a manger" (Luke 2:12). It is through Christ's mortal development that we have a picture of Adam's childhood, as he and Eve grew in stature, in the presence of their immortal parents.

1. In His likeness, Adam also grew, "And it came to pass that [Adam] grew up . . . And waxed strong, and waited upon the Lord for the time of his ministry to come" (JST Matthew 3:24).

2. "And the child grew . . . And all that heard him were astonished at his understanding and answers. . . . And he said unto them, how is it that ye sought me? wist ye not that I must be about my Father's business?" (Luke 2:40, 47, 49 [40–50]); "And the child grew . . . and was in [Eden/ the desert] till the day of his [partaking/shewing] unto [the Fall/Israel]" (Luke 1:80).

It is through professor Alonzo Gaskill that we find one early source who stated: "Be not deceived. Our father [Adam] was ignorant of nothing. Indeed, Judaism holds that prior to the Fall, God revealed to Adam the whole history of mankind . . . the tale of their years, the number of their days, the reckoning of their hours, and the measure of their steps, all were made known unto him."[273] Thus, Adam "waxed strong in spirit, filled with wisdom: and the grace of God was upon him" (Luke 2:40).

Elder Dallin H. Oaks also noted that "our first parents understood the necessity of the Fall."[274] Elder John A. Widtsoe wrote: "The gospel had been taught them during their sojourn in the Garden of Eden."[275]

"The Lord said unto Enoch: Behold these thy brethren; they are the workmanship of mine own hands, and I gave unto *them their* knowledge, in the day I created *them*; and in the Garden of Eden, gave I unto man his agency" (Moses 7:32; emphasis added).

Adam, being born into an immortal world to Heavenly Parents, was meticulously prepared for a mortal mission for the good of all mankind. Having grown in wisdom and power, Adam and Eve were married under the immortal hand of our Father and thus commanded to be fruitful and replenish the earth. In the image of God the Father and Mother, they were to set the stage of faith for the promised Messiah. In guarded obedience, they preserved our agency that we might return home through the infinite blood of Christ. "Adam began life as the human germ or embryo that becomes a man, that became the first man, chosen by God to show us the way."[276]

CHAPTER 29

BREATH OF LIFE

"And man became a living soul."
—*Abraham 5:7*

Breath of life" is a metaphor for the conception of the spirit as it enters the body of man. The metaphoric use of the word *breath* is a poetic way of comprehending a most sacred and holy act of creation by our Heavenly Parents. By the use of metaphors such as breath, dust, and rib, we are prompted to search for the greater love and power of God beyond that of mortal understanding.

The inadequate understanding of the mortal man is demonstrated in 3 Nephi as we try to perceive the heavenly works of God. It reads:

> The eye hath never seen, neither hath the ear heard, before, so great and marvelous things as we saw and heard Jesus speak unto the Father;
>
> And no tongue can speak, neither can there be written by any man, neither can the hearts of men conceive so great and marvelous things as we both saw and heard Jesus speak; and no one can conceive of the joy which filled our souls at the time we heard him pray for us unto the Father. (3 Nephi 17:16–17)

Creation of man is not done differently in immortality than in mortality; it is, however, done on an entirely different level of perfected obedience and love. The fact remains: we are all God's literal children through Adam's posterity, with the innate power to become like the Father ourselves. But searching these things in the minds of our own corruption, rather than by the Spirit, is grossly inadequate.

THE SPIRIT IS GIVEN BREATH

The account of Adam and the "breath of life" is about the spirit of man. President Joseph F. Smith noted that in this idea, "God 'breathed the breath of life into Adam and Eve,' we find support for the doctrine of a premortal life. Each of God's children lived as spirits, in His presence, before we were ever sent to this earth to inhabit mortal tabernacles. That which the Father places in Adam—namely his spirit—existed long before the mortal man was created."[277] "And I, the Lord God, formed man from the dust of the ground, and *breathed* into his nostrils the breath of life; and man became a living soul, the first flesh upon the earth, the first man also; nevertheless, all things were before created; but spiritually were they created and made according to my word" (Moses 3:7).

We acknowledge that "the elements are eternal" (D&C 93:33), so life is also eternal, and not created; *but life may be infused into organized matter.* Just as the spirit is conceived and enters the mortal body of an embryo, so the spirit was conceived and entered the embryo of the immortal bodies of Adam and Eve. Adam, like Christ, was conceived and given birth as an infant child.[278] That is the beginning of man. You and I also chose the breath of life, but is there more? Yes, there are three breaths that take us through this life, and into the eternities.

These three examples are in reference to:

- First, by the Father as the spirit entering the immortal bodies of Adam and Eve, "I God... *breathed into his nostrils the breath of life*; and man became a living soul" (Genesis 2:7).
- Second, the Spirit of the Holy Ghost entering the Apostles, "And when he had said this, *he breathed on them*, and saith unto them, *Receive ye the Holy Ghost*" (John 20:22).
- And third, by Christ, the Spirit reentering the bodies of those who have slept in the earth, "Thus saith the Lord God; Come

from the four winds, *O breath, and breathe* upon these slain, that they may live . . . and the *breath came into them*, and they lived, and stood up upon their feet, an exceeding great army" (Ezekiel 37:9, 10).

All three breaths are an infusion of the Spirit into our physical bodies. All three are vital gifts of the Spirit that we might attain immortality and eternal life. They are specific to the reigning Godhood, "Which the Father, Son, and Holy Ghost are one God, infinite and eternal, without end" (D&C 20:28). The apostles are therefore commanded to, "Go ye therefore, and teach all nations, baptizing them in the name of the Father, and the Son, and of the Holy Ghost" (Matthew 28:19).

Most interesting to me is that the breath of life given to Adam and Eve is specific to the Father. Breath of the spirit (of revelation) is of the Holy Ghost, and breath of the resurrection and eternal life is given by the Atonement of Jesus Christ. This is indicative of the Godhead and their specified missions as they pertain to the immortality and eternal life of man. These are three individual personages with distinct missions, but one in purpose.

Thus, "we believe in God, the Eternal Father, and in His Son, Jesus Christ, and in the Holy Ghost" (A of F 1:1). "And now, behold, this is the doctrine of Christ, and the only and true doctrine of the Father, and of the Son, and of the Holy Ghost, which is one God, without end" (2 Nephi 31:21). "For in [Christ] dwelleth all the fulness of the Godhead bodily. And ye are complete in him, which is the head of all principality and power" (Colossians 2:9–10).

Without question, these three infusions of the spirit into the body are our greatest gifts. It is by our agency that we are given the ability to apply these gifts of the spirit according to our discretion. Do we care for our bodies, seek the spirit of revelation, and obtain a remission of sins unto a perfect resurrection? Our object in coming into mortality is that we might receive each of these breaths and a fullness of joy in each of those combined powers. How disappointing it would be to return to Heavenly Father empty handed with a full realization of what we had not gain, with our agency, while on earth.

MAN IS AN IMMORTAL SPIRIT

President David O. McKay tells us:

Man's body, therefore, is but the tabernacle in which his spirit dwells. Too many, far too many, are prone to regard the body as the man, and consequently direct their efforts to the gratifying of the body's pleasures, its appetites, its whims, its desires, its passions. Too few recognize that the real man is an immortal spirit, which "intelligence or the light of truth," animated as an individual entity before the body was begotten, and that this spiritual entity with all its distinguishing traits will continue after the body ceases to respond to its earthly environment. Said the Savior: "I came forth from the Father, and am come into the world; again, I leave the world, and go to my Father (John 16:28)."[279] I personally, do not wish to forget, what I came so far a journey to obtain.

CHAPTER 30

DEEP SLEEP

"The Gods caused a deep sleep to fall upon Adam"
—Abraham 5:15; see also Moses 3:21, Genesis 2:21

The deep sleep that the gods caused to come upon Adam was in some way in preparation for receiving his help meet. That preparation, called a deep sleep, might well have been a time of learning and instruction as well as receiving priesthood ordinations for Adam to carry into mortality. This was not a sleep, but a *deep* sleep, perhaps indicating the paramount significance of that preparation. According to E. Douglas Clark, "The first notable feature of the rib story is its mention of sleep—not the normal Hebrew word for sleep, but 'an especially deep, wondrous sleep, a divine sleep' that God brought upon Adam, emphasizing that 'God's creation and activity always remain a secret [sacred].'"[280] As stated in scripture, "The order of this priesthood… was instituted in the days of Adam, and came down by lineage" (D&C 107:40, 41).

ABRAHAM ALSO FALLS INTO A DEEP SLEEP

I found similar references to deep sleep with Abraham: As a *deep sleep* fell upon Abram, he, like Adam, was being prepared to receive a covenant posterity.

> And when the sun was going down, a *deep sleep fell upon Abram*; and, lo, an horror of great darkness fell upon him. And he said unto Abram,

know of a surety that thy seed shall be a stranger in a land that is not theirs, and shall serve them; and they shall afflict them four hundred years; And also that nation, whom they shall serve, will I judge: and afterward shall they come out with great substance. And thou shalt go to thy fathers in peace; thou shalt be buried in a good old age. (Genesis 15:12–15; emphasis added)

The language used for Abraham might well be representative of what Adam's projected posterity and death would also be. Adam was also given fair warning of impending trials: "in the day that thou eatest thereof thou shalt surely die" (Genesis 2:17).

Like Adam, Abram, in his deep sleep, also received a covenanted Abrahamic mission, a promised land, a new name, a promised mother of a covenant nation: "in all that Sarah hath said unto thee, *hearken unto her voice;* for in Isaac shall thy seed be called" (Genesis 21:12; emphasis added). This compares to Adam being told to "cleave unto [thy] wife" (Genesis 2:24)—for in Seth shall thy seed be called.[281]

Isaac, Abraham's son, is perhaps a "mirror reflection" of Adam's promised posterity through Seth: "Adam knew his wife again, and she bare a son, and he called his name Seth" (Moses 6:2). Like Abraham, Adam also received a child to carry forth a priesthood lineage that brought a sure knowledge of Christ to ongoing generations, "Because he [Seth] was a perfect man, and his likeness was the express likeness of his father"[282] (D&C 107:43). Like Adam, the deep sleep of Abraham was in direct preparation for his covenanted Abrahamic mission and promised lineage. Through Adam, and then Abraham, we are promised the lineage of the priesthood through Adam, Seth, Noah, Shem (who is Melchizedek), Abraham, Isaac, Jacob, and even the promised Messiah.

JACOB'S DREAM

There is yet a third example of one who slept in the spirit of preparation and covenants. Jacob, also proclaimed to be the father of Israel, fell into a sleep in which he was given covenants pertaining to his posterity:

And he lighted upon a certain place, and tarried there all night, because the sun was set; and he took of the stones of that place, and put them for his pillows, and *lay down in that place to sleep.*

And he dreamed, and *behold a ladder set up on the earth, and the top of it reached to heaven: and behold the angels of God ascending and descending on it.*

And, behold, the Lord stood above it, and said, I *am* the Lord God of Abraham thy father, and the God of Isaac: the *land whereon thou liest, to thee will I give it,* and *to thy seed*; . . .

And Jacob awaked out of his sleep, and he said, surely the Lord is in this place; and I knew it not. . . .

And Jacob rose up early in the morning, and took the stone that he had put for his pillows, and set it up for a pillar, and poured oil upon the top of it. . . .

And Jacob vowed a vow, saying, If God will be with me . . .

So that I come again to my father's house in peace; then shall the Lord be my God. (Genesis 28:11–13, 16, 18, 20–21[11–22]; emphasis added)

"And he called the name of that place Beth-el" (Genesis 28:19). Bethel—Ugaritic: bt il, meaning "House of El" or "House of God."[283]

Elder Larry Y. Wilson, while serving at Church headquarters in the Temple Department, explained that the ladder that Jacob saw was in reference to the progressive ordinances of the temple.[284] Covenants were made between God and Jacob as Jacob was prepared to be the father of the twelve tribes of Israel, which also became the promised lineage of a covenant people. This sleep which fell upon Jacob is another example for the preparatory deep sleep which fell upon Adam and thus became his Adamic mission. Jacob likewise received a prophetic mission, promised covenant posterity, a new name, and a land of inheritance. We have Adam, the father of mankind, Abraham, the father of nations, and Jacob, the father of Israel. All received their new name, their ordination and priesthood lineage, a land of inheritance, and their posterity through a deep sleep.

The priesthood lineage that was passed down—through the keys given first to Adam—was connected by the new and everlasting covenant of marriage for Adam, Abraham, and Jacob. This lineage will be passed onto all the covenant generations throughout the earth. Abraham is the proclaimed linkage to this supernal priesthood from Adam to the ends of the earth (see Abraham 1:1–4).

> And I will bless them through thy name [patriarchal name]; for as many as receive this Gospel shall be *called after thy name*, and shall be accounted thy seed, and shall rise up and bless thee, as their father;
>
> And I will bless them that bless thee, and curse them that curse thee; and in thee (that is, in thy Priesthood) and in thy seed (that is, thy Priesthood), for I give unto thee a promise that this right shall continue in thee, and in thy seed after thee (that is to say, the literal seed, or the seed of the body) shall all the families of the earth be blessed, even with the blessings of the Gospel, which are the blessings of salvation, even of life eternal. (Abraham 2:10–11).

Priesthood, as seed, is connected by patriarchal order back to the Father. It is in this seed that we are all called to be fruitful and replenish the earth. This is why we came; this is what we seek for: for all the families of the earth to be linked back to our Father in Heaven, in covenant and promise. This linkage becomes the immortality and eternal life of man. The children of God. Adam, the father of all; Abraham, the father of nations; Jacob, the father of Israel. All of us come to the Lord God by way of priesthood lineage.

Adam, in a deep sleep, was carefully prepared for his required patriarchal journey through mortality. Adam's deep sleep was his preparation for receiving a wife, a new name, posterity, and a promised land through the ordination of the new and everlasting covenant of marriage. The rib was a covenant of marriage, which was also prerequisite to their anticipated posterity (seed): "And the Gods caused a deep sleep to fall upon Adam; and he slept, and they took one of his ribs, and closed up the flesh in the stead thereof; And of the rib which the Gods had taken from man, formed they a woman, and brought her unto the man" (Abraham 5:15–16). *God* gives Eve a name: woman; and also *Adam*, the great patriarch of the human family, gives Eve a name: woman. Woman, because of her characteristics. She is to be called "woman, because she was taken out of man" (Genesis 2:23; Abraham 5:17; Moses 3:23). (The origin of the word *woman* comes from the Old English *wifmon, -man* [wife man], a formation peculiar to English, *the ancient word being wife.*)

It does not, however, speak of Eve having fallen into a deep sleep. If Adam had been receiving the keys of the holy order of the priesthood at that time of preparation, what of Eve? The Lord said he took one of Adam's ribs during that deep sleep and made a woman, and brought her unto the man. Adam proclaimed that she shall be called woman, because she was *taken out of man.* The rib seems to be a relevant metaphor for beam, rod, inner structure, or bone, meaning power. "The term *bone* also connotes power and strength."[285] *This power and strength was taken out of man and presented to him as a woman.* The rib is a metaphor for priesthood power. It is this sealing power that *cannot* belong to man alone, nor to woman alone; only when the two are joined as one do they receive this priesthood ordinance. To be clear, Eve was not literally taken out of Adam. The term *rib* was not a literal term but a metaphorical term for the highest order of the priesthood that she would receive from Adam by way of the new and everlasting covenant of marriage (see chapter 16, Adam's Rib). Adam, having received the keys of that eternal companionship, then received Eve unto himself and they became joint heirs in that holy promise. Eve completed Adam in the priesthood order, becoming his help meet, purpose, and even the very life of man, which they now held together.

I suggest that this shared priesthood was also projected to be given to them as a power for procreation, for it was then that Adam called Eve to be the mother of all living (Moses 4:26). Only by her could his seed continue in that patriarchal order. Thus, "bone of my bone" is the sealing power of the families and "flesh of my flesh" might well be the power to procreate (Moses 3:23). That can only come by way of *mortal flesh and blood,* thus giving Adam and Eve the prescribed rite to transgress into mortality, being told, "thou mayest choose for thyself *for it is given unto thee*" (Moses 3:17). As man and wife, they were now ready for their destined Fall and proclaimed godhood. Armed with the power to procreate, Adam and Eve were then able to become physically, intellectually, and spiritually as their Father and Mother, who are exalted immortal beings. And God said, "the man is become as *one of us* to know good and evil" (Moses 4:28). Only after the marriage, the new and everlasting covenant, and clothed in salvation are they proclaimed to be "one of us [gods]."

This priesthood that they hold together in marriage eternally links their posterity together through the Abrahamic covenant, which becomes the prescribed lineage of the priesthood. The "welding together of dispensations, and keys, and powers, and glories should take place, and be revealed from the days of Adam even to the present time" (D&C 128:18). This everlasting covenant of eternal marriage was also proclaimed to come forth in the last days as a sealing covenant to the families of the earth: "Behold, I will send you Elijah the prophet before the coming of the great and dreadful day of the Lord: And he shall turn the heart of the fathers to the children, and the heart of the children to their fathers, lest I come and smite the earth with a curse" (Malachi 4:5–6).

When *Eve was taken out of Adam*, it was in similitude of her receiving that portion of the priesthood that is jointly man and woman's, which was first man's, for he holds the keys of that power. That power, however, could not be fulfilled without Eve as his eternal partner. She would be the life of that priesthood, as she was projected to become the mother of all living. This everlasting priesthood power is the order which keeps the curse of this world abated, until Christ comes in his glory the second time: "That my covenant people may be gathered in one in that day when I shall come to my temple. And this I do for the salvation of my people" (D&C 42:36). The holy order of the priesthood comes first from the Father, to Christ to Adam, then to Eve, then on to all their posterity, that *families* might receive it. Thus, by way of priesthood power, we are given the statement from Paul: "For Adam was first formed then Eve" (1 Timothy 2:13)— in the priesthood.

WALKING THROUGH THE SCRIPTURES FOR PERSPECTIVE

Adam and Eve came together in the scriptural rib story: all three scriptural renditions (Moses 3:15–25, Genesis 2:15–25 and Abraham 5:11–19) are almost exactly alike, with a few exceptions. Let's walk through the rib story in Eden using Abraham's rendition, which adds an extra concept in time and sequence.

Abraham's story starts with God putting Adam in the Garden of Eden, to dress and keep it. In the book of Moses, Adam names all the animals and in so doing finds that he does not have a help meet but is alone, unlike the animals that he is naming. In which "for Adam there was *not found* an help meet for him" (Genesis 2:20 and Moses 3:20).

However, in *Abraham's rendition*, the naming of the animals comes *after the rib story*, in which case it reads, "For Adam, there *was found* an help meet for him" (Abraham 5:21). This identifies a place in sequence for the rib or marriage of Adam and Eve. *Before the rib* story (in Moses and Genesis) there was *not* found a help meet, and *after the rib* story (in Abraham) there *was* found a help meet. Again, the sequence for Adam and Eve is pretty much the same in all three renditions of the rib ceremony, but written with different points to different sequences of the same story. The three stories may have been meant to be compiled for a full view of the spiritual interaction in this paramount story—as Bruce R. McConkie puts it, "interpolative."[286]

In all three renditions, Adam is offered the fruit of all the trees in the garden of which he may freely eat. But in pointing to the *tree of knowledge of good and evil*, God commands that Adam should *not eat of it*, lest he should die. In all three scriptural renditions, *forbidding Adam* to partake of the forbidden fruit occurs *before the rib ceremony*, while Adam was yet alone, perhaps indicating the importance of waiting upon Eve and her critical role as mother of all living. "For this cause shall a man leave father and mother, and shall cleave to his wife" (Matthew 19:5).

In Abraham's rendition, we find an extra insight for why Adam was not yet ready to partake of such a profound advancement into mortality, "Now I, Abraham, saw that it was after the Lord's time [purpose] . . . [see Abraham 3:4]; for as yet the Gods had not appointed unto Adam his reckoning [mortal probation]" (Abraham 5:13). To partake of mortality was untimely, for Adam was yet alone and in need of a help meet, a wife, a mother, that all righteousness might be fulfilled through the venue of mortality.

Only after the rib and before the Fall occurred, the gods pronounce a help meet for Adam, "the Gods said: Let us make a help meet for man, for it is not good that the man should be alone" (Abraham 5:14). In order for the gods to form a help meet for Adam, they caused a "deep sleep" to come upon him. This deep sleep that the gods caused to come upon Adam was in preparation for receiving his help meet, who was to be his wife and the mother of all the earth.

Out of the marriage ceremony, metaphorically called the "rib," was formed a sacred union, and Eve was brought unto Adam. "And the rib, which the Lord God had taken from man, made he a woman, and brought her unto the man" (Genesis 2:22). Adam acknowledged this union of marriage and expresses his acceptance: "This is now bone of my bones [bone metaphorically is power], and flesh of my flesh [flesh is mortality or more specifically procreation]; she shall be called Woman, because she was taken out of Man" (Genesis 2:23). Woman was taken out of man, in that she was presented to Adam ceremoniously by the Father, through the everlasting covenant of marriage. The keys to this holy order of the priesthood are given to man by design so that, by the power of those keys, man and woman might reign under the same family order, rather than two separate orders. Thus, the holy order of the priesthood, the everlasting covenant of marriage, is organized family. That's why God uses the phrase *one flesh* throughout the scriptures: "They are no more twain, but one flesh" (Mark 10:8) also meaning one priesthood. Thus, Eve was taken out of Adam's priesthood, to join him in that holy union, at which time God then proclaims in the book of Abraham, "For Adam, there *was found* an help meet for him" (Abraham 5:21).

Adam, having received the keys to the new and everlasting covenant of marriage, also recognizes Eve as mother of all living: "And Adam *called* his *wife's* name Eve, because she was the mother of all living; for thus have I, the Lord God, *called* the first of all women, which are many" (Moses 4:26; emphasis added). In which case God now "appointed unto Adam his reckoning [time of mortality]" (Abraham 5:13), that they might be fruitful and replenish the earth.

Eve accepts her call to become the mother of all living under the order of the covenant of marriage. And, under the ordination of family, Adam is prepared to leave his Father and Mother and cleave unto his wife as they choose mortality that men might be. So "when the woman saw that the tree was good for food, and that it was pleasant to the eyes, and a tree to be desired to make one wise, she took of the fruit thereof, and did eat, and gave also unto her *husband with her*; and he did eat" (Genesis 3:6; emphasis added).

Only after the marriage covenant was solemnized by the Father, which comes in anticipation of the projected Fall, were they ready to partake of mortality and be clothed in salvation. At that time, their eyes were opened as a dire need for the promised Messiah becomes evident. "Unto Adam, and also unto his wife, did I, the Lord God, make coats of skins, and clothed them" (Moses 4:27). Before sending His children into mortality, the Father adorned them with the robes of salvation that they might return with honor under the priesthood keys. "And let these, thine anointed ones, be clothed with salvation, and thy saints shout aloud for joy. Amen, and Amen" (D&C 109:80). "And Adam knew his wife, and she bare unto him sons and daughters, and they began to multiply and to replenish the earth" (Moses 5:2); thus fulfilling all the commandments of the Father.

THE TIME IS NOW

Under God's ordained keys, Adam was called upon to awake and arise. Adam with Eve would partake that men might be. The Fall was the beginning of the rise of man. Arising from his deep sleep, he and Eve stepped into their mortal journey. "Wherefore he saith, Awake thou that sleepest, and arise from the dead, and Christ shall give thee light" (Ephesians 5:14). An awakening by the Spirit brought Adam new advancements, new covenants, a new name, and a new opportunity for godhood as a new beginning unfolds. Adam and Eve accepted these covenants together, thus giving them a new sense of awareness, purpose, responsibility, and fulfillment.

Vivian M. Adams expresses her rendition of the rib *appropriately as a love story*:

Let me now more specifically suggest an interesting interpretation of the rib story. We read that the Lord caused, or designed in the natural scheme of things, a "deep sleep" to fall upon Adam (Moses 3:22–24). . . . Eve was not a mysterious extension of man, as women have supposed, but the companion who came in answer to his longing and was placed at his side.

Through his need, the man gave the woman being; in return, she gave purpose and being to him. There was now reason to survive, love, and labor, and in course of time there would come issue, the most precious gift, each to each. And thus the Lord closed the flesh in the stead of Adam's wound (Moses 3:21), suggesting that he closed or repaired the wound of Adam's yearning. "For as the woman is of the man," Paul said, "even so is the man also by the woman; but all things of God." (1 Corinthians 11:12)[287]

"Each was not entire. 'This [my companion],' Adam exulted, 'This I know now is bone of my bones'; that is, she is of my same order or genesis. Eve, continued Adam, is 'flesh of my flesh,' indicating a proper physical union drawing husband and wife together. 'Therefore,' Adam realized, 'shall a man leave his father and his mother, and shall cleave unto his wife' in faithful union" (Moses 3:23–24);[288] thus becoming as the gods.

CHAPTER 31

VEIL

A "veil of unbelief was being cast away from his mind"
—Alma 19:6

There are five types of veils that we will consider in this chapter: first, a *veil of forgetting*, in which Adam is induced to forget the events of the previous spirit world while in the garden; second, a *veil of separation* from an immortal God, where cherubim and a flaming sword are set to guard the way between God and man; third, a *veil of unbelief*, which is due to our lack of faith and obedience to the laws and ordinances of our Lord and Savior Jesus Christ while on the earth; fourth, the torn *veil of the temple at the time of Christ's crucifixion;* and fifth, the *veil* referenced by Paul, as an ordinance in 1 Corinthians 11:2–10, *to unite men and women as one in the priesthood.*

VEIL OF FORGETTING

According to Elder Jeffrey R. Holland, "*They* had full knowledge of the plan of salvation during their stay in Eden,"[289] as it was taught to them by the Father. Adam and Eve had, however, *a veil of forgetting* placed upon them in the garden. This forgetting caused Adam and Eve to no longer have a literal knowledge of the events of the spirit world from which they came; it had been erased from their minds. Having forgotten his previous experiences in the spirit, Adam was brought into a deeper state of innocence. He, like a child, was now fully dependent on being taught by the Father. This new knowledge came by faith as they now focused on the *word* of God. "In the beginning was the gospel preached through the Son. And the gospel was the word, and the word was with the Son, and the Son was with God, and the Son was of God" (JST John 1:1). Adam and Eve received the word of God as it was preached to them in the beginning, in Eden.

The forgetting was necessary for the eventful, mortal veil of separation, for the Fall could not have occurred without being preceded by a forgetting. *Only on faith could they transgress into a mortal world.* That faith was based on a promised Savior who would surely redeem them from a fallen world, not only to bring them safely back into God's presence, but to bring them back as gods. "For by grace are ye saved through faith; and that not of yourselves: it is the gift of God" (Ephesians 2:8).

Elder Maxwell explains, "We define the veil as the border between mortality and eternity; it is also a *film of forgetting* which covers the memories of earlier experiences. This forgetfulness will be lifted one day, and on that day we will see forever—rather than 'through a glass darkly.' . . . Thus the veil stands—not to forever shut us out—but as a reminder of God's tutoring and patient love for us."[290]

Adam and Eve had been obedient to the laws of God in a spirit world of *literal knowledge.* Now they needed to be trained in *faith* to believe in Christ, to gain a greater comprehension of truth by the spirit of truth. They needed to seek knowledge by faith, obedience and love. An example for this needed faith is given as Christ taught it to Thomas in the New Testament:

> The other disciples therefore said unto him, We have seen the Lord. But he said unto them, Except I shall see in his hands the print of the nails, and put my finger into the print of the nails, and thrust my hand into his side, I will not believe. . . .
>
> Then saith he [Jesus] to Thomas, Reach hither thy finger, and behold my hands; and reach hither thy hand, and thrust it into my side: and *be not faithless, but believing.*
>
> And Thomas answered and said unto him, My Lord and my God.

Jesus saith unto him, Thomas, because thou hast seen me, thou hast believed: blessed are they that have not seen, and yet have believed. (John 20:25, 27–29; emphasis added)

Literal truth and comprehensive truth by faith are two different types of knowledge. Literal knowledge is a physical witness of things as we see and know them to be true—denial of these events is not optional. Comprehensive truth comes by faith given by the Spirit of truth, "substance of things hoped for, the evidence of things not seen" (Hebrews 11:1). It is "by the power of the Holy Ghost ye may know the truth of all things" (Moroni 10:5). We must seek truth by faith, and we do so by experimenting on the word of truth through obedience.

One third part of heaven's spirit children, though they had literal knowledge of Christ and the Father, decided not to believe on the forthcoming Atonement of the chosen Savior. They saw Him, they knew Him, yet they denied His power and kept not His commandments. Only after the trial of our faith and obedience on His word can we obtain a full comprehension of truth. Within this new level of agency we were also able to obtain a higher awareness of truth by faith. Only by faith in Christ can we be saved and become as He is. We gain a higher level of truth by faith.

In this mortal world, my biggest problem is remembering the many spiritual witnesses which testify of Christ in a day-to-day experience. It is easy to forget. We must continually seek truth, making covenants to remember Him at all times. We seek witnesses by asking, for in that there is a promise: "And I say unto you, Ask, and it shall be given you; seek, and ye shall find; knock, and it shall be opened unto you. For every one that asketh receiveth; and he that seeketh findeth; and to him that knocketh it shall be opened" (Luke 11:9–10). *As with the biblical story of the ten virgins, we must continually fill our lamps of faith with a witness of truth and let that light guide us through the dark times. We need dark times in order to prove the power of the light; the power of the witness.* Having received this witness, "they are willing to take upon them the name of [His] Son, and *always remember him,* and keep his commandments which he hath given them, that *they may always have his Spirit to be with them*" (Moroni 4:3; emphasis added).

God the Father, in an immortal world, taught Adam and Eve by the testimony of His word, by faith, witnessing unto them that Jesus was the Christ who would come in the meridian of time and again in the end of time. Only on the name of Christ could they be saved and become as God is. Adam and Eve then, in faith, were commanded to teach these things unto their children that they, too, might be *saved*. We are taught "that all men must . . . endure in faith on his name to the end, or they cannot be saved in the kingdom of God" (D&C 20:29).

As promised, Jesus came in the meridian of time to teach the people and will yet come in the end of time. We, like Adam and Eve, are commanded to teach these things, standing as witnesses of Christ. Speaking to the Apostles, Jesus said, "But I have prayed for thee, that thy *faith fail not*: and when thou art converted, strengthen thy brethren" (Luke 22:32; emphasis added). It is by faith that we are saved.

VEIL OF SEPARATION

Before Adam and Eve were cast out of the Garden of Eden, according to the Prophet Joseph Smith, Adam was "lord or governor of all things on earth, and at the same time enjoying communion with his Maker, *without a Veil between*."[291] Our first parents "could converse with God face to face as we converse with our friends: [with] *no intervening veil*."[292] Elder Parley P. Pratt, President John Taylor, and President Joseph Fielding Smith[293] each stated that in Eden there was no '*dimming veil* between Adam and God."[294] There was no separation from God in Eden. The veil of separation from God occurred after Adam and Eve partook of the tree of knowledge of good and evil, at which time they were then sent out of the Garden of Eden and out of God's presence. Cherubim and the flaming sword were then set to guard the way of the tree of life, and thus, became their veil of separation.

VEIL OF UNBELIEF

It was important for me to understand that a forgetting is not the same as a veil of separation. The forgetting is a spiritual impairment, while the veil of being sent out of God's presence is more of a physical impairment (the veil of separation). The physical veil occurred only after the Fall, when they were cut off from the presence of God by cherubim and a flaming sword. However, this veil of forgetting and the veil of separation also prompted a third veil, which is called a *veil of unbelief.* Only by repentance, through a broken heart and contrite spirit, can this veil of unbelief be recompensed in full measure. A broken heart becomes an open heart. Pride becomes the veil of unbelief as it is the difference between pride and humility that blocks or allows the light of Christ to enter our hearts.

There are those who would choose to hide from truth and light and would rather perish in the dark. The Lord was rejected by the Hebrew nation that were led out of Egypt and out of captivity. Moses's face was lighted when filled with the Spirit, but the people, unable to accept the light, required Moses to place a veil upon his face. As with Abinadi, "the Spirit of the Lord was upon him; and his face shone with exceeding luster" (Mosiah 13:5), "and they were afraid to come nigh him" (Exodus 30:35). "But even unto this day, when Moses is read, the veil is upon their heart. Nevertheless when [we] shall turn to the Lord, the veil shall be taken away. Now the Lord is that Spirit: and where the Spirit of the Lord is, there is liberty" (2 Corinthians 3:15-17).

> Being sent from God's presence brought on a veil of unbelief among many of the children of Adam. But there was a restoration and in the Kirtland temple, Joseph says, "The veil was taken from our minds, and the eyes of our understanding were opened" (Doctrine and Covenants 110:1). Much like the Book of Mormon, when King Lamoni was taught the law of repentance, in which "*a veil of unbelief* was being cast from his mind" (Ether 4:15). Now, this was what Ammon desired, for he knew that king Lamoni was under the power of God; he knew that the dark *veil of unbelief* was being cast away from his mind, and the light which did light up his mind, which was the light of the glory of God, which was a marvelous light of his goodness—yea, this light had infused such joy into his soul, the cloud of darkness having been dispelled, and that the light of everlasting life was lit up in his soul, yea, he knew that this had overcome his natural frame, and he was carried away in God. (Alma 19:6; emphasis added)

With a broken heart and contrite spirit,

> Behold, when ye shall rend that veil of unbelief which doth cause you to remain in your awful state of wickedness, and hardness of heart, and blindness of mind, then shall the great and marvelous things which have been hid up from the foundation of the world from you—yea, when ye shall call upon the Father in my name, *with a broken heart and a contrite spirit,* then shall ye know that the Father hath remembered the covenant which he made unto your fathers, O house of Israel. (Ether 4:15; emphasis added; see also D&C 38:8)

VEIL OF THE TEMPLE

A fourth veil is represented in the *veil of the temple*: "And, behold, the veil of the temple was rent in twain from the top to the bottom; and the earth did quake, and the rocks rent, 'causing many to exclaim, 'The God of nature suffers.' Finally, even the seemingly unbearable had been borne, and Jesus said, 'It is finished.' 'Father, into thy hands I commend my spirit.' Someday, somewhere, every human tongue will be called upon to confess as did a Roman centurion who witnessed all of this, 'Truly this was the Son of God.'"[295]

La Mar Adams, professor emeritus at BYU, teaches, "But the day soon cometh that ye shall see me, and know that I am; for the *veil of darkness shall soon be rent* and he that is not purified shall not abide the day. When the veil of the temple was "rent in twain" (torn in two) at the death of Jesus Christ (Matthew 27:51), it was a dramatic symbol that the Savior, the Great High Priest, had passed through the veil of death and would shortly enter into the presence of God."[296]

"Paul, in expressive language (Hebrews 9 and 10), shows how the ordinances performed through the veil of the ancient temple were in similitude of what Christ was to do, which he now having done, *all men become eligible to pass through the veil* into the presence of the Lord to inherit full exaltation."[297]

"The Apostle Paul taught that just as the torn veil of the temple allowed symbolic entrance into the Holy of Holies, *it is the torn flesh of Jesus Christ that opens the way for us to enter into the presence of the Father* (Hebrews 10:12, 19–20; emphasis added)."[298]

It is within the trial of these four veils that we shall once again be given a remembrance of all things, having a perfect comprehension of all truth. "But the Comforter, which is the Holy Ghost, whom the Father will send in my name, he shall teach you all things, and bring all things to your remembrance, whatsoever I have said unto you" (John 14:26). "Wherefore, fear not even unto death; for in this world your joy is not full, but in me your joy is full" (D&C 101:36).

PRIESTHOOD VEIL

There is one other veil, a fifth veil, and that is the veil between the priesthood and Eve. Though Adam and Eve possessed the same high priesthood with equal power as they obtain their ordinance of marriage, that priesthood came first to Adam, who held the keys of that priesthood, and then Eve. Thus giving her equal authority in their relationship, "For Adam was first formed, then Eve" (1 Timothy 2:13). Or, I would say, Eve was veiled from the priesthood, except she should obtain it through Adam's ordained keys. There is a uniting purpose in this sacred veiling for Adam and Eve.

This veil of the priesthood between God and woman is vaguely expressed as Paul speaks to the Corinthians. "Now I praise you, brethren, that ye remember me in all things, and *keep the ordinances*, as I delivered them to you" (1 Corinthians 11:2; emphasis added). In reference to keeping the *ordinances*, Paul explains the priesthood relationship between men and women. The priesthood is given first to Adam and then to Eve, in that "the head of every man is Christ; and the head of the woman is the man; and the head of Christ is God. . . . . But every woman that *prayeth* or prophesieth with her head *uncovered* [unauthorized] dishonoureth her *head* [keys of the priesthood]" (1 Corinthians 11:3, 5; emphasis added). Under the priesthood keys of the new and everlasting covenant of marriage, which came first to Adam and then to Eve, Eve is then given full authority to fulfill her calling as mother and help meet in equal partnership to Adam: *"For this cause ought the woman to have power on her head because of the angels"* (1 Corinthians 11:10 [2–10]; emphasis added). Many believe that because Eve partook first, she could not receive the priesthood. On the contrary, Eve received the power of priesthood because she acted in faith, under divine authority. Thus, she was the mother of all living.

Read Paul's words in 1 Corinthians chapter 11:2–10:

> Now I praise you, brethren, that ye remember me in all things, and *keep the ordinances*, as *I delivered them to you* [temple ordinance].

But I would have you know, that *the head of every man is Christ; and the head of the woman is the man*; and the head of Christ is God [express priesthood lineage from God].

Every man praying or prophesying, having his head covered, *dishonoureth his head* [His head being represented as Christ or the keys of the priesthood].

But every *woman* that *prayeth* or prophesieth with her *head uncovered* [without authority under the designated key of the priesthood] *dishonoureth her head* [dishonoureth the keys by which the priesthood was given to her]: for that is even all one as if she were *shaven* [naked or without covenants].

For if the woman be not *covered* [authorized], let her also be *shorn* [removed]: but if it be a shame for a woman to be shorn or shaven, let her be *covered* [retaining that priesthood through proper keys].

For a man indeed ought not to cover his head, forasmuch as *he is the image and glory of God* [Priesthood keys]: but the *woman is the glory of the man.* [Completes that same priesthood by her covenants]

For the man is not of the woman; but the woman of the man [in the priesthood].

Neither was the man created for the woman; but the woman *for the man* [she is equal companion to his ordained priesthood].

For this cause ought the woman to have power *on her head because of the angels.* [She receives full and equal power through temple ordinances and prescribed keys.] (emphasis added)

Bishop Whitney urged the women to stay focused on the work of the Lord and prepare to receive His power. 'Without the female, all things cannot be restored to the earth,' he declared."[299] In the writings of Ambrosiaster, "the veil signifies power."[300] The veil implies that "the woman should have Authority on her head."[301] "Far from being a symbol of the woman's subjection to man, therefore, her head-covering is what Paul calls it—authority: in prayer and prophecy she, like the man, is [acting] under the authority of God."[302] Her power, however, cannot be independent from those keys by which she is authorized. I think this is what Paul meant when he said, "But I suffer not a woman to teach, nor to *usurp authority* over the man" (1 Timothy 2:12; emphasis added). I think Paul is saying that she is not to teach or practice unauthorized doctrine or unauthorized authority (nor is the man). Her authority must come from the presiding keys given first to Adam in the name of Christ. In the beginning it came from the Father to the Son, to Adam, to Eve, to the families. This is an increase in power not a lessoning of it.

While man is given the priesthood keys *directly* by God, woman is given that same priesthood *indirectly* from God, through man, or the keys of the priesthood that a worthy man might hold. This is her veil. Her *indirect* priesthood authority is symbolized by a head covering worn by the woman as she receives it from her husband or authorized priesthood keys of God (1 Corinthians 11:5). (Note: this covering is also evidenced in secular tradition as symbolized by a bridal veil.) Though this covering is channeled through her husband's priesthood to her, it is, nevertheless, equal to his.

This uniting power between husband and wife—the new and everlasting covenant of marriage—is the eternal ordinance of families. Children are then born under that sacred covenant of marriage. It is by this ordinance of marriage that "they twain shall be one flesh" (Mark 10:8). "This is now bone of my bones, and flesh of my flesh" (Genesis 2:23). Elder M. Russell Ballard gave these teachings: "Our Church doctrine places women equal to and yet different from men. God does not regard either gender as better or more important than the other."[303]

However, Dallin H. Oaks goes on to explain, "The Lord has directed that only men will be ordained to *offices in the priesthood*. But, as various Church leaders have emphasized, men are not 'the priesthood.' Men hold the priesthood, with a sacred duty to use it for the blessing of all of the children of God. . . . As stated in the family proclamation, the father presides in the family and he and the mother have separate responsibilities, but they are 'obligated to help one another as *equal* partners.'"[304]

Eve is told to hearken unto her husband: "Thy desire shall be to thy husband" (Genesis 3:16). This unites *their* priesthood under one head (Christ), becoming an *equal partnership* in that family order. The authority of the priesthood is given to women: "We are not accustomed to speaking of women having the authority of the priesthood in their Church callings, but what other authority can it be?[305]

With each veil a weakness is implemented. By faith in Jesus Christ those weaknesses become our strengths, even power, even the joy of our redemption as we seek for His guiding hand in all things; "And he shall be called Jesus Christ, the Son of God, the Father of heaven and earth, the Creator of all things from the beginning; and his mother shall be called Mary" (Mosiah 3:8).

CHAPTER 32

TREE OF LIFE

"To him that overcometh will I give to eat of the tree of life"
—*Revelation 2:7*

The tree of life is central to the doctrine of Jesus Christ. Because of this, scriptures are full of references to the tree of life. It is seen by Lehi in 1 Nephi 8; Nephi sees the tree of life in 1 Nephi 11; Nephi teaches his brothers about the tree of life in 1 Nephi 15:21–22 [21–36]. The tree of life and the partaking of the tree of knowledge of good and evil are depicted in Genesis 2 and 3, Moses 3 and 4, and in Abraham 5. Alma speaks to a chief ruler on the purpose of both trees in Alma 12:20–33; John the Revelator also speaks of the tree of life in Revelations 2:7 and 22:14. John the Revelator, in speaking of the tree of life, said: "Blessed are they that do his commandments that they may have right to the tree of life, and may enter in through the gates into the city" (Revelation 22:14).

The tree of life is as literal as the New Jerusalem, with actual fruit that can be eaten and enjoyed. Adam and Eve partook of it liberally in the garden while they were yet in the presence of God. "And I, the Lord God, commanded the man, saying: Of *every tree* of the garden thou mayest freely eat, But of the tree of the knowledge of good and evil, thou shalt not eat of it" (Moses 3:16–17; emphasis added). The tree of life in Eden represents immortality in the presence of God, as opposed to the tree of knowledge of good and evil, which represents mortality and being sent out of God's presence. Thus, partaking of the tree of knowledge was forbidden in Eden. After the Fall we were given a promise that we will yet again partake of the tree of life, by way of Christ's Atonement. The tree of life is representative of the love of God, which is the greatest of all gifts. Likewise, the sacramental bread and wine is literal as was the sacrificial lamb, both representative of the Atonement of our Lord and Savior Jesus Christ.

The tree of knowledge of good and evil was also literal to Adam and Eve. The nutrient value cannot be calculated by the mortal man, and the transformation of either tree cannot be comprehended, just as the redeeming effects of the bread and wine cannot be fully comprehended. These trees have a physical and spiritual countenance, which Nephi says about the tree of life, "is most precious and most desirable above all other fruits, yea, and it is the greatest of all the gifts of God" (1 Nephi 15:36). "To him that overcometh will I give to *eat* of the tree of life, which is in the midst of the paradise of God" (Revelations 2:7; emphasis added). To *"eat"* is also representative of covenant making, as was the partaking of the bread and wine at the last supper (see Luke 22:19–20).

ALL THINGS HAVE THEIR LIKENESS

Throughout the scriptures, food often becomes a tutorial in the use of sacred symbols. Such examples include the use of lamb, bread, wine, fruit, fish, bitter herbs, water, manna, milk and honey, feast and hunger, and clean and unclean animals. Food is often a significant part of obedience and covenant making and, though it is a physical partaking, it is effectively used as a spiritual focus to remember our covenants and the goodness of God. Why is this so? Moses explains: "And behold, all things have their likeness, and all things are *created and made to bear record of me,* both things which are *temporal,* and things which are *spiritual*" (Moses 6:63; emphasis added).

The tree of life and the tree of good and evil, though physically created, also became paramount symbols of spiritual laws. "And out of the ground made I, the Lord God, to grow every tree, naturally, that is pleasant to the sight of man; and man could behold it. And it became also a *living soul*. For it was spiritual in the day that I created it" (Moses 3:9; emphasis added).

"But behold, I say unto you, that all these things were types of things to come. And now, did they understand the law? I say unto you, Nay, they did not all understand the law; and this because of the hardness of their hearts; for they understood not that there could not any man be saved except it were through the redemption of God" (Mosiah 13:31–32).

Because mortality breeds a natural man, God uses natural, or literal, senses to communicate spiritual commitments by our natural hunger. "A person who chooses to be influenced by the passions, desires, appetites, and senses of the flesh rather than by the promptings of the Holy Spirit. Such a person can comprehend physical things but not spiritual things."[306] We are taught spiritual senses by the physical needs of the mortal body. God teaches by hunger, thirst, fast, feast, and famine, often brought on as a direct result of man's obedience or disobedience. This effectively teaches the existence of God, His justice, and His mercy. "All things are created and made to bear record of me, both things which are temporal, and things which are spiritual" (Moses 6:63).

In the Doctrine and Covenants, we are told,

First spiritual, secondly temporal, which is the beginning of my work; and again, first temporal, and secondly spiritual, which is the last of my work—Speaking unto you that you may *naturally understand*; but unto myself my works have no end, neither beginning; but it is given unto you that ye may understand, because ye have asked it of me and are agreed. Wherefore, verily I say unto you that all things unto me are spiritual, and not at any time have I given unto you a law which was temporal; neither any man, nor the children of men; neither Adam, your father, whom I created. (D&C 29:32–34; emphasis added)

Obedience to the physical laws of God becomes key to spiritual understanding. These things are not about the fruit, bread, wine, and meat; these are about covenants made in the Garden of Eden, that a Savior would be provided. The physical laws teach us about the spiritual concepts of truth and light. As seen in the Mosaic law,

"Wherefore the law was our schoolmaster to bring us unto Christ, that we might be justified by faith. But after that faith is come, we are no longer under a schoolmaster" (Galatians 3:24, 25).

Unlike the Israelite people, it was the converted Lamanite nation that understood the importance of the Law of Moses,

> Yea, and they did keep the law of Moses; for it was expedient that they should keep the law of Moses as yet, for it was not all fulfilled. But notwithstanding the law of Moses, they did look forward to the coming of Christ, considering that the law of Moses was a type of his coming, and believing that they must keep those outward performances until the time that he should be revealed unto them.
>
> Now they did not suppose that salvation came by the law of Moses; but the law of Moses did serve to strengthen their faith in Christ; and thus they did retain a hope through faith, unto eternal salvation, relying upon the spirit of prophecy, which spake of those things to come. (Alma 25:15,16)

Unfortunately, the Israelite nation often missed the message provided by the sacrifices required, which would point them to Christ as the Savior. It was King Hezekiah who "brake the images, and cut down the groves, and brake in pieces the *brazen serpent that Moses had made*: for unto those days the children of Israel did burn incense to it" (2 Kings 18:4; emphasis added). The chosen Israelites had begun to idolize the object—the brazen serpent—as the healer, rather than Christ. These people, seeing only the object, rejected truth and light. Again, it's not about the bread, the wine, the meat, the trees, or the brazen serpent. These things are about Christ, in whom lies all power. Perhaps that is why we don't consider the cross as being an appropriate object for worship, the danger being that we too often make our worship about the objects as having power rather than the eternal teachings they represent.

Even in baptism we are told, "Come and be baptized unto repentance, that ye . . . may be partakers of the fruit of the tree of life" (Alma 5:62). Is baptism a physical or spiritual commandment and reward? One is not without the other. As in baptism, by obedience to physical law we become spiritually born of God. Talmage tells us, "The water baptism is not alone the means provided for gaining remission of sins, but is also an indispensable ordinance established in righteousness and required of all mankind as an essential condition for membership in the kingdom of God."[307] Because John's baptism was unto repentance, he forbade the sinless Christ, saying, "I have need to be baptized of thee . . . Jesus answering said . . . for thus it becometh us to fulfill all righteousness" (Matthew 3:14,15). There are no fast tracks to entering into God's kingdom. Obedience to physical ordinances is a requirement for all. "Jesus answered, Verily, verily, I say unto thee, except a man be born of the *water and of the Spirit*, he cannot enter into the kingdom of God" (John 3:5). When John obeyed and baptized Jesus, "John bare record, saying, I saw the Spirit descending from heaven like a dove, and it abode upon him" (John 1:32). The Spirit comes because of obedience to physical requirements.

In this same obedience, man and woman, in the ordinance of the everlasting covenant of marriage, become a spiritual power. So also by partaking of the tree of life—the Atonement of Jesus Christ—we are once again admitted into the presence of God. These are physical ordinances for eternal salvation, but without the Spirit they have no effect.

ESSENTIAL DOCTRINE

Vivian M. Adams explained, "To facilitate the Fall, God placed two trees in the midst of the garden, the tree of life and the tree of the knowledge of good and evil. The significance of the trees extended beyond that of natural or physical fruit: their importance lay in the figures provided. The trees, with their spreading branches and fruit, *represented essential doctrines.*"[308]

As written by Joseph Fielding McConkie and Robert L. Millet, the scriptural tree of life is "the *symbol*, even from the time of paradise, of the central and saving role of Jesus Christ."[309] "For it was spiritual in the day that I created it" (D&C 29:32–34). Its mission had been preordained.

A RECURRING SYMBOL

Delbert A. Stapley, an ordained Apostle in 1950, tells us,

The tree of life was not unknown to the descendants of Lehi, part of whom are the Indian tribes of the Americas, for it is found in the pictorial hieroglyphics that were carved upon rocks in regions of the past civilizations of Lehi's posterity. The tree of life is not something new taught in our day, for there are many references to it in the scriptures. The significance of this representation may not be understood fully, except by few, yet it has real and important spiritual value. In the book of Revelation 2:7 we learn that 'the tree of life . . . is in the midst of the paradise of God.' In Genesis 2:9 we are informed that a tree of life was placed by God in the midst of the Garden of Eden. Adam and Eve were privileged *to partake of the fruit of this tree until they transgressed God's law.* Thereafter the fruit of the tree was denied them, if they had partaken, they would have lived forever in their fallen state (Moses 4:28). Death was in the great plan of God, and the hope of man became centered in Jesus Christ, who gave his life on Calvary to redeem and save man from the effects of the fall.[310]

Alma quotes Christ, saying, "Come unto me and ye shall partake of the fruit of the tree of life" (Alma 5:34). Nephi advises, "Wherefore, the wicked are rejected from the righteous, and also from that tree of life, whose fruit is most precious and most desirable above all other fruits, yea, and it is the greatest of all the gifts of God" (1 Nephi 15:36).

ALMA ON THE TREE OF LIFE

Alma, in contending with Antionah (a chief ruler), explains the impact that the tree of life would have had on Adam and Eve had they partaken of it after the Fall:

And now behold, I say unto you that if it had been possible for Adam to have partaken of the fruit of the tree of life at that time, there would have been no death, and the word would have been void, making God a liar, for he said: If thou eat thou shalt surely die.

And we see that death comes upon mankind, yea, the death which has been spoken of by Amulek, which is the temporal death; nevertheless there was a space granted unto man in which he might repent; therefore this life became a probationary state; a time to prepare to meet God; a time to prepare for that endless state which has been spoken of by us . . .

But there was a plan of redemption laid, which shall bring to pass the resurrection of the dead, of which has been spoken. . . .

Therefore he sent angels to converse with them, who caused men to behold of his glory. . . .

And this he made known unto them according to their faith and repentance and their holy works. . . .

Therefore God gave unto them commandments, after having made known unto them the plan of redemption, that they should not do evil, the penalty thereof being a second death. . . .

But God did call on men, in the name of his son, (this being the plan of redemption which was laid) saying: If ye will repent, and harden not your hearts, then will I have mercy upon you, through mine Only Begotten Son. (Alma 12:23–25, 29–33)

If they had partaken of the tree of life after the Fall, without first gaining it through the blood of Christ, they would have made salvation void. The tree of knowledge of good and evil gives us that needed choice, "And thus did I, the Lord God, appoint unto man the days of his probation—that by his mortal death he might be raised in immortality unto eternal life, even as many as would believe" (D&C 29:43). It is immortality and eternal life, the Atonement of Jesus Christ, the tree of life, that is offered through the partaking of the tree knowledge of good and evil.

THE SACRAMENT, THE TREE OF LIFE, AND THE CROSS

Similar to the careful guarding of the tree of life, we are also warned to not partake of the sacrament unworthily (unrepentant of outstanding sin), as it is a precursor for the tree of life. "For whoso eateth and drinketh my flesh and blood unworthily eateth and drinketh damnation to his soul; therefore if ye know that a man is unworthy to eat and drink of my flesh and blood ye shall forbid him" (3 Nephi 18:29). We must not partake of the symbolic reference of the Atonement lightly. The Lord's salvation and the price he paid for us must not be mocked or scoffed at, lest we find ourselves required to pay full price for our sins.

Susan Easton Black wrote: "The tree of life is connected with the cross, the two having somewhat the same significance. Both related to the resurrection, eternal life, the Lord, and the 'Love of God.'"[311] When Nephi wished to know the meaning of the tree that his father saw in his dream (1 Nephi 11:9–24), the angel showed him a vision of the birth of Christ: "It is the love of God." "For God so loved the world, that he gave his only begotten Son, that whosoever believeth in him should not perish, but have everlasting life" (John 3:16).

The tree of life, bread, wine, and water *represent what we hunger for.* Christ is the living bread; He is the tree of life. Hunger after righteousness; feast upon the words of Christ. "Take, eat; this is in remembrance of my body which I give a ransom for you" (JST Matthew 26:22).

CHAPTER 33

CHERUBIM AND A FLAMING SWORD

"I placed . . .cherubim and a flaming sword which turned every way to keep the way."

—*Moses 4:31*

What is "cherubim and the flaming sword"? Having been forbidden and blocked, is there another door back into the presence of God? It would seem that cherubim guard the gate of heaven: "Blessed are they that do his commandments that they may have right to the tree of life, and may enter in through the gates into the city" (Revelation 22:14). Are cherubim the same as porters at the gate (2 Chronicles 23:19); keys of the kingdom (Matthew 16:19); the gate of heaven (Helaman 3:28); or more commonly called the Pearly Gates, or St. Peter's gate? We are told that the strait and narrow path leads to the gate. These all might be in reference to the gate guarded by cherubim and the flaming sword.

> Wherefore, do the things which I have told you; . . . for, for this cause have they been shown unto me, *that ye might know the gate* by which ye should enter. For the gate by which ye should enter is repentance and baptism by water; and then cometh a remission of your sins by fire and by the Holy Ghost. And then are ye in this *strait and narrow path* which leads to eternal life; yea, ye have entered in by the gate; ye have done according to the commandments of the Father and the Son. (2 Nephi 31:17, 18–20)

The Garden of Eden account could not be complete without adding a compilation as to what cherubim and a flaming sword are, "to keep the way of the tree of life" (Genesis 3:24). Not finding a full explanation, I pulled together various scriptures that define who or what the guarding of the tree of life is.

In the book *The Man Adam*, we are told that "cherubim and a flaming sword, which turned every way to protect the tree of life (Moses 4:31), constituted a symbolic announcement; that the earth could not return to its paradisiacal state while death reigned. Until that great millennial day, the earth would be subject to corruption."[312]

From the sculpted edifices in Solomon's temple to the elaborate symbolic descriptions of Ezekiel, we find creatures in Ezekiel, beasts in Revelations, seraphim in Isaiah, and cherubim sculptures in Moses's Holy of Holies and in Solomon's temple. These all have similar descriptions and character, which relate to the guarding of the tree of life but in symbolic relevance.

I also found angelic messengers with sword in hand throughout the Old Testament, wielding a godly vengeance for righteousness. These angels of light seem similar to the cherubim and flaming sword that guarded the tree of life. Therefore, justice and mercy hang in the balance upon this earth with the watchful vigilance of heavenly cherubim.

Cherubim are angelic guardians, probably men, though their description in Ezekiel and depiction in sculpted form is more of a symbolic representation of their *godly gifts and powers*. Cherubim are angelic beings involved in the worship and praise of God (cherub being singular and cherubim being plural). The cherubim are first mentioned in the Bible: "So I drove out the man, and I placed at the east of the Garden of Eden, cherubim and a flaming sword, which turned every way to keep the way of the tree of life" (Genesis 3:24). The cherubim which protected the tree of life are found in Genesis 3:24; Moses 4:31; Alma 12:21–29; and Alma 42:2–3. To solidify in our minds what cherubim are, I have gathered examples of what seems representative of the cherubim that guarded the tree of life.

SATAN, PRIOR TO HIS REBELLION

"Thou art the *anointed cherub* that covereth; and I have set thee so: thou wast upon the holy mountain of God; thou hast walked up and down in the midst of the stones of fire. Thou wast perfect in thy ways from the day that thou wast created, till iniquity was found in thee" (Ezekiel 28:12–15).

BALAAM AND THE ANGEL

The angel that stood before Balaam is a biblical example of a cherub and a flaming sword. The angel was sent to protect the Israelite people from a prophetic curse by an apostate prophet:

> And Balaam rose up in the morning, and saddled his ass, and went with the princes of Moab.
>
> And God's anger was kindled because he went: and *the angel of the Lord stood in the way for an adversary against him.* . . .
>
> And *the ass saw the angel of the Lord standing in the way, and his sword drawn in his hand:* . . .
>
> And the *angel of the Lord went further, and stood in a narrow place, where was no way to turn either to the right hand or to the left.* . . .
>
> *Then the Lord opened the eyes of Balaam, and he saw the angel of the Lord standing in the way, and his sword drawn in his hand:* . . .
>
> And the *angel of the Lord* said unto him, . . . *And the ass saw me, and turned from me these three times: unless she had turned from me, surely now also I had slain thee, and saved her alive.* . . .
>
> *Go with the men: but only the word that I shall speak unto thee, that thou shalt speak.* (Numbers 22:21–23, 26, 31–33, 35; emphasis added)

Similarly, we find "cherubim and a flaming sword flashing back and forth to guard the way to the tree of life" (Genesis 3:24).

KING DAVID'S VISION

King David disobeyed the laws of the Lord by numbering the people: "And Satan stood up against Israel, and provoked David to number Israel" (I Chronicles 21:1). "And David lifted up his eyes, and saw *the angel of the Lord stand between the earth and the heaven, having a drawn sword in his hand* stretched out over Jerusalem. Then David and the elders of Israel, who were clothed in sackcloth, fell upon their faces" (1 Chronicles 21:16).

JOSHUA'S ENCOUNTER

Joshua witnessed an angelic guardian to the Israelite nation as they prepared for war,

> And it came to pass, when Joshua was by Jericho, that he lifted up his eyes and looked, and, behold, *there stood a man over against him with his sword drawn in his hand*: and Joshua went unto him, and said unto him, Art thou for us, or for our adversaries?
>
> And he said, nay; but as *captain of the host of the* Lord am I now come. And Joshua fell on his face to the earth, and did worship, and said unto him, what saith my lord unto his servant?
>
> And the captain of the Lord's host said unto Joshua, Loose thy shoe from off thy foot; for the place whereon thou standest is holy. And Joshua did so. (Joshua 5:13–15)

Could the captain of the Lord's host be "Michael . . . even the archangel" (D&C 112–13)? The same as the "Mighty Michael, the eternal captain of Jehovah's army."[313]

CHERUBIM

We are not alone in our defense of Christ, because cherubim are waiting upon the Saints of God in their course of righteousness. "Topologist Patrick Fairbairn indicated that they are the angels who have become like God and dwell in His presence in eternity."[314] "One theological dictionary noted that the Hebrew word cherub is likely related to the idea of an 'intercessor.'"[315] Dictionaries, religious and secular alike, often define cherubim as "celestial beings."[316] Joseph Fielding McConkie wrote that cherubim are placed to ensure that the "holiness of God is not violated by those in transgression or those who have not complied with the proper rituals."[317]

IN CARVED FORM

These representations are described in some detail. As symbolic representation, these cherubim were carved for the temple in the wilderness in the Holy of Holies, on the ark of the covenant, and on the mercy seat in Exodus 25:19, 20.[318] These symbols are intricately described in the building of Solomon's temple in 1 Kings 6 and in Chronicles 3.

"And make one cherub on the one end, and the other cherub on the other end: even of the mercy seat shall ye make the cherubim on the two ends thereof. And the cherubims shall stretch forth their wings on high, covering the mercy seat with their wings, and their faces shall look one to another; toward the mercy seat shall the faces of the cherubims be" (Exodus 25:19–20). These carved cherubim were symbolic guardians to the sacred ordinances performed in the early temple.

ANGELIC CREATURES IN EZEKIEL

Angelic creatures, as in Ezekiel 1 and 10, have a similar likeness, as do the beasts and seraphim. The beasts, creatures, and seraphim are more specific in their commonalities to each other than that of cherubim but are, nevertheless, guardians of righteousness. In Ezekiel 10, as in chapter 1, each creature had *four faces*—that of a *man*, a *lion*, an *ox*, and an *eagle* (see Ezekiel 1:10; also 10:14)—and each had four *wings*. The dramatic symbology of these guardians in Ezekiel, Isaiah, and Revelation brings both fear and wonder to the heart and mind. These ideological references are illustrations of specified powers which the angelic creatures posses.

BEASTS IN REVELATION

Beasts, much like cherubim at the tree of life, represent sentinels upon the throne of God, "And before the throne *there was* a sea of glass like unto crystal: and in the midst of the throne, and round about the throne, were *four beasts full of eyes* before and behind. . . . and they rest not day and night, saying, Holy, holy, holy, Lord God Almighty, which was, and is, and is to come. And when those beasts give glory and honour and thanks to him that sat on the throne, who liveth forever and ever" (Revelation 4:6–9). These angelic creatures, like cherubim, have specified powers and callings. Where do they come from? "The angels do not reside on a planet like this earth; but they reside in the presence of God, on a globe like a sea of glass and fire, where all things for their glory are manifest, past, present, and future, and are continually before the Lord" (D&C 29:23).

Joseph Smith gave us some comprehensive explanations for the beasts mentioned in Revelation in D&C 77:2–4. With these comments and by the spirit of prayer we can better understand their watchful care over our mortal lives.

The carved cherubim in Solomon's temple take on a symbolic form to demonstrate godly powers, as do the beasts, creatures, and seraphim. The cherubim at the tree of life seem to be presented in angelic human form, as are other angels, while carrying a flaming sword to demonstrate a protective stance for God's ordained laws. All, however, seem to have great power given them to accomplish the Lord's errand. "Are they not all ministering spirits, sent forth to minister for them who shall be heirs of salvation?" (Hebrews 1:14)

WHAT IS A FLAMING SWORD?

I found no reference to a "flaming sword" except in the Garden of Eden, so I referenced the words *flaming* and *sword* separately, hoping to better understand the meaning of a flaming sword by picking up keywords and statements such as found in the following scriptures:

FLAMING: "Therefore I will make him as *flaming fire* and a ministering angel" (D&C 7:6). And "the justice . . . and the brightness thereof was like unto the brightness of a *flaming fire*, which ascendeth up unto God forever and ever, and hath no end" (1 Nephi 15:30). "Thy God is a consuming *fire*" (Deut. 4:24). "And this is my gospel—repentance and baptism by water, and then cometh the baptism of *fire* and the Holy Ghost, even the Comforter, which showeth all things, and teacheth the peaceable things of the kingdom" (D&C 39:6).

SWORD: "And he said unto them: Behold . . . the *sword* of justice hangeth over this people" (Helaman 13:5). "Hearken to the voice of the Lord your God, whose *word* is quick and powerful, sharper than a two-edged *sword*, to the dividing asunder of the joints and marrow, soul and spirit; and is a discerner of the thoughts and intents of the heart" (D&C 33:1). "Yea, a *sword* shall pierce through thy own soul also, that the thoughts of many hearts may be revealed" (Luke 2:35). "And he hath made my mouth like a sharp *sword*" (1 Nephi 21:2). "And out of his mouth went a sharp two edged *sword*" (Revelation 1:16). "For the *word of God* is quick, and powerful, and sharper than any two-edged *sword*" (Hebrews 4:12). In Ephesians 6:17 we are taught that the *sword* of the Spirit is *the word of God.*

Flames represent illumination, inspiration, enlightenment, purification, and the Holy Ghost. Sword represents word of God, protection, covenants, commandments, teachings, and discernment, which separates.

"The symbolism of the sword as the *word of God* is enshrined in the word *Sword,* (se-word) is a word [meaning] *'the fire or light of the word.'* The Anglo-Saxon for a sword was seax [which meant] *'the fire of the great fire.'*"[319] Putting all these thoughts together, I would say that these sentinels stand armed with the all-powerful word of God, as an irrevocable truth. God's word stands eternal; His judgments are true and sure.

AN ACT OF LOVE

In reference to cherubim and a flaming sword, Brad Wilcox explains,

> At times, all of us run into closed doors. They are rarely pleasant and seldom wanted. However, when seen in an eternal perspective, closed doors may actually be helpful to us as they lead us to open windows of even greater opportunities. Adam and Eve faced one of the first closed doors: Cherubim and a flaming sword were placed to keep them from the tree of life. The cherubim and flaming sword were not evidence of God's anger and rejection. Rather, they were evidence of his benevolence and love. This "closed door" existed not to bar Adam and Eve from God but to point them toward the open window of Christ's atonement, which would enable them to return to God and live with him forever.[320]

CONCLUSION
FROM EVERLASTING TO EVERLASTING

Eve is the final touch to Adam's power, purpose, and might. She takes him forward into an onward course. Without accolades, she becomes the very life of man.

Who is Eve? She is Adam. She is his completion; he is not without her. "They twain shall be one" (Moses 5:13). Adam and Eve as one are articulated in the following scriptures:

> In the image of his own body, *male and female*, created he *them*, and blessed *them*, and called *their* name *Adam*, in the day when *they* were created and became a *living soul* in the land upon the footstool of God. (Moses 6:9; emphasis added)
>
> Then shall *they* be gods, because *they* have no end; therefore shall *they* be from everlasting, because *they* continue; then shall *they* be above all, because all things are subject unto *them*. Then shall *they* be gods, because *they* have all power. (D&C 132:20; emphasis added)

The fullness of Adam's life can be reflected in the words, "And Adam said, this is now bone of my bones, and flesh of my flesh: she shall be called Woman, because she was taken out of Man" (Genesis 2:23).

President Packer spoke those same sentiments of his wife:

> Sister Donna Smith Packer and I have been side by side in marriage for nearly 70 years. When it comes to my wife, the mother of our

children, I am without words. The feeling is so deep and the gratitude so powerful that I am left almost without expression. . . . Toward the end of our mortal days together, I am grateful for each moment I am with her side by side and for the promise the Lord has given, that there will be no end.[321]

OUR TEMPLES ARE AN EVERLASTING ENSIGN

Historically, the righteousness (or lack of it) in a culture or society is directly related to how the relationship between men and women in that society (or home) are conducted. The new and everlasting covenant of marriage is based on oneness and love, and that becomes significant in how we perfectly perceive godhood and the priesthood.

"Verily I say unto you, blessed are you for receiving mine everlasting covenant, even the fullness of my gospel, sent forth unto the children of men, that they might have life and be made partakers of the glories which are to be revealed in the last days, as it was written by the prophets and apostles in days of old" (D&C 66:2). Adam and Eve have shown that family is the beginning and the end of our connective rights to God's throne—inherently becoming His sons and daughters.

I have gained an abiding love for our first parents. Eve is my mother, and by such, is also my sister, and my daughter; she is of Adam; therefore, she is also my strength. I, too, am Eve, "For thus have I, the Lord God, called the first of all women, which are many" (Moses 4:26).

ENDNOTES

1. Jeffrey R. Holland, *Christ and the New Covenant: The Messianic Message of the Book of Mormon* (Salt Lake City: Deseret Book, 1997), 204.

2. Bruce C. Hafen, *The Broken Heart: Applying the Atonement to Life's Experiences* (Salt Lake City: Deseret Book, 1989), 37.

3. Robert L. Millet, *The Man Adam*, eds. Joseph Fielding McConkie and Robert L. Millet (Salt Lake City: Bookcraft, 1990), 25.

4. Robert L. Millet (1992), 2:724; quoted in Alonzo L. Gaskill, *The Savior and the Serpent* (Salt Lake City: Deseret Book, 2005), 134.

5. Alonzo L. Gaskill, *The Savior and the Serpent* (Salt Lake City: Deseret Book, 2005), 134–35; emphasis added.

6. Bruce C. Hafen, *The Broken Heart: Applying the Atonement to Life's Experiences* (Salt Lake City: Deseret Book, 1989), 212; quoted in BYU Studies, Vol. 30 (1990).

7. Jeffrey R. Holland, *Christ and the New Covenant: The Messianic Message of the Book of Mormon* (Salt Lake City: Deseret Book, 2006), 202–3; emphasis added.

8. Brigham Young, "*Journal of Discourses*," 4:373.

9. Orson F. Whitney, *Cowley and Whitney on Doctrine* (Salt Lake City: Bookcraft, 1963), 287; quoted in *Select Writings of Robert L. Matthews*: Gospel Scholars Series, Chapter 14, 480.

10. Joseph Fielding Smith, *The Words of Joseph Smith*, eds. Andrew F. Ehat and Lyndon W. Cook (Salt Lake City: Bookcraft, 1980), 63; emphasis added.

11. Matthew L. Davis to Mrs. Matthew [Mary] L. Davis, Feb. 6, 1840, Church History Library; Bushman, Rough Stone Rolling, 394-95. Quoted in "Saint; Standard of Truth" 1815-1846, Vol. 1, Ch. 34, 412."

12. Joseph Fielding Smith, *"Fall—Atonement—Resurrection—Sacrament"* (presentation, LDS Institute of Religion, Salt Lake City, UT, January 14, 1961), 125.

13. Karen Jensen, "Quotes by Karen Jensen," at https://www.google.com/search?q=goodreads.com&rlz

14. James E. Talmage, *Jesus the Christ* (Salt Lake City: Deseret Book, 1981), 527.

15. Joseph Fielding Smith, *The Man Adam*, eds. Joseph Fielding McConkie and Robert L. Millet (Salt Lake City: Bookcraft), 63; emphasis added.

16. Bruce R. McConkie, *Mormon Doctrine*, 2nd ed. (Salt Lake City: Bookcraft, 1966), 289; emphasis added.

17. Vivian M. Adams, *The Man Adam*, eds. Joseph Fielding McConkie and Robert L. Millet (Salt Lake City: Bookcraft), 102; emphasis added.

18. Bruce R. McConkie, "Chapter 10: Matthew 27–28," New Testament Student Manual (2014).

19. Ibid; emphasis added.

20. Niddah 45b, Epstein, Babylonian Talmud, quoted in E. Douglas Clark, *Echoes of Eden* (Salt Lake City: Covenant Communications), 27.

21. Brigham Young, *"Journal of Discourses,"* 12:194 (correcting "that" to "than").

22. Ibid., 18:233.

23. J. Reuben Clark, "Our Wives and Mothers in the Eternal Plan," 801, quoted in E. Douglas Clark, *Echoes of Eden* (Salt Lake City: Covenant Communications), 28.

24. Gordon B. Hinckley, "Daughters of God," *Ensign*, November 2011, 97.

25. Rodney Turner, *Pearl of Great Price: Revelations from God*, eds. H. Donl Peterson and Charles D. Tate Jr. (Salt Lake City: Deseret Book), 94.

26. Dallin H. Oaks, "The Great Plan of Happiness," *Ensign*, November 1993, 73.

27. Al-Kisa'i, *Tale of the Prophets*, 39, quoted in E. Douglas Clark, *Echoes of Eden* (Salt Lake City: Covenant Communications), 51.

28. Harold B. Lee, *Teachings of Harold B. Lee*, ed. Clyde J. Williams, (Salt Lake City: Bookcraft, 1996), 36.

29. Hyrum L. Andrus, *Doctrinal Commentary on the Pearl of Great Price* (Salt Lake City: Deseret Book, 1972), 78; emphasis added.

30. Joseph F. Smith, *Teachings of Presidents of the Church* (1998), 87; emphasis added.

31. Alonzo L. Gaskill, *The Savior and the Serpent* (Salt Lake City: Deseret Book, 2005), 154.

32. Alonzo L. Gaskill, *The Truth about Eden: Understanding the Fall and Our Temple Experience* (Springville, UT: Cedar Fork Publishing, 2013), 67.

33. Harold B. Lee, *Teachings of the Presidents of the Church*: Harold B. Lee (Salt Lake City: Deseret Book), 36.

34. Dieter F. Uchtdorf, "Are You Sleeping through the Restoration?" *Ensign*, May 2014, 61–62.

35. Joseph F. Smith, *Teachings of Presidents of the Church*: Joseph F. Smith (1998), 141; Joseph Smith Translation, Genesis 14:28–31, in Bible appendix; quoted by Boyd K. Packer, "The Power of the Priesthood," *Ensign*, May 2010, 7.

36. Larry E. Dahl, "Adam's Role from the Fall to the End—and Beyond," *The Man Adam*, eds. Joseph Fielding McConkie and Robert L. Millet (Salt Lake City: Bookcraft), 121–22; emphasis added.

37. Ibid., 122.

38. Ibid., 123. Also see Bruce R. McConkie, Doctrinal New Testament Commentary, 3 vols. (Salt Lake City: Bookcraft, 1965–73), 3:423; *The Man Adam*, 223; emphasis added.

39. Ibid., 122. Also see Joseph Fielding Smith, *Teachings of the Prophet Joseph Smith* (Salt Lake City: Deseret Book), 208.

40. John A. Widtsoe, *Evidences and Reconciliations* (Salt Lake City: Bookcraft), 193–94.

41. Daniel H. Ludlow, "Fall of Adam," *Encyclopedia of Mormonism*, 4 vols.

42. Ibid., "JD", 13:145.

43. Ibid., "Widtsoe", 194.

44. David H. Yarn, Jr., "The Messianic Expectation," *Ensign*, April 1972.

45. James E. Talmage, *Jesus the Christ* (Salt Lake City: Covenant Communications), 43.

46. Daniel H. Ludlow, The Pearl of Great Price Student Manual (2000), 3–27.

47.   Daniel H. Ludlow, "Eve," *Encyclopedia of Mormonism*, 4 vols.

48.   Hugh W. Nibley, "LDS Women's Treasury," *Patriarchy and Matriarchy*, 38–39.

49.   Robert L. Millet and Kent P. Jackson, *Studies in Scripture: The Pearl of Great Price*, Vol. 2; emphasis added.

50.   "Bridegroom," *Guide to the Scriptures*, lds.org.

51.   Spencer W. Kimball, *Teachings of Presidents of the Church*: Spencer W. Kimball (2006), 222–23.

52.   Bruce R. McConkie, "Eve and the Fall," *Sermons and Writings of Bruce R. McConkie* (Salt Lake City: Bookcraft), 68.

53.   Vivian M. Adams, *The Man Adam*, eds. Joseph Fielding McConkie and Robert L. Millet (Salt Lake City: Bookcraft), 107.

54.   Jeffrey R. Holland, *Christ and the New Covenant* (Salt Lake City: Deseret Book, 1997), 204; original emphasis.

55.   Dallin H. Oaks, "The Keys and Authority of the Priesthood," *Ensign*, May 2014, section 5.

56.   Joseph Fielding Smith, "Fall—Atonement—Resurrection—Sacrament" (presentation, LDS Institute of Religion, Salt Lake City, UT, January 14, 1961), 125.

57.   Matthew Holland, "Wrong Roads and Revelation," *New Era*, July 2005; emphasis in original.

58.   Dallin H. Oaks, "The Great Plan of Happiness," *Ensign*, (November 1993), 73.

59.   Joseph Fielding Smith, "Doctrines of Salvation," 1:115; see also *Ensign*, February 1994: "It is widely taught in the world that when Adam and Eve 'Partook of the forbidden fruit' they committed sexual sin. What is the Latter-day Saint view on the 'forbidden fruit?"

60.   Dr. Nehama Aschkenasy, quoted in "Re-discovering the Divine Nature of Pregnancy and Birth," (Madison & West Publishers, 2012), 2–3.

61.   Henry B. Eyring "The Lord Leads His Church," *Ensign*, November 2017; emphasis in original.

62.   Joseph Smith, Journal, Aug. 31, 1842, in JSP, J2:124; Nauvoo Relief Society Minute Book, Aug. 31, 1842, in Derr and others, First Fifty Years of Relief Society, 93. Quoted in "Saints"; The Standard of Truth 1815-1846, Vol. 1, Ch. 39, 475.

63. George Q. Cannon, *Gospel Truth* (Salt Lake City: Deseret Book, 1987), 1:24; emphasis added.

64. Marion G. Romney, address to seminary and institute personnel, (July 13, 1966), 20, 193.

65. Bruce R. McConkie, *Sermons and Writings of Bruce R. McConkie* (Salt Lake City: Bookcraft, 1989), 202. See also Bruce R. McConkie, Eve and the Fall (Salt Lake City: Deseret Book, 1979), 64, quoted in Beverly Campbell, *Eve and the Choice Made in Eden* (Salt Lake City: Deseret Book), 60.

66. Russell M. Nelson, "Life After Life," *Ensign*, May 1987.

67. Spencer W. Kimball, as quoted in Dallin H. Oaks, "The Keys and Authority of the Priesthood," *Ensign*, May 2014; emphasis added. See also Spencer W. Kimball, "Our Great Potential," *Ensign*, May 1977, 49.

68. James E. Talmage, *"Articles of Faith"*, Deseret Book, Unabridged version 1981, 46–47; emphasis added.

69. James E. Talmage, as quoted in "Young Woman's Journal," Oct. 1914, 602–3.

70. Ibid., 48; emphasis added.

71. "Doctrines of the Gospel Student Manual," 2000, 19–21; emphasis added.

72. Bruce R. McConkie, *Mormon Doctrine* (Salt Lake City: Bookcraft), 268.

73. Alonzo L. Gaskill, *The Savior and the Serpent* (Salt Lake City: Deseret Book), 20; emphasis added.

74. Ibid.

75. Dallin H. Oaks, "The Great Plan of Happiness," *Ensign*, November 1993; emphasis added.

76. Jeffrey R. Holland (1997), 202–3, as quoted in Alonzo Gaskill, *Savior and Serpent* (Salt Lake City: Deseret Book), 9.

77. Brigham Young, "Discourses of Brigham Young," 104.

78. Alonzo L. Gaskill, *The Truth about Eden: Understanding the Fall and Our Temple Experience* (Salt Lake City: Bookcraft, 2013), 14. See also Speiser (1962), 26.

79. Ibid. See Maxwell (1985), 72.

80. Ibid. See Pratt (2000), 81.

81. Joseph Smith, "Adam, the Archangel," Mark E. Peterson, *Ensign*, November 1980. See also Teachings, pp. 157–58.

82. Joseph Fielding Smith, *The Man Adam* (1990), eds. Joseph Fielding McConkie and Robert L. Millet; emphasis in original.

83. "There is no other way," See also Alma 38:9; Helaman 5:9; see also Mosiah 3:17; 2 Nephi 9:41.

84. Joseph Fielding McConkie, *Here We Stand* (Salt Lake City: Deseret Book, 1995), 119.

85. Henry B. Eyring, "The Holy Ghost as Your Companion," *Ensign*, Nov. 2015, 106–07, 105–106; emphasis added.

86. Erik Peterson, quoted in Stephen D. Ricks and Donald W. Parry, "Temples of the Ancient World: Ritual and Symbolism," *The Garment of Adam as a Primordial Creation*, 709–710.

87. Hugh Nibley, Gen. 3:1, in Richard Elliott Friedman, "Commentary on the Torah with a New English Translation," quoted in E. Douglas Clark, *Echoes of Eden*, 68.

88. Dale G. Renlund, "Choose You This Day," *Ensign*, Nov. 2018.

89. Alonzo L. Gaskill, *Paradise Lost: Understanding the Symbolic Message of the Fall* (2011), 173–74; emphasis added.

90. Alonzo Gaskill, *The Lost Language of Symbols* (Salt Lake City: Deseret Book), 62–63.

91. Ibid., 64.

92. Joseph Smith, as quoted in Hyrum L. Andrus, "Doctrines of the Kingdom," *Restoring the Divine Patriarchal Order* (Salt Lake City: Bookcraft), 532.

93. Joseph Smith, "History of the Church," Deseret Book, 4:555.

94. Brown, Driver, and Briggs (1999), 497–98, quoted in Alonzo Gaskill, *The Savior and the Serpent* (Salt Lake City: Deseret Book, 2005), 91.

95. Hugh Nibley, *Temples and Cosmos: Beyond This Ignorant Present* (Salt Lake City: Deseret Book), 136–7, quoted in Beverly Campbell, *Eve and the Choice Made in Eden*, (Salt Lake City: Deseret Book), 55.

96. Beverly Campbell, *"Eve and the Choice Made in Heaven,"* Deseret Book, 55.

97. Benjamin H. Harry, John J. Hay, and Fred Astren, "Judaism and Islam Boundaries, Communication, and Interaction," *Brill's Series in Jewish Studies*, 206.

98. "Church" (1992), New International Bible, 12; original emphasis.

99. Brigham Young, *Journal of Discourses*, 17:143.

100. Hugh Nibley, Old Testament and Related Studies, eds. John W. Welch, Gary P. Gillum, and Don E. Norton (1986), 89–90.

101. "How Firm a Foundation," *Hymns*, no. 85.

102. Heber J. Grant, "The Sanctifying Powers of Distress," *Improvement Era*, February 1922, 194.

103. Elder Jeffrey R. Holland, "Hope After Sandy Hook," *LDS Living*, November 2017.

104. Joseph Smith, "Shem Was Melchizedek," *Lectures on Faith* (Salt Lake City: Deseret Book), 93.

105. C. S. Lewis, *Letters of C. S. Lewis*, reissue edition (Harper One, 1966), 440.

106. Joseph Smith, *Lectures on Faith* (Salt Lake City: Deseret Book, 1985), 69; emphasis added.

107. Sailhamer (1992), 108; Sailhamer (1976–1992), 2:56, quoted in Alonzo Gaskill, *Savior and the Serpent* (Salt Lake City: Deseret Book), 83.

108. Alonzo L. Gaskill, *The Truth about Eden: Understanding the Fall and Our Temple Experience* (Salt Lake City: Deseret Book, 2013), 79.

109. Augustine, "Two Books on Genesis against the Manicheans," 2.19.29, in Oden (2001), 93; quoted in Alonzo Gaskill, *Savior and the Serpent* (Salt Lake City: Deseret Book), 83.

110. Howard W. Hunter, *Teachings of Presidents of the Church*: Howard W. Hunter (Salt Lake City: Church of Jesus Christ of Latter-day Saints, 2015), 46.

111. Beverly Campbell, *Eve and the Choice Made in Heaven* (Salt Lake City: Deseret Book), 105.

112. Spencer W. Kimball, "The Blessings and Responsibilities of Womanhood," *Ensign*, March 1976, 72.

113. "The Family: A Proclamation to the World," *Ensign* or *Liahona*, Nov. 2010, 129.

114. Bruce C. Hafen and Marie Hafen, "Equal Partnership in Marriage," Valerie M. Hudson and Richard B. Miller, *Ensign*, April 2013.

115. Spencer W. Kimball, "The Blessings and Responsibilities of Womanhood," *Ensign*, March 1976.

116. Alonzo Gaskill, *The Truth about Eden* (Springville, UT: Cedar Fort Publishers), 167.

117. Sister Tarasevich, "Be Like Ammon," *Ensign*, July 2014.

118. Rodney Turner, *Woman and the Priesthood*, Deseret Book (Salt Lake City, 1978), 29.

119. Alonzo Gaskill, *The Truth about Eden* (Springville, UT: Cedar Fort Publishers), 166.

120. Vivian M. Adams, *The Man Adam*, eds. Joseph Fielding McConkie and Robert L. Millet, 91; emphasis added.

121. Earl C. Tingey, "The Simple Truths from Heaven: The Lord's Pattern" (Church Educational System fireside for young adults, Jan. 13, 2008), speeches.byu.edu; emphasis added.

122. Bruce R. McConkie, *"Sermons and Writings of Bruce R. McConkie,"* The Fall of Adam, Bookcraft, 203.

123. Vivian M. Adams, *The Man Adam*, eds. Joseph Fielding McConkie and Robert L. Millet (Salt Lake City: Bookcraft), 97; emphasis added.

124. Russell M. Nelson, "Salvation and Exaltation," *Ensign*, May 2008.

125. M. Russell Ballard, "Men and Women and Priesthood Power," *Ensign*, September 2014; emphasis added.

126. James E Talmage, *Articles of Faith* (Salt Lake City: Deseret Book), 138.

127. Russell M. Nelson, "Perfection Pending, and Other Favorite Discourses," *Jesus Christ: Our Master and More* (Salt Lake City: Deseret Book, 2000), 154; emphasis added.

128. Jaynann Payne, "Lucy Mack Smith," *Ensign*, November 1972.

129. Lucy Mack Smith, "My Great-Great-Grandmother, Emma Hale Smith," Gracia N. Jones, *Ensign*, August 1992.

130. Eliza R. Snow, "To the Branches of the Relief Society," Sept. 12, 1884, Woman's Exponent (Salt Lake City, UT), Sept. 15, 1884, vol. 13, no. 8, p. 61. (See image of the original document at lib.byu.edu, courtesy of Harold B. Lee Library, Brigham Young University, Provo, UT.)

131. Joseph Smith, Saints; The Standard of Truth 1815-1846, Vol. 1, Ch. 37, 448.

132. Ibid., Ch. 42, 510.

133. Brigham Young, "Traditions," *Journal of Discourses*, 26 vol. (Liverpool: Latter Day Saints' Book Depot, 1855–86), 14:102.

134. Hyrum L. Andrus, *God, Man, and the Universe*, (Salt Lake City: Bookcraft), 354.

135. John A. Widtsoe, *Understandable Religion* (Salt Lake City: Deseret Book, 2009), 134.

136. Hugh Nibley, *Eve and the Choice Made in Eden*, Beverly Campbell, (Salt Lake City: Deseret Book), 52. Jeremiah 20:10; Lexicon: H 6763, Strong's- tsela

137. Hugh Nibley, *LDS Women's Treasury: Insights and Inspiration for Today's Woman* (Salt Lake City: Deseret Book), 34–35; emphasis added.

138. Joseph Fielding Smith and Bruce R. McConkie, *The Man Adam*, eds. Joseph Fielding McConkie and Robert L. Millet (Salt Lake City: Bookcraft), 26; emphasis added.

139. Freedmon, "Women & Power Equal to Man," 56–58.

140. Jolene Edmund Rockwood, "Eve's Role in the Creation and Fall to Mortality," *From Women and the Power Within* (Salt Lake City: Deseret Book, 1991), 17–18.

141. Joseph Smith, "History of the Church," 2:320, quoted in Joseph Fielding Smith, "The Perfect Marriage Covenant," *New Era*, 1931.

142. Dallin H. Oaks, "The Great Plan of Happiness," *Ensign*, November 1993.

143. Vivian M. Adams, "Our Glorious Mother Eve," *The Man Adam* (Salt Lake City: Bookcraft), 88.

144. Howard W. Hunter, "Reading the Scriptures," *Ensign*, November 1979.

145. Joseph Smith to Emma, Oct. 13, 1832, in JSP, D2:313. Joseph Smith's Polygamy, 1:201-2. Quoted in "Saints"; The Standard of Truth 1815-1846, Vol. 1, Ch. 34, 413.

146. "Perfect" (English Term), CRI/Voice; http://www.crivoice.org/terms/t-perfec.html

147. Joseph Smith, *"Lectures on Faith,"* compiled by N. B. Lundwall, (1834–35), 2:18.

148. Brigham Young, *"Journal of Discourses,"* vol. 26, [Liverpool, England: Albert Carrington and others, 1853–1886], 9:38.), quoted in *LDS Women's Treasury: Insights and Inspirations for Today's Woman* (Salt Lake City: Deseret Book), 445.

149. Bruce C. Hafen, *Covenant Hearts: The Moral Influence of Women* (Salt Lake City: Deseret Book), 190.

150. Joseph F. Smith, *Gospel Doctrine: Sermons and Writings of*

President Joseph F. Smith (Salt Lake City: Deseret Book), 315.

151.   Joseph Smith, Young Woman's Journal 2 (November 1890): 81. Quoted in *Women and the Priesthood*, Sheri Dew (Salt Lake City: Deseret Book), 154.

152.   Ibid.

153.   Mary Case, "LDS Church News," Canoga Park, CA, 05/09/98.

154.   David O. McKay, "Man May Know for Himself: Teachings of President David O. McKay," ed. Clare Middlemiss, 263.

155.   "Patriarchs and Patriarchal Blessings," Duties and Blessings of the Priesthood: Basic Manual for Priesthood Holders, Part A, (2000), 69–76.

156.   Joseph Smith, *"Teachings of the Prophet Joseph Smith,"* 301, quoted by Vivian Adams, *The Man Adam*, eds. Joseph Fielding McConkie and Robert L. Millett (Salt Lake City: Bookcraft), 103.

157.   Boyd K. Packer, "A Tribute to Women," *Ensign*, July 1989.

158.   Bruce R. McConkie, "Eve and the Fall," *Sermons and Writings of Bruce R. McConkie* (Salt Lake City: Bookcraft), 64.

159.   Heber C. Kimball to Parley P. Pratt, June 17, 1842, Parley P. Pratt Correspondence, Church History Library; Historian's office, Joseph Smith History, draft notes, May 4, 1842; Joseph Smith History, 1838-56, volume C-1, 1328. Topic: Anointed Quorum ("Holy Order"). Quoted in "Saints"; the Standard of Truth 1815- 1846, Vol. 1, Ch. 37, 454

160.   Dallin H. Oaks, "The Keys and Authority of the Priesthood," *Ensign*, May 2014.

161.   M. Russell Ballard, "The Sacred Responsibilities of Parenthood," *Ensign*, March 2006, 29–30.

162.   Boyd K. Packer, "The Power of the Priesthood," *Ensign*, May 2010; emphasis in original.

163.   James E. Faust, "The Prophetic Voice," *Ensign*, May 1996.

164.   Joseph Smith, *Teachings of the Prophet Joseph Smith*, (Salt Lake City: Deseret Book, 157–58.

165.   James E. Talmage, "House of the Lord," 79.

166.   M. Russell Ballard, "Men and Women in the Work of the Lord," *New Era*, April 2014; emphasis added.

167.   M. Russell Ballard, "The Relief Society," *Ensign*, May 1998.

168.   Joseph Fielding Smith, *Conference Report*, Apr. 1970, 59, quoted

in *Teachings of the Presidents of the Church*: Joseph Fielding Smith, 163; emphasis added.

169. Dallin H. Oaks, "The Keys and Authority of the Priesthood," *Ensign*, April 2014.

170. John A. Widtsoe, *Priesthood and the Church Government*, Salt Lake City: Deseret Book, 1939, 83. Quoted in "Participate Fully In Receiving the Blessings of the Priesthood," *Ensign*, January 1994.

171. Russell M. Nelson, "Love Your Wife," *Ensign*, January 2014, 31.

172. L. Tom Perry, as quoted in Valerie M. Hudson and Richard B. Miller, "Equal Partnership in Marriage," *Ensign*, April 2013; emphasis added.

173. Joseph Smith, quoted in "Presidents of the Church Speak on Temple Marriage," *New Era*, June 1971.

174. L. Tom Perry, "Fatherhood, an Eternal Calling," *Ensign*, May 2004, 71.

175. Robert L. Millet, *"The Man Adam,"* *Ensign*, January 1994.

176. Joseph Smith, *"Teachings of the Prophet Joseph Smith,"* Joseph Fielding Smith (Salt Lake City: Deseret Book, 1976), 357; cited hereafter as Teachings.

177. Robert L Millet, *"The Man Adam,"* *Ensign*, January 1994.

178. Ibid.

179. Ibid.

180. Bruce R. McConkie, *The Promised Messiah* (Salt Lake City: Deseret Book, 1976), 365.

181. Joseph Smith, "The Fulness of Times," Robert J. Matthews, *Ensign*, December 1989.

182. Robert L Millet, *"The Man Adam,"* *Ensign*, January 1994.

183. Bruce R. McConkie, *The Mortal Messiah: From Bethlehem to Calvary*, 4 volumes (Salt Lake City: Deseret Book, 1979–81), 4:125. See also *Conference Report*, Apr. 1985, 10.

184. Alonzo Gaskill, *The Truth about Eden* (Springville, UT: Cedar Fort Publishers), 165.

185. Joseph Smith, *"Teachings of the Prophet Joseph Smith,"* 369–374. See also John 10:34–36; Psalm 82:6); emphasis added.

186. Talmage, *Jesus the Christ* (Salt Lake City: Covenant Communications), 38.

187. Old Testament Student Manual, "Genesis–2 Samuel," (1980), 45–46.

188.   Robert D. Hales, "Seeking to Know God, Our Heavenly Father, and His Son, Jesus Christ," *Ensign*, October 2009; emphasis added.

189.   James E. Talmage, *Jesus the Christ* (Salt Lake City: Covenant Communications), 38.

190.   Russell M. Nelson, "The Correct Name of the Church," *Ensign*, November 2018.

191.   Robert D. Hales, "Seeking to Know God, Our Heavenly Father, and His Son, Jesus Christ," *Ensign*, November 2009. see "To Speak About God," Harvard Divinity Bulletin, Krister Stendahl vol. 36, no. 2, 2008: 8–9.

192.   Joseph Smith Jr., "The King Follett Sermon," *Ensign*, April 1971; emphasis added.

193.   Boyd K. Packer, "The Pattern of Our Parentage," *Ensign*, Nov. 1984.

194.   Lorenzo Snow, "Becoming Like God," lds.org. Also see Eliza R. Snow, Biography and Family Record of Lorenzo Snow (1884), 46. See also "The Teachings of Lorenzo Snow," ed. Clyde J. Williams (1996), 1–9.

195.   Ibid. Gordon B. Hinckley. Also see Don Lattin, "Musings of the Main Mormon," San Francisco Chronicle, Apr. 13, 1997.

196.   Rudger Clawson, "Our Mother in Heaven," Latter-day Saints' Millennial Star, 72, no. 39 (Sept. 29, 1910), 620. Rudger Clawson was the editor of the periodical and likely author of this editorial. "Mother in Heaven," Gospel Topics, https://www.lds.org/topics/mother-in-heaven?lang=eng.

197.   M. Russell Ballard, *When Thou Art Converted: Continuing Our Search for Happiness* (Salt Lake City: Deseret Book, 2001), 62.

198.   Harold B. Lee, "The Influence and Responsibility of Women," Relief Society Magazine, 51, no. 2 (Feb. 1964), 85; See also "Mother"; Topics, https://www.lds.org/topics/mother-in-heaven?lang=eng.

199.   Genesis 1:26–27; Moses 3:4–7; Romans 8:16–17; Psalm 82:6; Doctrine and Covenants 132:19–20.

200.   "Becoming Like God." Also Elaine Anderson Cannon, "Mother in Heaven," in *Encyclopedia of Mormonism*, ed. Daniel H. Ludlow, 5 vols. (New York: Macmillan, 1992), 2:961. For an extensive survey of these teachings, see David L. Paulsen and Martin Pulido, "'A Mother There': A Survey of Historical Teachings about Mother in Heaven," BYU Studies, 50, no. 1 (2011): 70–97.

201. "The Origin of Man: Male and Female," *Improvement Era* 13, no. 1 (Nov. 1909): 78

202. Susa Young Gates, "The Vision Beautiful," *Improvement Era*, 23, no. 6 (Apr. 1920): 542; emphasis added. At this time, Gates was the recording secretary of the Relief Society General Presidency, also a writer, periodical editor, and women's rights advocate in Utah.

203. Joseph Smith, Saints, The Standard of Truth 1815-1846, Vol. 1, Ch. 34, 404.

204. "The Family: A Proclamation to the World," *Ensign*, Nov. 2010, 129; emphasis added.

205. Spencer W. Kimball, "The True Way of Life and Salvation," *Ensign*, May 1978, 6.

206. 3 Nephi 18:19–21; Matthew 6:6–9; John 17:1, 5, 21, 24–25; see also Matthew 4:10; Luke 4:8; and 3 Nephi 13:9; 17:15.

207. Gordon B. Hinckley, "Daughters of God," *Ensign*, Nov. 1991, 100.

208. Dallin H. Oaks, "Apostasy and Restoration," *Ensign*, May 1995, 84; emphasis added.

209. Robert J. Matthews, *The Man Adam*, eds. Joseph Fielding McConkie and Robert L. Millet, 78.

210. "Transgress," Random House Webster's College Dictionary (1996), 1415.

211. Alonzo Gaskill, *Savior and the Serpent* (Salt Lake City: Deseret Book), 16.

212. Dallin H. Oaks, "Great Plan of Happiness," 73, quoted in Valerie M. Hudson and Richard B. Miller, "Equal Partnership in Marriage," *Ensign*, April 2013.

213. Bruce R. McConkie, "The Fall of Adam," Sermons and Writings of Bruce R. McConkie (Salt Lake City: Bookcraft), 201.

214. Robert J. Matthews, *The Man Adam*, eds. Joseph Fielding, McConkie and Robert L. Millet, 74, 75.

215. James E. Talmage, *The Broken Heart*, Bruce C. Hafen, Deseret Book (2009), 32.

216. Bruce D. Porter, "A Broken Heart and a Contrite Spirit," *Ensign*, November 2007.

217. Bruce R. McConkie, "Who is the Author of the Plan of Salvation?" (May 1953), *Improvement Era*, 56; emphasis added.

218. Robert J. Matthews, *The Man Adam*, eds. Joseph Fielding, McConkie and Robert L. Millet, 83, 84.

219. D. Todd Christofferson, "Free Forever, to Act for themselves," *Ensign*, November 2014.

220. Joseph Fielding McConkie, "The Mystery of Eden," *The Man Adam* eds. Joseph Fielding McConkie and Robert L. Millet (Salt Lake City: Bookcraft), 30.

221. Matthew Henry, "Genesis Chapter One: Genesis 3:21," Commentaries on Genesis.

222. Hamilton (1982), 48, quoted in Alonzo Gaskill, *Savior and the Serpent*, (Salt Lake City: Deseret Book), 162.

223. Historian's office, Joseph Smith History, draft notes, May 4, 1842. Topic: Temple endowment. Quoted in "Saints"; the Standard of Truth 1815- 1846, Vol. 1, Ch. 37, 453.

224. James E. Talmage, *Jesus the Christ*, 608.

225. Doctrine and Covenants Encyclopedia, by Hoyt W. Brewster, 340.

226. Hugh Nibley, Gen. 3:1 in "Commentary on the Torah with a New English Translation," Richard Elliott Friedman. quoted in *"Echoes of Eden,"* E. Douglas Clark, 68.

227. Brigham Young, Journal, Feb 3, 1846. Quoted in Saints; The Standard of Truth 1815- 1846, Vol. 1, Ch. 46, 583.

228. Robert J. Matthews, *The Man Adam*, eds. Joseph Fielding Smith McConkie and Robert L. Millet (Salt Lake City: Bookcraft), 46.

229. Joseph Smith, *"Teachings of the Prophet Joseph Smith,"* 200, 367, 326.

230. Robert J. Matthews, *The Man Adam*, eds. Joseph Fielding McConkie and Robert L. Millet, 45.

231. Ibid., 46.

232. Ibid., 44.

233. Ibid., 45; emphasis added.

234. Ibid., 48.

235. Ibid., 60; emphasis added. Teachings of Prophet Joseph Smith, 12.

236. "Cowley and Whitney on Doctrine," Bookcraft (1963). Quoted in "The Man Adam", Robert J. Matthews (Salt Lake City: Bookcraft, 1963), 287; emphasis added.

237. Joseph Smith, *Teachings of the Prophet Joseph Smith*, 12; emphasis added.

238. Robert J. Matthews, *The Man Adam*, eds. Joseph Fielding McConkie and Robert L. Millet, 60; emphasis added.

239. Bruce R McConkie, "The Purifying Power of Gethsemane," *Ensign*, April 2011, 57.

240. Brigham Young, *"Journal of Discourses,"* 2:6; 3:319; 7:285.

241. Botterweck, Theological Dictionary of the Old Testament, 2:245–46, quoted in E. Douglas Clark, *Echoes of Eden* (Salt Lake City: Covenant Communications), 21.

242. Pratt (1978), 30, also quoted in Alonzo Gaskill, *The Savior and the Serpent*, footnote 9, 184.

243. Bruce R. McConkie, *Mormon Doctrine* (Salt Lake City: Bookcraft), 589.

244. Joseph Smith Jr. "The King Follett Sermon," *Ensign*, April 1971; emphasis added.

245. Joseph F. Smith, "The Father and the Son: A Doctrinal Exposition by the First Presidency and The Twelve," June 30, 1916, in Clark (1965–75), 5:26; emphasis added.

246. Also Gen. 2:7; Moses 3:7; Abraham 5:7; D&C 77:12.

247. "Moses", The Pearl of Great Price Student Manual (2000), 3–27; emphasis added. Also Bruce R. McConkie, *Mormon Doctrine*, 209.

248. Genesis 1:28; Genesis 9:1; Moses 2:28; and Abraham 4:28.

249. "Spirit," Guide to the Scriptures; https://www.lds.org; emphasis added.

250. D&C 138:17; Lev. 17:11; 1 Cor. 15:50; *Teachings of Presidents of the Church*: Joseph Smith, 199–200, 326.

251. "Resurrection," Guide to the Scriptures, https://www.lds.org.

252. Alonzo Gaskill, *The Savior and the Serpent*, 45. See also Spicer (1962), 16; Cornwall and Smith (1998), 6, S.V. "Adam"; Sweet (1995), 15; Hertz (1962) 5; Neusner (1985), 183.

253. Philo of Alexandria, "Allegorical Interpretations" 1:29 quoted in Yonge (1997), 35. Quoted in *"The Savior and the Serpent,"* Alonzo Gaskill, 45.

254. Alonzo Gaskill, *The Savior and the Serpent*, 45, 46; emphasis added. See also Fontana (1994), 34; Todeschi (1995), 289, and Spicer (1962), 46.

255. Bruce R. McConkie, "Christ and the Creation," *Ensign*, June 1982, 13.

256. Robert L. Millet, *The Man Adam*, eds. Joseph Fielding McConkie and Robert L. Millet, 19.

257. Ibid., 20.

258. Orson Pratt, *Journal of Discourses*, Vol. 1, 280–284. See also Joseph Fielding Smith, *Man: His Origin and Destiny*, 391–92.

259. Joseph Fielding Smith, *Man: His Origin and Destiny* (Salt Lake City: Deseret Book, 1954), 367, 376–77; emphasis added.

260. Joseph Fielding Smith, *The Man Adam*, eds. Joseph Fielding McConkie and Robert L. Millet, 18.

261. Bruce R. McConkie, *Mormon Doctrine*, 268, 211.

262. Caesarius of Arles, "Sermons," 136, quoted in Alonzo Gaskill, *The Savior and the Serpent*, 81.

263. Spencer W. Kimball, *Conference Report*, April 1978, 7.

264. Jeffrey R. Holland, "Where Justice, Love, and Mercy Meet," *Ensign*, May 2015.

265. Bruce R. McConkie "Eve and the Fall," *Mormon Doctrine*, 60–61; emphasis added.

266. Spencer W. Kimball (1998) 170; Kimball (1969), 286.

267. Ezra Taft Benson, *Teachings of Ezra Taft Benson* (1998), 21.

268. Joseph F. Smith, "The Origin of Man," *Improvement Era*, November 1909, 80; emphasis added.

269. Bruce R. McConkie, *A New Witness of the Articles of Faith* (Salt Lake City: Deseret Book), 63.

270. Joseph Smith, *Teachings of the Prophet Joseph Smith*, 157, 158, 167–169.

271. J. Reuben Clark, *Behold the Lamb of God* (Salt Lake City: Deseret Book), 53.

272. Joseph F. Smith, "The Origin of Man", *Improvement Era*, November 1909, 80; emphasis added.

273. Roberts and Donaldson (1990), The Clementine Homilies, 3:18, 8:241, quoted in Alonzo Gaskill, *The Savior and the Serpent*, 11, 12.

274. Dallin H Oaks, "The Great Plan of Happiness," *Ensign*, October 1993.

275. John A. Widtsoe, "Evidences and Reconciliations," *Improvement Era*, 193–195.

276. Joseph F. Smith, "Sons and Daughters of the Eternal Father," in *Teachings of Presidents of the Church*: Joseph F. Smith, https://www.lds.org/?lang=eng.

277. Joseph F. Smith, quoted in Alonzo Gaskill, *The Savior and the Serpent*, 131. See also Joseph F. Smith, John R. Winder, and

Anthon H. Lund, in Clark (1965–1975), 4:205; Clark (1965–1975), 5:26; Ludlow (1981), 109; Rasmussen (1993), 10.

278. Joseph F. Smith, "Sons and Daughters of the Eternal Father," Teachings of Presidents, Chapter 37, https://www.lds.org/?lang=eng.

279. David O. McKay, *Steppingstones to an Abundant Life* (Salt Lake City: Deseret Book), 5.

280. Gunkel, Genesis 12, quoted in E. Douglas Clark, *Echoes of Eden* (Salt Lake City: Covenant Communications), 26.

281. Genesis 5:4–29. The only posterity give in the Bible about Adam's posterity was a patriarchal lineage of the priesthood through Seth, which followed down to Noah and to Shem and on to Abraham. Abraham's lineage is given in Genesis 11:24–28, 31–32.

282. Joseph Smith, "Shem was Melchizedek," quoted in *Lectures on Faith*, Dr. John A. Widtsoe, Orson Pratt, N.B. Lundwall, 93.

283. Bethel, Genesis 28:19, https://en.wikipedia.org/wiki/Bethel.

284. Larry Y. Wilson, "Provo Temple Employee Devotional," Director of Temple Department, November 13, 2015.

285. Vivian M. Adams, *The Man Adam*, eds. Joseph Fielding McConkie and Robert L. Millet, 98.

286. Bruce R. McConkie, "Christ and the Creation," *Ensign*, June 1982, 13. Interpolative: is to introduce something in addition to another subject. Interject; interpose; intercalate.

287. Vivian M. Adams, *The Man Adam*, eds. Joseph Fielding McConkie and Robert L. Millet, 97.

288. Ibid., 97–98.

289. Jeffrey R. Holland, as quoted in Alonzo Gaskill, *The Savior and the Serpent*, 9. See also Holland (1997), 202–3; emphasis added.

290. Neal A. Maxwell, "Patience," *Ensign*, October 1980; emphasis added.

291. Joseph Smith, "*Lectures on Faith*," 2:12.

292. Parley P. Pratt, "Times and Seasons," (1843), 672.

293. Elder Parley P. Pratt (1978), 85; President John Taylor (1852), 108–9; and President Joseph Fielding Smith (1954), 383–84.

294. Parley P. Pratt, John Taylor and Joseph Fielding Smith, as quoted in Alonzo Gaskill, *The Savior and the Serpent*, 11.

295. Jeffrey R. Holland, "The Atonement of Jesus Christ," *Ensign*, March 2008.

296.   L. LaMar Adams, "The Man and His Message," *Ensign*, March 1982; emphasis added.

297.   Daniel H. Ludlow, DNTC 1:830; "Companion to Your Study of the New Testament: The Four Gospels," 202.

298.   "Chapter 10," New Testament Student Manual, 2014.

299.   Newel Whitney, Quoted in "Saints"; The Standard of Truth 1815- 1846, Vol. 1, Ch. 38, 464; emphasis added. Nauvoo Relief Society Minute Book, May 27, 1842, in Derr and others, First Fifty Years of Relief Society, 75-76; see also 75, note 188.

300.   Ambrosiaster, Ancient Christian Commentary on Scripture, Bray, 108, quoted in Alonzo Gaskill, *The Lost Language of Symbolism*, 81.

301.   The NIV, NRSV, Jerusalem Bible, quoted in Alonzo Gaskill, *The Lost Language of Symbolism*, 81.

302.   Alonzo Gaskill, *The Lost Language of Symbolism*, Morris, 1 Corinthians, 152; 81.

303.   M. Russell Ballard, "Men and Women in the Work of the Lord," *Ensign*, April 2014.

304.   Dallin H. Oaks, "The Keys and Authority of the Priesthood," *Ensign*, May 2014.

305.   Ibid.

306.   "Natural man," The Guide to the Scriptures, https://www.lds.org.

307.   James E. Talmage, *Jesus the Christ*, 126.

308.   Vivian M. Adams, *The Man Adam*, eds. Joseph Fielding, McConkie and Robert L. Millet, 99.

309.   Ibid., 100.

310.   Delbert A. Stapley, "The Tree of Life a Recurring Symbol," *Conference Report*, April 1966, p. 23-27.

311.   Susan Easton Black, quoted in Alonzo Gaskill, *The Lost Language of Symbolism* (Salt Lake City: Deseret Book, 1988), 123, n. 7.

312.   Joseph Fielding McConkie, *The Man Adam*, eds. Joseph Fielding McConkie and Robert L. Millet (Salt Lake City: Bookcraft), 31.

313.   Robert L Millet, *The Man Adam*, eds. Joseph Fielding McConkie and Robert L. Millet (Salt Lake City: Bookcraft).

314.   Patrick Fairbairn, (1989), 1227, quoted in Alonzo Gaskill, *Savior and the Serpent*, 94.

315.   Ibid.; see also Myers (1987), 204.

316.   Ibid.; see also Unger (1966), 192; Random House, Webster's College Dictionary (1996), 233, s. v., "cherub"; Douglas (1971), 208.

317.   Joseph Fielding McConkie, quoted in *The Truth about Eden*, Alonzo Gaskill, (Springville, Utah: Cedar Fort, Inc.) 89. See J. McConkie (1985), 256.

318.   "Old Testament Video Presentation" (53224), which describe Moses's tabernacle.

319.   Bayley (1990), 2:74, quoted in Alonzo Gaskill, *Savior and the Serpent*, 95.

320.   Brad Wilcox, "Closed Doors and Open Windows," *Ensign*, December 1993.

321.   Boyd K. Packer, "The Plan of Happiness," *Ensign*, May 2015, 28.

ACKNOWLEDGMENTS

To all who have assisted with this eight-year journey of discovery and insight. Your reviews, edits, and suggestions have been invaluable. Every comment was significant to the development of this book. I have gleaned from some excellent editors who have taught me what it takes to write a book. A special thanks to Bridgewood Publishing for their patience and care to details. They have made this book possible. Friends and family who took the time to read, review and add substance through the entire book in particular are: Niki Hendershot, Eileen Knudsen, Ashley Reid, Morgan Lechtenberg, and Heather Gibbons.

I thank the Lord for keeping me enlightened and focused through this entire process. It has been a learning experience and great joy.

ABOUT THE
AUTHOR

M arla Whitman is a mother of fourteen beautiful children, with wonderful sons- and daughters-in-law, culminating into 47 (and counting) grandchildren. Born in 1948, she is of pioneer stock. She is the youngest of twelve children, the daughter of George and Ruby Adams, and the great-great-granddaughter of Levi Ward Hancock.

Deeply imbedded in the gospel of Jesus Christ of Latter-day Saints, her passion for truth has led her on a path of inquiry and study about Adam and particularly about the elusive truths concerning Mother Eve. Recognizing a need to clarify what took place in Eden for herself, the author realized that there were many who have similar questions and hopes to help them as well. Her research has been comprehensive, and she wishes to pass this knowledge onto her posterity and others who are inquisitive about Eve in Eden.